Tim Price Plays 2

For Martha
What a wonderful place it is to be,
wrapped around your little finger.
Love,
Dad x

Tim Price Plays 2

Odyssey '84
Nye
Isla
Force Majeure
Teh Internet Is Serious Business

TIM PRICE

methuen | drama
LONDON • NEW YORK • OXFORD • NEW DELHI • SYDNEY

METHUEN DRAMA
Bloomsbury Publishing Plc
50 Bedford Square, London, WC1B 3DP, UK
1359 Broadway, New York, NY 10018, USA
29 Earlsfort Terrace, Dublin 2, Ireland

BLOOMSBURY, METHUEN DRAMA and the Methuen Drama logo are
trademarks of Bloomsbury Publishing Plc

First published in Great Britain 2025

Copyright © Tim Price, 2025

Tim Price has asserted his right under the Copyright, Designs
and Patents Act, 1988, to be identified as author of this work.

Cover artwork © Ross Walker

All rights reserved. No part of this publication may be: i) reproduced or
transmitted in any form, electronic or mechanical, including photocopying,
recording or by means of any information storage or retrieval system without
prior permission in writing from the publishers; or ii) used or reproduced in
any way for the training, development or operation of artificial intelligence (AI)
technologies, including generative AI technologies. The rights holders expressly
reserve this publication from the text and data mining exception as per Article
4(3) of the Digital Single Market Directive (EU) 2019/790.

Bloomsbury Publishing Plc does not have any control over, or responsibility
for, any third-party websites referred to or in this book. All internet addresses
given in this book were correct at the time of going to press. The author and
publisher regret any inconvenience caused if addresses have changed or sites
have ceased to exist, but can accept no responsibility for any such changes.
No rights in incidental music or songs contained in the work are hereby
granted and performance rights for any performance /presentation
whatsoever must be obtained from the respective copyright owners.

All rights whatsoever in these plays are strictly reserved and application
for performance etc. should be made before rehearsals to 42, Palladium
House, Argyll Street, London W1F 7TA. No performance may be given
unless a licence has been obtained.

A catalogue record for this book is available from the British Library.

Library of Congress Control Number: 2025939508

ISBN: PB: 978-1-3505-4753-7
ePDF: 978-1-3505-4755-1
eBook: 978-1-3505-4754-4

Series: Modern Plays

Ceripeset by Mark Heslington Ltd, Scarborough, North Yorkshire
Printed and bound in Great Britain

For product safety related questions contact productsafety@bloomsbury.com.

To find out more about our authors and books visit
www.bloomsbury.com and sign up for our newsletters.

Contents

Introduction vii
Odyssey '84 1
Nye 133
Isla 249
Force Majeure 321
Teh Internet Is Serious Business 439

methuen | drama
LONDON · NEW YORK · OXFORD · NEW DELHI · SYDNEY

Introduction

Odyssey '84 – from the new Modern Play
Nye – from the 2025 edition
Isla – from the Modern Play
Force Majeure – from the Modern Play
Teh Internet Is Serious Business – from the Modern Classic

Plays Collection 2

Introduction

This collection of plays bridges two periods of writing. *Teh Internet Is Serious Business* is the oldest – produced in 2014 downstairs at the Royal Court directed by Hamish Pirie and represents the high point of my first professional creative writing period. This play built on what I had learned from the *Radicalisation of Bradley Manning* and *Protest Song* from my first collection and sits with those two plays as a story inspired by the explosion of anti-censorship and anti-authority protest that Wikileaks inspired between 2011 and 2014.

At this point, trolling hadn't evolved into fake news or populism and hacking was performed by gifted teenagers, rather than nation states. The Internet was young, and for a short time the kids understood it better than anyone else. This is what *Teh Internet Is Serious Business* captured, that period where teenagers ran rings around governments and corporations, for no reason other than to prove they could. The challenge of putting the Internet on stage was made easier, as most things are, when we gave ourselves limitations – the key limitation being that there were to be no screens in this show. Actors became memes and webpages, lasers were digital security, brass instruments a DDOS attack and a ball pool became a search engine.

The show brought a large crowd of digital natives into the theatre for the first time and I had the satisfying experience of watching the cast dramatize a scene in a chatroom from the rise of Anonymous, and heard an audience member whisper to a friend 'I was in that chatroom'.

Despite the Royal Court's relatively generous commissioning fees, *Teh Internet is Serious Business* had cost me dearly, the opportunity to have a show downstairs at the Court meant that I worked solely on the play for just over a year getting it ready and I had overstretched myself financially. There was a moment where with my name in lights over Sloane Square, I went to the train station to buy a ticket to London from Liverpool to go and watch it, and none of my bank cards worked. With reality biting, after that play I stepped away from theatre and focused on better paid work in television and teaching. Eventually the bruising experience in television brought me back to the Royal Court, where *Isla* was commissioned. Eventually this show came to life in 2021 at Theatr Clwyd, directed by Tamara Harvey, during a period of socially distanced performances. The play set during the first lockdown explored how digital voice assistants were being abused by their owners with sexist and misogynistic language and how programmers had been forced to change how these devices responded, as unchecked verbal violence was leading to increased violence at home. Lockdown provided a perfect pressure cooker for this story.

Force Majure, directed by Michael Longhurst at the Donmar Warehouse, followed fairly quickly at the end of 2021. At this point social distancing measures had been abandoned just in time to maximize the impact of the Omicron Covid variant. We lost nearly all of our previews, shut down for nearly two weeks and returned with new heads of department after Christmas. Somehow, the show did go on. During that period the tremendous work of understudies, swings and the willingness of crew and stage management to undertake roles they were neither trained nor paid for kept the whole industry working.

Throughout both *Isla* and *Force Majeure* I was also working on *Nye*. I knew when it was commissioned at the National Theatre that this would be my big one. If I am gifted at anything it is biting off more than I can chew and with this one, I truly outdid myself. It took me ten years to write, and when I eventually clicked 'send' I burst into tears of relief. Emily Mclaughlin was at the NT Studio at that point and Nina Steiger joined soon after; they both championed the play as did Ben Power who had originally commissioned it. I was summoned to a meeting at the NT where I was to meet Rufus Norris, for what I felt was an unnecessarily elaborate rejection. In the meeting Nina, Ben and Rufus talked about how enormous, unhinged and unstageable it was, which I heartily agreed with. At some point Rufus said despite all that, it was also the kind of the play the National Theatre is desperate for and the kind of play writers tend to avoid. So now they have one, they felt compelled to see if they could make it work. He said: 'There's only a handful of directors in the country who could do this play, and I'm one of them. Would working with me be something you'd be open to?' Like Nye Bevan, I have a stutter but somehow 'yes, yes, that would be fine', came out, thankfully, without hesitation. I looked over to Ben and Nina who beamed like proud parents watching a gormless son who has just passed a very simple test and given the *right answer*.

And so Rufus and I wrestled *Nye* into a stageable shape. I tend to write a lot of drafts and throw out a lot of material, so a large part of our process was trying to find the draft where a scene did work and figuring out why we threw it out in the first place. Rufus would ask for forgiveness for his 'dramaturgical enthusiasm' but very quickly we found that neither of us were particularly precious about either of our respective crafts and were both very open to suggestion from each other. Our disagreements were so few that on the rare occasion it happened, there was a frisson of excitement.

With brilliant work from Vicky Mortimer, Paule Constable, Will Mortimer, Donnato Wharton, Jess Williams and Stephen Hogget we staged what I'd written and 'made' what I hadn't and the show opened in spring 2024. Rufus's masterful stewardship meant we were able to support Michael Sheen's lightening performance and tell Nye's story with the heart and conviction it deserved. It is the only play that I have burst into tears on first preview. The stress and strain got to me combined with the joy of seeing a huge cast of Welsh actors telling a Welsh story on the Olivier stage overwhelmed me. I am hugely proud of *Nye*; it is a good play, but it was Rufus's soaring vision for his final show as AD at the National that made this show the success it was.

Three months after *Nye* closed at the Wales Millennium Centre I was at the Sherman Theatre in Cardiff for *Odyssey '84*, directed by Joe Murphy. I had neglected *Odyssey '84*, due to *Nye* going in to production the same year. Joe was relentlessly patient with my missed deadlines and underdeveloped thinking. The idea came from having interviewed miners when I was a local journalist for the twentieth anniversary of the Miners' Strike in 2004. And with the fortieth anniversary looming in 2024, I contacted Joe and said I had an idea for telling the story of the strike but using the structure of the *Odyssey*. I'd always loved the *Odyssey* and when I thought about the incredible tales from the international fundraising committee, I could see a new way to tell the Miners' Strike story without it being one of drudgery and poverty. I have always, on some level, resented how the Miners' Strike seemed to be something that only happened in the north of England, that there wasn't a great piece of popular storytelling that told the Welsh experience. The film *Pride* came closest but really the heroes in that story were from the LGBT community and the Welsh community provided a context for their heroism. I wanted Welsh characters to take centre stage and with Joe's careful dramaturgy we were able to tell a story that felt representative of Valleys culture with all its communal bravery, comedy and suffering.

Odyssey '84

List of Characters

John O'Donnell, *30s, male, Welsh*
Penny O'Donnell, *30s, female, Welsh*
Billy Lewis, *30s, male, Welsh*
Dai Morgan, *30s, male, Welsh*
Shaz Lewis, *30s, female, Welsh*
Aiden McGinty, *20s, male, Irish*
Con O'Hare, *20s, male, Irish*
Ceri Watts, *50s, male, Welsh*
Kev Hulse, *40s, male, Welsh*
Vinny Olsen, *30s, male, Welsh*
Simon Billsborrow, *40s, male, Welsh*
Helen Gavin, *20s, female, Welsh*
Sara Smith, *20s, female, Welsh*
Liam Gerrard, *40s, male, Welsh*
Lucy Hughes, *40s, female, Welsh*
Vicky Corcoran, *30s, female, Welsh*
LGBT Community Members 1, 2, 3, *various ages, queer*
Hannah Murphy, *any age, female, English*
Lily DeValley, *any age, drag queen, Londoner*
WPC Richards, *30s, female, Welsh*
Mounted Officer, *any age, male, Londoner*
Miners, 1, 2, 3, *any age, Northern*
Riot Police Officers, *any*
News Reporter, *any*
Barry Collins, *50s, male, Australian*
Nadia Hussaini, *40s, female, Afghan*
Marco Santini, *any, male, Italian*
Mathilde Ramirez, *any, female, Spanish*
Arnaud Barbier, *any, male, French*
Artem Babenko, *any, male, Ukrainian*
Dieter Becker, *any, male, German*
Lars Storhaug, *any, male, Norwegian*
Translator, *any*
Rania Salem, *40s, female, Libyan*
Colonel Gaddafi, *42, male, Libyan*
Rory Owens, *20s, male, Welsh*

David Jones, *24, male, Yorkshire*
Joe Green, *55, male, Yorkshire*
David Wilkie, *40s, male, Welsh*
Huw Smith, *40s, male, Welsh*
Yura Ivanov, *any, female, Russian*
PC Roger Hopkins, *30s, male, Welsh*

Note

An / oblique indicates when the next line should be spoken.

A // double oblique indicates when the line after the next line should be spoken.

A – dash indicates an interruption of thought or hesitation.

Parenthesis (...) indicates words or phrases that can be left unspoken, at the discretion of the director or cast.

Thanks

Joe Murphy, Julia Barry, Davina Moss and all the Sherman Theatre, the cast, crew and creatives of Odyssey '84, *The Sherman Players, Cathy King and all at 42, Ceri Thompson, Benjamin Price and all at National Museum Wales Big Pit, Paul O'Sullivan, Lara McMillan, Mawgaine Tarrant-Cornish, Dom O'Hanlon and all at Methuen, Mark Jefferies, Gary Marsh, Menna, Phil, Matt, Maryline, Sophia and Joe Price, Chloë Moss, Franklin and Martha Moss Price.*

Odyssey '84 received its world premiere at Sherman Theatre on 11 October 2024.

For Franklin
The journey that stirs you now is not far off
Love,
Dad x

Act One

Scene One

IRA hideout

At a table, with a bag over his head, **O'Donnell** *sits restrained.*

A number of men in balaclavas stand around.

The bag is whisked from **O'Donnell**'s *head and a harsh light is shone on him.*

O'Donnell *blinks.*

McGinty   Can you see?

O'Donnell *nods.*

McGinty   Take your time.

O'Donnell *nods.*

O'Donnell   I can see.

McGinty   Good. Can you see him?

McGinty *points to* **Con**.

O'Donnell *nods.*

McGinty   Can you see what he's doing?

O'Donnell *nods.*

McGinty   What's he doing?

O'Donnell   He's holding a hammer and a chisel, to my knee.

McGinty   You know why?

O'Donnell   I don't.

McGinty   Guess.

O'Donnell   I don't know.

McGinty GUESS.

O'Donnell I DON'T FUCKING KNOW.

McGinty He's gonna hammer that fucking chisel into your knee if he thinks you're lying to us.

O'Donnell *nods.*

McGinty One fucking wrong word.

O'Donnell OK.

McGinty That chisel will go through to the back of your knee.

O'Donnell OK.

McGinty Did the Brits send you?

O'Donnell No.

O'Donnell *shakes his head.*

McGinty Did, the, Brits, send you?

O'Donnell *shakes his head.*

McGinty *looks to* **Con** *– are they convinced? Not so sure.*

Con *moves.*

O'Donnell They didn't!

McGinty Then how the fuck did you find us?

O'Donnell Well, it's …

McGinty How do you know my name?

O'Donnell I was given it by …

McGinty What the fuck are you doing out here anyway? Wandering around pubs asking after me?

O'Donnell Well, uhm … Well, it's

McGinty This already sounds like bullshit.

O'Donnell No, wait / … wait wait!

McGinty What do you say, Con?

Con I say bullshit.

Con *raises the hammer.*

O'Donnell WAIT, no! Wait / wait! Please listen listen.

McGinty You better start talking.

O'Donnell I just. It would be much easier if we could just put the …

McGinty You better start talking.

O'Donnell It's hard to think straight with a fucking chisel on my knee. Please.

McGinty *signals for* **Con** *to lower the tools.*

O'Donnell *breathes …*

O'Donnell Liam, Flaherty gave me your name.

McGinty How'd you know Liam?

O'Donnell Moscow.

Beat.

McGinty What the fuck are you talking about?

O'Donnell Revolutionary college. We were paired up in the international / program. I met him via the solidarity exchange.

McGinty Whoa whoa whoa. Stop. Stop. Stop. Go back to the beginning.

O'Donnell The beginning beginning?

McGinty Yes, man of many fucking turns, the beginning beginning. Tell us everything.

O'Donnell Everything?

McGinty Everything.

Silence.

O'Donnell Well, I suppose it all started … with the letter.

Scene Two

O'Donnell's home

O'Donnell *takes a letter from* **Penny***'s hand.*

Penny Are you done?

O'Donnell Nearly.

Beat.

Penny Now?

O'Donnell Nearly.

Penny *waits what feels like an age.*

Penny Are you done now?

O'Donnell Nea /rly.

Penny OH FUCKING HELL, / JOHN! HOW LONG DOES IT TAKE TO READ A FUCKING LETTER?

O'Donnell *nearly falls off his chair in fright.*

O'Donnell Jesus Christ! What are you shouting at me for? You scared the crap out of me, I'm trying to read this bloody thing.

Penny It's only / a page long, why's it taking you so long?

O'Donnell I can't bloody read it / with you asking me if I've read it every five seconds, can I?

Penny Just get on with it, / it's only a page!

O'Donnell Well, stop shouting at me then and let me get on with it, I would have read it by now!

Penny ...

A stand off.

O'Donnell *goes back to his letter.*

O'Donnell Lost my place / now.

Penny JESUS FUCKING / CHRIST, JOHN!

O'Donnell Stop shouting at me! You know I hate fighting!

Penny They want you to go on strike.

O'Donnell Where does it say that?

Penny Just read it.

Penny *silently combusts, dies and resurrects herself.*

Finally **O'Donnell** *puts the paper down.*

Penny *opens her mouth.*

O'Donnell *picks up the paper again.*

Penny *closes her mouth.*

O'Donnell *re- reads a section before putting it down.*

Penny *indicates she'd like a response.*

Penny Are you gonna say anything?

O'Donnell What do you want me to say?

Penny Are you gonna go on strike or not? Why are you making this so hard?

O'Donnell I dunno! We haven't voted yet. They say they want us to hold a vote in our individual pits.

Penny So, how are you gonna vote?

O'Donnell I dunno, I've just woken up and you've shoved a letter in my face.

Penny What do you think?

O'Donnell Well. I dunno.

Penny I want you to vote no.

O'Donnell OK.

Penny Do you want to strike?

O'Donnell No.

Penny Because you haven't got to do it. They can't make you.

O'Donnell I'm not gonna break a strike if the majority vote yes.

Penny They're not your boss, that's the whole point of a union, no one's in charge.

O'Donnell That's not / technically true.

He looks at the letter again before folding it up and putting it into his pocket.

Penny What if you get arrested?

O'Donnell For picketing?

Penny If you get arrested / doing this you'll get sacked and the Coal Board won't let you go back to work, even if they do back down. Remember what happened to Leanne's fella? He's a hospital porter now.

O'Donnell Why would they arrest me for picketing?

Penny Pushing people around in wheelchairs. How are we gonna get the house finished on that kind of money?

O'Donnell I've just woke up, I haven't even had a piss yet / and already you've got me pushing people round in wheelchairs.

Penny We can't afford you to lose your job.

O'Donnell It sounds like you wanna fight, so how about I just sit here in silence and you fight with yourself?

Penny You must have known this was happening. Did you?

O'Donnell Did I know that Thatcher planned to shut down twenty mines overnight? No, unfortunately I wasn't invited to that meeting.

Penny Don't be a dick, John.

O'Donnell You've got Thatcher and MacGregor and Scargill up here, and I'm all the way down here. Lower. I'm under the ground. I don't know what's going on, no one tells me nothing. And I'm glad 'cause I don't wanna know all this shit. I just wanna do my job.

Penny This is the worst, the *worst* possible time for us. The worst possible time for us.

O'Donnell I know.

Penny We're homeowners now. I'm trying to make this place nice, a home we can be proud of that we can have people around. But we've got leaks, we've got damp, what are people going to think, if we've been living here a year and we still haven't fixed the damp?

O'Donnell Who cares what people think?

Penny We've got two kids.

O'Donnell Who cares what people think?

Penny What people think of us, that's what we are.

O'Donnell I don't know if that's true.

Penny You don't understand, you're not a woman. How can we fix any of this if you're not working?

O'Donnell Might come to nothing.

Penny Mam came round yesterday to see Tommy because he got a merit in school, you know what she was wearing?

O'Donnell Nipple tassels, googly eyes and a fez?

Off **Penny**.

O'Donnell Sorry.

Penny I'm glad you find this funny.

O'Donnell What did she wear?

Penny Wellies. I wanted to *die*.

O'Donnell Why was she wearing wellies?

Penny Because our kitchen is like a pond with the leaking pipes.

O'Donnell Oh, it's not that bad.

Penny She's got wet feet so many times she said she thought it was easier. Everyone can see her coming and going in wellies.

O'Donnell When I get paid I'll get all the piping done.

Penny You're on strike!

O'Donnell I'm not!

Beat.

Yet.

Beat.

Might not happen.

(*Off* **Penny**.)

O'Donnell It might not.

Beat.

But y'know. If the boys / come out -

Penny This is Yorkshire's issue, they're not closing / any pits in Wales.

O'Donnell But if the boys come out what am I supposed to do?

Penny Persuade them to stay working.

O'Donnell It's not / that easy.

Penny You think Yorkshire would come out / for us? I don't think so.

O'Donnell You know I hate all this shit. I can't be arsed with it all.

Penny Promise me this one thing. Put us first.

O'Donnell I always do that.

Penny No you don't, but I want you to this time. Will you vote against going on strike?

Scene Three

Penrikyber Pit

O'Donnell *approaches a few* **Miners** *picketing outside the pit gates.*

Billy Here he is!

Dai Look who's shown his face.

O'Donnell What's going on?

Billy Get the letter?

O'Donnell Yeah. Where's your shoes?

Billy What did Penny say? Did she hit the roof? / She hit the roof, didn't she?

O'Donnell She was fine.

Billy   She hit the roof, / didn't she?

O'Donnell   No, she was fine, she's fine.

Dai   She hit the roof though, didn't she?

O'Donnell   No. She was fine.

Dai   Was she though?

O'Donnell *takes a moment before realising he can't keep up the pretence.*

O'Donnell   She went fucking mental, / she's been chewing my ear off all morning, / / she started before I even had a shit.

Billy   I knew it!

Dai   Cathy was shouting so much the dog wouldn't come out from behind the sofa.

O'Donnell   What about Lisa? / What did she say?

Billy   I didn't wait for her to read it, I just grabbed it and ran out of the house. Still got my slippers on.

The three laugh.

O'Donnell   Right, come on, we'd better head in and do this ballot then.

Dai   Oh you're too late, Johnny boy.

Widespread laughter which **O'Donnell** *joins in with.*

O'Donnell   What?

Billy   Ceri. John's wondering when we're gonna have a ballot.

Ceri   John-ow! Good to see you. So the news is, we had a meeting, and we actually had a vote on whether we should have a vote on striking or not.

Beat.

O'Donnell Right.

Ceri And we democratically decided, by consensus, in a formal motion, ratified by the committee of Penrikyber Colliery Lodge, that we didn't want to hold a vote on whether to strike or not.

Pause.

O'Donnell Let me get this right. You lot, had a vote on whether you should have a vote or not, and you voted against having a vote?

Ceri That's right.

O'Donnell That is the Welshest thing I have ever heard.

Ceri Point being. We're not voting on whether we support miners whose jobs are on the line. No debate.

Billy No debate.

Ceri No discussion.

Dai No discussion.

Ceri We're out.

Ceri *goes back to painting signs.*

Billy Yay! Striking.

The boys dress **O'Donnell** *as a picket with arm bands, pin badges and placard.*

Dai Penny's gonna / kill you.

O'Donnell What about a national ballot?

Ceri Scargill's not gonna call a national ballot.

O'Donnell Why not?

Billy It's the threshold, innit.

O'Donnell   The what?

Ceri   Don't you go to any of the meetings?

Billy   He can't be arsed, Ceri, he'd rather be in the garden.

O'Donnell *whacks* **Billy**.

Ceri   They changed the threshold for it to be legal for the NUM to strike, we have to get fifty-five per cent of members voting yes, not just a majority, and we've not hit it the last three times we've balloted.

Dai   She never threatens a Nottingham pit, so Nottingham never votes to strike.

Ceri   Thatcher *wants* us to ballot because …

Billy   We always lose.

Dai   We always lose.

O'Donnell   I'll bloody vote this time.

Ceri   So rather than holding a national ballot we're going pit to pit on whether to go on strike or not.

Billy   Picket the pits who want to work, and then we get a national strike without calling it a national strike.

Ceri   Thatcher shifted the goal posts, so Scargill shifted the penalty spot.

Billy   Yay! Striking.

Ceri   Bill.

Billy   What?

Ceri   Grab these signs by here. No one's coming in today, let's get over the mountain to Deep Navigation, make sure they're coming out too. / I want the whole of the South Wales coalfield shut down today.

Billy   Dai, give me a hand with these.

Dai *helps* **Billy** *pick up the signs and they follow the others.*

O'Donnell *remains.*

Billy   John grab those ones will you?

A beat as **O'Donnell** *doesn't move.*

Dai   Come on, we'll miss the bus.

Can **O'Donnell** *turn his back on his friends?*

Billy   John? Hurry up!

O'Donnell *picks up the signs and follows them off-stage.*

Scene Four

Picketing in Wales

Billy, **Dai**, **O'Donnell** *and* **Ceri** *picket a mine. A* **Miner** (**Kev**) *approaches.*

Ceri   Alright, this is an official NUM picket line, we're asking you not to cross.

Kev   But. We voted to go back to work.

Ceri   We voted to go out on strike.

Kev   Well, go on strike then.

Ceri   We're asking you to come out.

Kev   Picket your own pit.

Ceri   We have and we're all out because we've got a sense of solidarity / with our comrades in Yorkshire.

O'Donnell   Maybe we should …

Kev   I 've gotta work!

Ceri   Have you really though?

Kev   Yes.

Ceri   You'll be labelled a scab / forever.

Kev *goes for* **Ceri** -

Kev Don't you fucking / dare! Scargill said we can all decide ourselves!

Dai Whoa / whoa whoa!

Billy Easy! / Calm down!

Ceri You gonna / cross a picket line then, are you? Is that what you're gonna do?

Kev I fucking will because we've voted to work!

Ceri Then you're a scab!

A fight breaks out. Ad lib as **Kev** *and* **Ceri** *wrestle and* **Billy** *and* **Dai** *and the others try to separate them.*

O'Donnell Fuck this, I'm going home.

O'Donnell *starts to walk away.*

Ad lib the next exchange.

Kev Who are you / calling a scab? I'll fucking smash your face in.

Ceri Come on / then, you fucking scab! Let's have it.

Dai Ceri! / Fucking hell, leave it, leave it, lads.

Billy Whoa! Knock it off! / John! Grab him! Grab him!

Billy *and* **Dai** *are pulling* **Ceri** *and* **Kev** *apart.*

Billy John! John! Give us a hand! JOHN!

O'Donnell *watches them, he looks to his exit and back to them.*

He can't leave them.

O'Donnell *runs back and holds* **Ceri**.

Billy *gets between them.*

Billy Everyone, calm / down. Calm down.

Ceri He's a scab!

O'Donnell CERI!

Dai Knock it off. / Fucking hell.

O'Donnell Everyone calm down. / Fighting's not gonna solve nothing.

Ceri This is an official / picket!

Kev We voted / to work!

Billy He's not striking, / Ceri.

Ceri He bloody should be! / We're the South Wales miners.

We're the leaders of this union.

Kev Don't tell me what I should / be doing.

Billy Look! OK. OK. OK. Stop. Stop it, everyone. Listen. I'm Billy, this is Dai, John and Ceri. (*Add any other names if we have ensemble.*)

What's yours?

Kev Kev.

Billy Kev. I don't wanna strike neither. I don't.

Dai Nor me.

O'Donnell Nor me.

Billy None of us do.

Ceri I do.

Pause.

Kev I don't wanna be an arsehole. / But this one's different.

Billy No one thinks you're an arsehole.

Ceri I do.

Billy None of us do. Everyone's gotta make their own choices and put their own families first.

Beat.

You got kids?

Kev Two.

Billy Same as us, we've got two.

Beat.

We're not together, we've got two with our wives, we've all got wives individually, / individual wives, three // wives between us. And two children each, six in total, six. I've got two, he's got two, he's got two with our own separate wives.

O'Donnell Bill. Bill.

Dai We're all. We're …

Beat.

We're all thinking about our kids. Aren't we?

Kev Yeah.

Dai But going to work today means something it didn't yesterday.

This lands with **O'Donnell**.

Dai Lines have been drawn. Not by us. But they've been drawn. And there's a battle ahead. So we've just come to ask; whose side are you on?

Dai, **Billy** *and* **O'Donnell** *make space for* **Kev** *to cross the line, eventually* **Ceri** *joins them.*

A moment as **Kev** *weighs this up. He looks everyone in the eye.*

He offers a hand to **Dai**, *then* **Billy**, *then* **O'Donnell** *and finally after a pause …* **Ceri**.

Billy Thank you.

Kev Thanks, butt.

Kev *turns to walk away.*

O'Donnell Do you really think there's a battle ahead? Not just gonna be a couple days' strike.

Ceri I dunno. Remember all that business with the coal cutter teeth? Maybe they've been planning this for ages.

A moment for **O'Donnell**.

They see more **Miners** *approaching ...*

Dai Come on then.

Billy *and* **Dai** *intercept* **Miners**:

A conversation, a handshake and a turn, a coming together between our heroes and strangers. **O'Donnell** *watches.*

More **Miners** *approach,* **O'Donnell** *watches as a conversation, a handshake and a turn with* **Billy** *becomes a beautiful moment of solidarity between* **Billy** *and a stranger.*

A **Miner** *approaches and* **Billy**, **Dai** *and* **Ceri** *are occupied so* **O'Donnell** *finds himself stepping forward, he takes the stranger's hand, a conversation, a handshake and turn and solidarity is forged.* **O'Donnell** *begins to find his place in this fight. The harmony with a stranger is inspiring.*

Scene Five

A phone box / O'Donnell's home - night time

O'Donnell Hey.

Penny Hey.

O'Donnell I'm guessing you heard.

Penny Yup.

O'Donnell We're all out. Every pit in South Wales is out on strike.

Penny Jesus Christ.

O'Donnell Yeah.

Penny How long for?

O'Donnell Well, no one knows.

Penny What are people saying?

O'Donnell Three weeks. Six weeks tops.

Penny *exhales.*

O'Donnell Can we not fight about this?

Penny OK, let's celebrate it, shall we?

Silence.

O'Donnell I love you.

Penny Don't.

O'Donnell I love you.

Penny No.

O'Donnell I love you. You have to say it. That's the rules.

Penny Let me be angry with you, at least give me that.

O'Donnell Say it.

Penny I love you. And you're a twat.

O'Donnell Thank you.

Penny I just feel like in these things, I don't count.

O'Donnell That's not true. I'm doing it for you.

Penny I don't want you to do it.

Beat.

O'Donnell The only way we'll win is if we turn the lights off. And the only way we'll do that is if every miner goes on strike. Scargill said, if your coalfield is out and the strike in your area is solid, he wants us to go and picket the mines that voted to stay open.

Penny So you're picketing? Where?

O'Donnell Nottingham.

Penny You're going to picket mines in Nottingham.

O'Donnell I think so, yeah.

Penny You think, or you are?

O'Donnell Yeah … well, yeah I, think I am. If that's OK?

Penny It's not OK.

Silence.

O'Donnell I really think I should.

Penny Let someone else picket, someone without kids and a mortgage.

Silence.

O'Donnell I think I should go.

Penny You mean you want to go.

O'Donnell I'm a miner.

Penny And a husband and a father. What's more important?

O'Donnell That's not fair. Obviously you and the kids.

Silence.

But today. I realised. I wouldn't have any of you if it wasn't for this job.

Penny I'm not with you for the money.

O'Donnell No, I know that, I know that. I'm not saying that about you, I'm saying it about me. I would never, have got you, if I wasn't / a miner.

Penny I don't *care* that you're a miner.

O'Donnell I do! I care. I've got two O levels and one of them is in gardening. And somehow, I got you.

Beat.

And two gorgeous kids.

Beat.

And a home. And I got that, because one day I walked up to the gates of Penrikyber and asked if they had any apprenticeships and the next day I had a locker with my name on it and three pairs of overalls. I would never have got the guts to speak to you if I wasn't a miner. I've always known it, but today brought it all home.

Beat.

What am If I'm not a miner? Nothing.

Penny Don't say that.

O'Donnell If I lose my job, I'll lose everything.

Penny That's not true, and anyway, they're not coming for your job.

O'Donnell Well.

Penny Well, what? Have you heard something? Is your pit under threat?

O'Donnell They've been sending us equipment. The wrong equipment. For months.

Penny So?

O'Donnell It goes down as a cost. Against the pit. If we send it back or store it, whatever, it still goes down as a cost against our pit.

Penny Right.

O'Donnell The more random bits of new kit we have, the more our costs go up and our profits go down.

Penny I don't follow.

O'Donnell They've been falsely inflating our costs for the best part of a year.

Penny What would be the point in that?

O'Donnell To *make* our pit unprofitable.

Silence.

Penny No, that's paranoia.

O'Donnell I thought so too, but now …

Penny These Yorkshire pits are unprofitable.

O'Donnell That's what they say. But are they really?

Penny No, this is NUM paranoia; they've got into your head after one day. You sound like Ceri.

O'Donnell Right, we've needed new teeth for the coal cutter since June last year. The coal cutter's slowing right down. We've ordered new teeth over and over again. They keep sending us all sorts of crap, everything except new teeth. So the cutter's slowing right down and we're fetching up less coal. Costs going up, productivity going down for months. I thought we were going mad. So we asked Clive in Deep Duffryn to order the same coal cutter teeth that we needed.

Penny And?

O'Donnell They came the next day.

Penny How can they get them but you can't?

O'Donnell You tell me. But the Coal Board won't give us the equipment we need. The only reason we're profitable is because we dug an underground road into Deep Duffryn's mine and they passed us the equipment through a hole in the wall. If they hadn't, we'd be on that list too.

Penny Why would the Coal Board try to shut down a profitable pit?

O'Donnell We've toppled two prime ministers. She'd rather shut down a whole industry than live in fear of the NUM. And we're the militant pit in South Wales.

Penny You really believe this?

O'Donnell I didn't. But I'm starting to, yeah.

Beat.

Penny You think she'd take your job away to keep hers safe?

O'Donnell I do, yeah.

Beat.

Are you still angry?

Penny Yes. No. I don't know, John. I don't know what to think.

O'Donnell I've run out of coins, Penny.

Penny OK. Promise me you -

The line is dead.

Penny *hangs up.*

Suddenly she heaves. She runs off.

Lights down.

Scene Six

Picketing Nottingham

Movement sequence to 'Only You' by the Flying Pickets or something similar.

O'Donnell, **Billy** *and* **Dai** *discover picketing a contested coalfield is a different matter. They enter with their placards from South Wales.*

The boys attempt their peaceful approaches to **Miners** *but they are pushed and shoved away -* **Miners** *wanting to work tear down their placards and destroy them.*

O'Donnell *tries to broker a peace between the* **Miners** *and* **Billy** *and* **Dai** *but can't contain the aggression.*

Fights break out and **O'Donnell** *is thumped and knocked to the floor - he crawls away and spits blood.*

Looking back at the melee, **O'Donnell** *weighs up what to do - does he walk away or does he fight?*

O'Donnell *runs into the melee and before he knows it, he throws some punches,* **O'Donnell** *knocks a man to the ground, and then another. The other* **Miners** *back off, intimidated by* **O'Donnell**.

O'Donnell *looks at his fists - he's good at this.*

Police *arrive and escort the working* **Miners** *away.*

O'Donnell *is left alone on stage, victorious but with blood drawn - he is becoming hardened to the battle.*

Scene Seven

O'Donnell's home

Penny *mops up* **O'Donnell***'s spit.*

Penny   The place is a tip.

Shaz   It's fine.

Penny   Don't look at the sink, I'm bleaching it.

Shaz   It's fine.

Penny   I'm trying to ration the washing up liquid, so.

Shaz   Stop fussing.

Penny   I wasn't expecting anyone.

Shaz   The place is spotless, you should see mine.

Penny   I don't have anything in.

Shaz   It looks lovely. You, on the other hand.

Penny What?

Shaz You look awful.

Penny Thanks.

Shaz Not sleeping?

Beat.

Have you heard from him?

Penny *shakes her head.*

Shaz Dean called and said they'd eaten chips eight days in a row. Between that and the drinking, Iesu Mawr. God knows what shape they'll be in when they get back.

Penny John said six weeks and that was six weeks ago.

Shaz Dean said four. But then, four pints to Dean is eight. So take from that what you will.

Penny He hasn't called in days.

Shaz This lot, when they get together they think they can beat the bloody Nazis with some pin badges and a brass band.

Penny Can't be much longer, can it?

Shaz I dunno.

Penny What have you heard?

Shaz I haven't heard nothing.

Penny Why'd you think it's gonna be longer, then? Last time it was six weeks.

Shaz Last time it was autumn. Can't turn the lights off if no one's putting them on.

Penny *is in some discomfort.*

Shaz You OK?

Penny Fine. Just feel a bit …

Shaz   How far gone are you?

Penny *stops.*

Penny   You haven't told him.

Beat.

Are you gonna tell him?

Penny   I'm scared.

Beat.

I can't have a third. I'm so embarrassed.

Shaz   Nothing to be embarrassed about.

Penny   Not being careful at our age. And - I feel sick. I'm wasting food. I cook something and then it's - I can't face eating it but I can't be throwing away food, not now.

Shaz   There's never a good time to have a baby, come on.

Penny   What if we lose everything?

Shaz   Come on.

Penny   If we didn't have his strike pay we'd lose everything in weeks. I don't want to be poor or homeless.

Shaz   They'll be back before we know it.

Penny   I lie in bed and I just watch the clock go round. / Another night, another night and I think …

Shaz   It's just whoever can swallow their bloody pride first.

Penny   I don't love him. I don't love him for doing this to us. To me. To the kids.

Beat.

I worry that the feeling will go. That'll he come back, but it'll be too late. Something will break in me.

Beat.

And I won't be able to pull it back.

Beat.

What if he comes back and I love him, but I don't want him anymore?

Silence.

Shaz You need to come down the club.

Penny I'm not drinking.

Shaz You need to come down the club.

Scene Eight

Northern Workingmen's Club

A bandaged **O'Donnell** *unfolds a map on a pub table.* **Miners** *stand around and listen.*

Dai The police have closed the roads here and here.

Dai *marks the map with a pen.*

Billy Tomorrow morning, the boys from Deep Navigation are going to set out early and head down this alleyway here. They're gonna try and pull the police from this road by here.

Beat.

But if we can't get down the road before the set up, then we're gonna be trapped and sitting ducks all day.

O'Donnell What if we can get the Trelewis Drift boys to come here? This cross roads. Give me the pen.

O'Donnell *starts marking up.*

If they can get there and create a barricade here. Tyrone and the Tower boys can get there. That's the main route they're using to get to the gates.

O'Donnell *notices* **Ceri** *enter, stressed.*

O'Donnell With, with a barricade there - that means we'll have time, we'll have time to get through this alleyway and to the gates.

Billy Alright, Napoleon.

O'Donnell Here, carry on.

O'Donnell *hands* **Billy** *the pen.*

O'Donnell *heads over to* **Ceri**.

O'Donnell Everything alright, Ceri?

Ceri What?

O'Donnell You OK?

Ceri I'm fine.

Ceri *takes a shot of whisky.*

O'Donnell *sits with him.*

Ceri *takes a deep breath and then discreetly confesses to* **O'Donnell**.

Ceri We're running out of strike pay.

Saying it out loud means **Ceri** *needs another drink.*

O'Donnell We've only been out ten weeks. How are we running out of money?

Ceri Every move we make, she's ahead of us. Every move. She's there. We shut down South Wales, turns out she's been stockpiling coal for years. We thought we had her with the ballot, but now she's changed the law to stop picketing.

O'Donnell What?

Ceri Oh, we can picket, yeah - with a maximum of six men.

O'Donnell *laughs.*

O'Donnell You're joking?

Off **Ceri**.

O'Donnell She can't do that. We can't shut anything down with six people at the gate. We can't. We'll just ignore it. What are they gonna do, arrest every one of us?

Ceri No. She'll fine us. She's been fining us. South Wales District is getting fined every time we picket with more than six people. And it's South Wales miners running this strike.

O'Donnell That's every bloody picket.

Ceri The fines are getting bigger and bigger, we're not paying them. We're paying lawyers to fight it but it's costing a bloody fortune. South Wales District is gonna run out of strike pay in two weeks.

Ceri *takes another drink.*

O'Donnell *pours himself a drink and takes a drink.*

Ceri I'm gonna sound like an idiot now. But I thought this was gonna be fun.

Beat.

I thought we were gonna stick it to them again.

Beat.

Another victory for the miners.

Beat.

But they're sticking it to us.

Ceri *drinks.*

I led a lot of people into this. It's my fault they're here.

O'Donnell We're all grown ups, we all made our own choices. Hey. We did.

Ceri Thank you.

Beat.

I'm just so tired. I'm exhausted, I fell asleep in a meeting earlier.

O'Donnell   You need to rest, you've been on the go for weeks.

Ceri   I suppose the one benefit of the strike collapsing is that at least there won't *be* any more meetings.

O'Donnell   Hey, come on.

Ceri   I'm serious. If the Government doesn't kill me with dirty tricks, the NUM will with one very long agenda-less meeting.

O'Donnell   What are we gonna do about the strike pay?

Ceri   I don't know.

Beat.

Ponty wants three volunteers for the fundraising committee but I can't even think about that now.

Billy   John! Look at this.

O'Donnell *gets up and heads over to the boys looking at a map.*

Something stops him. He looks back to **Ceri** *who has his head in his hands.*

He goes back to **Ceri**.

O'Donnell   Ceri.

Beat.

If you want. I'll do it.

Ceri   Do what?

O'Donnell   The fundraising. I'll volunteer. If we're gonna keep the boys out we need money. I'll do my bit getting the donations. If that's what Ponty wants.

Ceri   Oh that's brilliant, John. I just need two more.

O'Donnell   Billy! Dai!

Billy *and* **Dai** *come over.*

O'Donnell   They've volunteered as well.

Ceri   Brilliant.

Dai   What?

Billy   Hang on, what are we doing?

O'Donnell   Fundraising committee.

Dai   Fundraising for what?

Ceri   The strike, Dai. The strike.

Billy   What's going on?

O'Donnell   Ponty needs three men to go round collecting money, and collecting sharpish.

Ceri   Here's the address of the first fundraiser.

O'Donnell *reads it.*

Billy   Hang on, what about the picket tomorrow?

Ceri   You're not doing that you're going to …

O'Donnell   Perth.

Dai   Where the fuck is that?

Ceri   Listen now. The Government might seize our bank accounts. So none of this can go through NUM accounts. We have to keep this a secret. Don't tell anyone where you're going, especially the wives. Our phones are getting tapped and there's informers in the NUM. Collect the money and then there'll be a secret network of people who will smuggle it back to South Wales without the police knowing.

Billy   So we were soldiers, and now we're spies.

Ceri   Yes. You're now spies.

Billy   Champion.

Dai So it's just pick up the money and drop off it off to someone else.

Ceri Exactly.

Dai We can do that.

O'Donnell Pick up, drop off done.

Dai Pick up, drop off done.

O'Donnell *makes to leave followed by* **Billy** *and* **Dai**.

Ceri Pick up, little speech say thanks drop off. Done.

O'Donnell, **Billy** *and* **Dai** *stop.*

O'Donnell What did you say?

Ceri Pick up drop off done.

O'Donnell You said something else.

Ceri No I didn't.

O'Donnell You said, 'little speech'.

Ceri Yeah, pick up little speech, drop off done.

O'Donnell What you mean 'little speech?'

Ceri It's a fundraiser.

Beat.

There'll be hundreds of people there.

O'Donnell So.

Ceri You're striking miners at a striking miners fundraiser where they're gonna give you money. You're gonna have to give a little speech.

Billy Whoa whoa whoa, / hang on, // now hang on, I thought we were spies.

Ceri What? What did I say? What's the big deal?

O'Donnell   What do you / mean 'give a speech'? You didn't say nothing about a speech.

Dai   I'm not making a speech / I'm not doing nothing like that.

Ceri   A little speech / saying thanks that's all.

O'Donnell   What are you talking about / 'speech'?

Ceri   Nothing / special.

Dai   Hang on hang / on hang on hang on

Ceri   Nothing / special.

Billy   Hang on. / No speeches.

Dai   No / speeches.

Billy   We're not / doing speeches.

Ceri   It's nothing special, just say thank you and tell them why the money's so important.

Billy   Hang on! / Tell them why the money's so important?

Dai   Whoa! Why've we got to / say why it's so important?

Ceri   We've got to say why we need it or they won't give any more will they? So a little speech saying thank you this money is very much important, and telling them exactly what's going on for us. The real side of things / not what's in the papers.

Billy   First it's pick up and drop off then it's just say thanks, then it's a little speech on why the money's so important now it's tell them what's going on? We're not bloody politicians.

Ceri   No even better - you're miners.

Dai   We can't do public speaking. I can barely get the kids to listen to me. We're heading men, he's a spark.

Ceri You're striking miners. It is the miners' destiny to lead this country on the road to socialism. Go out there and inspire them to support us.

Scene Nine

Cynon Valley Workingmen's Hall

There are boxes stacked up and **Women** *working, packing boxes.*

Shaz Penny's here.

Lucy Hiya, love!

Shaz Where's the food parcels?

Lucy Over by there.

Shaz By here?

Lucy By there.

Shaz By here?

Lucy By there, yeah.

Another woman, **Vicky**, *enters the club and is looking at food parcels.*

Penny What's this?

Shaz This is the ... what are - what are we? Penrhiwceiber, Women ... Support / the Miners' Committee.

Lucy Women's / Committee for ...

Shaz For Supporting / the

Lucy Solidarity with / the Women and Wives.

Shaz Women and Wives / Solidarity with the Miners Committee.

Lucy The / Committee for ...

Shaz For Christ's sake. We're the women, that's all you need to know. We're the women we organise food parcels, coal, toys for the kids, clothing, sanitary products, when everyone's struggling. We struggle together.

Shaz *holds out some parcels.*

Penny Oh no, keep this for those people who need it.

Shaz Take it.

Penny No, no, we're fine. You keep this for people who need it. I don't need it.

Shaz You need it.

Penny I'm fine.

Beat.

Honestly, I'm fine.

Shaz *takes* **Penny** *to one side.*

Shaz I take parcels. We all take parcels. And we all make up parcels for other people. Nothing to be embarrassed about.

Beat.

The only person here making you feel bad is you.

Beat.

It's not forever.

Vicky *staggers on her feet, she's about to faint. Everyone rushes around her.*

Penny Whoa, whoa. Here we are, you're alright, you're alright, I've got you. You're OK.

Lucy I'll get some water.

Vicky I'm so sorry. I don't know what came over me.

Shaz That's alright, love.

Vicky Just felt all light headed.

Lucy Here you go. Try that.

Vicky *drinks some water.*

Lucy When was the last time you ate, love?

Vicky I don't know.

Shaz What's your name?

Vicky Vicky.

Shaz You eaten today, Vicky?

Vicky No.

Shaz You eat yesterday?

Vicky No.

Shaz You think you've eaten this week at all?

Vicky I've got three kids.

Lucy It's a shock seeing all the food.

Vicky I feel so stupid.

Lucy N / o!

Shaz Don't / be daft!

Lucy Don't be so silly.

Penny It's fine.

Shaz Do you think you could manage a biscuit?

Vicky Umm … I don't know.

Penny We'll all have one. We'll have one, / let's have a biscuit. Shall we have a biscuit?

Shaz Yes, let's all have a biscuit.

Lucy I fancy a biscuit. All this packing, worked up an appetite.

Lucy *gets a pack of biscuits out and hands one to everyone, including* **Vicky**.

Penny There we are.

Shaz I love these ones.

Vicky *holds the biscuit and looks at it, everyone watches.*

Eventually **Vicky** *takes a bite. She eats the biscuit and a sob escapes her.*

Penny *puts an arm around her.*

Shaz Dean likes Hobnobs but I don't like the bits.

Lucy Oh, the oaty ones. They get in your teeth.

Shaz It's like eating sand.

Vicky James likes those ones. Thank you. Sorry, I'm so embarrassed.

Penny That's alright. We're all just trying our best.

Shaz *smiles.*

Scene Ten

Fundraising Montage

A microphone is placed on stage.

Spotlight on **Dai**, **O'Donnell** *and* **Billy**, *one of them holds a cheque.*

O'Donnell *smiles, he sees* **Dai** *and* **Billy** *looking terrified, he nudges them and both try to fix their smiles.*

O'Donnell *clears his throat.*

Dai *and* **Billy** *clear their throats.*

Some comedy business with a mic being too short, too high, feedbacking. **Billy** *adjusts the mic and it whacks him in the face, causing his swearing to be amplified.*

Billy (*amplified*)   ffUCKING thing.

Long silence.

O'Donnell *clears his throat.*

O'Donnell   Alright?

Dai   Alright or wha'?

Billy   Alright or wha'?

O'Donnell *clears his throat.*

O'Donnell   Yeah. Uh. So. Well. Um, what it is, is. Me. And the boys by here. Are.

Dai   We're on strike, like.

Billy   On strike, like.

O'Donnell   Yeah what it is, is, we're on strike like. And well. Y'know. Like. It's, y'know.

O'Donnell *entirely loses his nerve.*

He turns his back on the mic and heads towards **Billy** *and* **Dai** *who spin him around and comically push him back to the mic.*

O'Donnell *opens him mouth but his mouth is dry, he has nothing.*

Billy *sidles up.*

Billy   Say thank you.

O'Donnell   Thank you.

Billy   Not to me to them.

O'Donnell   Oh yeah. Thank you.

Billy *implores him.*

O'Donnell   For, this, cheque.

Billy *implores him to be more enthusiastic.*

O'Donnell   It's. It's. Well, it's *fucking* brilliant is what it is.

Billy *and* **Dai** *put their heads in their hands.*

O'Donnell *turns to look at the oversized cheque they are holding.*

O'Donnell   To have the support of **Dai** *moves his hand so* **O'Donnell** *can read*

O'Donnell   The Christian Mother's Union, Perth.

O'Donnell *hangs his head in disastrous shame.*

SFX Flash.

A new angle, a new cheque. **Dai** *and* **Billy** *bundle* **O'Donnell** *to the mic.*

O'Donnell   Uh uh uh uh. Yeah, thank you. Yeah, thanks to …

Reads cheque

The workers of Amrex, Plastic Mouldings Factory, Lancashire.

Beat.

Yeah. Thanks. It's … great to. Um. Yeah. Have the, y'know money. It's great - money. Is. You know.

O'Donnell *searches for a word, with his hands he makes a shape although it's not clear what the shape is.*

(*To* **Dai**.) Say something. Say something political.

Dai   Free Nelson Mandela.

O'Donnell   About the strike! Bill! Say something! Anything.

Billy   No!

O'Donnell *pushes him to the mic.*

Billy *has nothing, and then, a thought strikes him.*

Billy   Coming here, we went on a road and it was the B470! B470. Amazing.

O'Donnell Alright.

Billy Single carriageway.

SFX Flash - New cheque, new angle. Printworkers Union London Branch. New banner at the back.

O'Donnell So what I'm trying to say is, sometimes, you're the hammer and sometimes you're the nail.

Billy And sometimes you just get screwed.

SFX Flash - New cheque, new angle. Lesbian and Gay Men Support the Miners. New banner at the back.

O'Donnell This is. It's. You know. Yeah. We're. We're. Uh. We're in the fight of our lives here we are. So, yeah. It means a lot. The Miners! / United! Will never be defeated!

Billy United! // Will never be defeated!

Dai United! Will never be defeated!

*They all raise a fist in solidarity, but **Dai** gets the wrong hand and has to correct himself.*

O'Donnell Thank you, thank you very much.

Scene Eleven

London

O'Donnell, **Dai** *and* **Billy** *step away from the mic and colourful*

Members of the Queer Community *shake their hands and hand them drinks etc.*

Community Member One Good luck, boys.

O'Donnell Thank you.

Community Member Two Stay strong.

Dai Thank you.

Community Member Three All my family are Welsh.

Billy Oh, very good.

Community Member Three My dear old grandmother was from (*pronounced poorly*) Tonyrefail!

Billy Oh, Tonyrefail! Not far from us.

Community Member Three Yes, she was the sweetest old lady. And ever since I was little she used to say 'fuck the Tories, they're a pack of lying bastards'.

Pause.

Billy Well, that's lovely.

Community Member Three She's dead now.

Community Member Three *leaves.*

O'Donnell OK. So, stay sharp. We're in London now.

Money in you socks and you piss in the cubicles. No talking to strangers.

A drag queen, **Lily***, approaches the boys.*

Lily Are you OK, boys? Can I get you anything?

O'Donnell No / no, we're fine … we're fine, thanks.

Dai Cham /pion, thanks.

Billy Super, thanks.

Lily Do you guys want a joint?

Silence.

A smoke?

O'Donnell Um …

Billy Cannabis?

Lily Yes, cannabis.

O'Donnell We're / OK, / / thanks.

Lily Yeah.

Billy   Yes please, yeah.

O'Donnell   Boys? What are you doing?

Billy   Just a little one. No harm in that.

Dai   Yeah, it's fine. Relax.

Billy   Relax. One little toke before bed.

O'Donnell (*to* **Billy**)   One toke.

Billy   Yeah, yeah.

O'Donnell (*to* **Dai**)   You. One fucking toke.

Dai   Yeah.

Lily *holds out a joint.*

O'Donnell   I'm going to get a drink.

O'Donnell *heads to the bar.*

O'Donnell   Pint of lager, please.

Hannah *the barmaid pours a lager for* **O'Donnell**.

Hannah   I enjoyed your speech.

O'Donnell   It wasn't a speech. I'm no good at this stuff.

Hannah   You were great. Genuine.

O'Donnell   Genuinely awful.

Hannah   You're being daft. How's the strike going for you?

O'Donnell   I'm exhausted. Want to get home. It's been months on the road. Just want it all over now.

Hannah   Even if she backs down this time, it won't be over.

O'Donnell   She'll back down, and then she'll have to stand down. New Prime Minister by Christmas.

Hannah   And you think that'll be the end of it?

O'Donnell *shrugs.*

O'Donnell You don't think so?

Hannah The men here have only been allowed to be gay for the past seventeen years. Before that, they would have jailed them just for being themselves. Not just for defending a job but for existing.

O'Donnell You fought, you won. It's legal now.

Hannah Go ask any one of them if they feel safe.

Silence.

O'Donnell We just want to go back to the way things were.

Hannah Then you're a fucking idiot.

O'Donnell Excuse me?

Hannah There is a reason why every marginalised and disenfranchised group is throwing money at you and supporting your cause.

O'Donnell Because what's happened to us is totally unfair.

Hannah You're the biggest group out there. Hundreds of thousands of straight white men; you're an army. You can break things the rest of us can only dream of. Yeah, protect your jobs but don't forget about us. If you can put people before profits in your community, maybe you can do that for the rest of us.

O'Donnell It's about more than jobs?

Hannah Yes, it's about people.

Lily Which one of you's the top and which one of you's the bottom?

Dai Well I'm the driver and he's the tail.

Billy Depends who's on shift.

Dai But we're both heading men. Well we're supposed to be.

Lily But *is* that what you are, darlings?

Dai That's what we're paid to do.

Billy We're not paid anymore.

Billy No. Well I dunno. What are we?

Lily Are we *more* than our jobs?

Dai Wow. Are we more than our jobs?

Billy Fucking hell.

Dai Is this strike - are we making the biggest mistake of our lives by defining ourselves by what we get *paid* to do rather than who we *really* are? But who are we really?

Billy Billy and, Dai?

Dai Maybe we're brilliant at, formula one driving. Or being an astronaut. We've never done nothing else.

Billy We've never done anything else.

Dai We've never done nothing else right. What if we're terrible miners?

Billy *bursts out laughing.*

Billy We might be shit.

Dai We might be shit! What if we're shit?

They piss themselves laughing.

If we were terrible, I hope someone would say.

Lily They might be too embarrassed. Here comes Billy and Dai; quick, everyone get some coal for them to push around.

Billy and **Dai** *are howling.*

Dai Someone would say. Someone would say.

Billy I hope so.

Lily I expect so, I can't imagine anyone worrying about your feelings down the pit.

Dai What do you mean?

Lily Mining. It's not famous for being a very, feelings- orientated industry. I can't imagine you two sitting around talking about your deepest darkest fears, I might be wrong.

Dai Yeah, you might be wrong.

Lily Might I?

Dai Yeah.

Lily Convince me.

Dai Well. Have you ever seen a friend die, right in front of you?

Long silence.

Lily Yes, I have unfortunately.

Dai Oh. Sorry to hear that. Was it someone old or …

Lily My age. My friend.

Dai Then you get it. We lost our friend Rory, underground.

Billy *raises his glass in a non- verbal cheers.*

Without looking, **Dai** *clinks* **Billy**'s *glass.*

Dai Brutal death. But we can't talk to our wives or family about it. So we have to keep it between ourselves.

Dai If we told them what really happened.

Billy They'd try to stop us working.

Dai So we keep it between us.

Billy He can tell when my head's gone. I can tell him to fuck off and it's fine. 'Cause he knows.

Beat.

And 'cause he knows, being with him helps. Don't have to talk. Just him walking with me is enough sometimes. Being by my side. I'm blessed to have him.

Lily When I lost my, friend. I didn't want to talk about it, but I couldn't be around people who didn't know either. Thank God for my gay family.

Dai What's a gay family?

Billy Yeah, what's a gay family?

Lily Well, they're friends who come to your rescue.

Pause.

Billy Maybe we're a gay family, Dai?

Dai Yeah, sounds just like us. Can we be one?

Lily Of course, we come in all shapes and sizes. You've just got to promise to always be there for each other.

Billy I promise.

Dai I promise.

Lily Well now, you're a big gay family.

Billy *and* **Dai** *clink glasses.*

Billy Tidy.

Lily *raises a glass and* **Billy** *and* **Dai** *toast it.*

Dai So, what do you do then?

Lily Darling, I'm professionally fabulous.

Billy How'd you get into that then?

Lily Somebody get me a blanket and a shoebox - I'm gonna have to take these two home. I sing, darling. I sing, I entertain, I bring a touch of class to this shithole. Shall I sing a song for you?

Billy Yeah, crack on, take your belt off.

Lily JORGE, YOU CUNT, we're going hard on Bonnie tonight.

Music starts up!

Lily *starts to perform a raucous number like 'I Need a Hero' which gets everyone dancing.*

O'Donnell *turns back to* **Dai** *and* **Billy***, they are now smoking massive bongs and giggling.*

O'Donnell OK guys, that's enough … Come on, time to go.

Dai Relax.

O'Donnell It's time.

Billy John. Chill. Just relax. Have a smoke.

O'Donnell No. We've got to go.

Billy We don't wanna go.

Dai We're having a great time!

Billy Yeah, come on! Loosen up, Dad.

Dai *guffaws.*

Dai Yeah, Dad.

Much hilarity between **Billy** *and* **Dai***.*

O'Donnell I think you two have had enough.

Smoke is exhaled around **O'Donnell** *who covers his mouth.*

Lily*'s show swells and* **O'Donnell***,* **Billy** *and* **Dai** *and community slip into a dumb show.*

It's a movement sequence.

As **O'Donnell** *tries to get* **Dai** *and* **Billy** *out of the club. They resist.*

O'Donnell *tries to take them out. They resist.*

Dai *and* **Billy** *dance with some colourful characters from the community.*

O'Donnell *is pulled back in. He tries to escape but he's pulled back in.*

Someone puts a joint in **O'Donnell***'s mouth and he desperately pulls it out.*

O'Donnell *is lifted up and spun around and there's smoke everywhere.*

Eventually **O'Donnell** *crawls free -* **Dai** *and* **Billy** *are lost to the hedonism of the community.*

O'Donnell *sees his chance to escape through the fire exit - hanging by the fire exit he sees a feather boa. He takes it down, wraps it around himself. Taking a deep breath* **O'Donnell** *steps into the melee. He acts like he's joining in, he might even put a joint in his mouth to make them feel at ease. He wraps the feather boa around himself,* **Billy** *and* **Dai***, they think it's fun! Carefully he dances them towards the fire exit, and eventually, once close, he pushes them down it and out!*

Scene Twelve

Fundraising in Inverness

Spotlight on **O'Donnell** *holding a new cheque.*

O'Donnell Thank you, to the Congregation of the St Joseph's Church, Inverness.

Beat.

We're in the fight of our lives here.

O'Donnell *is about to step away from the mic. He stops. And turns back.*

Can I ask you to do something for me?

Beat.

Do you mind closing your eyes for me? Just for a minute. Imagine yourself stepping out of a house in Penrhiwceiber in the Cynon Valley. A house identical to every other one in the street. Built with cold grey stone. You step out and you smell the coconut gorse from the mountain behind you and you can hear children laughing as they play tag in the street.

Beat.

You could knock on the door of twenty houses in both directions and know the names of everyone living there. You don't pass the time of day with anyone because you're too busy sharing your lives, whether it's a landline or a piano, or fears about poor health. You borrow and lend, share and care and you *all* rely on the coal industry.

Beat.

Your street goes from the town at the bottom of the mountain to the pit at the top. Hundreds and hundreds of streets twist up the mountainsides like veins and arteries because mining isn't an industry, it's not even our life-blood, it's the reason we exist.

Beat.

It's the reason our villages are where they are, the reason we've got roads and canals and chapels and pubs. But not only that, it's the reason why we play team sports, why we sing together, why our kids have twenty houses they can run into. Coal is the reason we exist.

Beat.

You can open your eyes now. When they say they don't want our coal no more. They are saying they don't want us no more. My street. My neighbours. My family.

Beat.

But I do.

Beat.

That's why I'm striking, that's why I'm here. And that's why your money is so, so important. Because yes, it helps us to keep striking, feeding the kids and heating our homes.

Beat.

But what it really does is tell me that *you* want us to exist. And that is the real gift you've given us.

Beat.

Thank you.

Billy *and* **Dai** *look at him - inspired.*

More money pours around them.

Scene Thirteen
Money smuggling sequence

Movement sequence as money is moved and passed around the country - for example:

A sports bag is filled with money by **O'Donnell**.

Sports bag is put down at a bus stop and someone else picks it up and puts it inside a pram and walks off.

A pram is pushed on and someone leans in and rather than picking up a baby, pulls out wads of cash and puts it inside a cat basket before walking off.

Someone enters with a cat basket. Another person comes along and the cat basket is opened and the cash is pulled out and put into a toolbox.

Someone with a toolbox enters and the cash is swapped into a box of washing powder.

The box of washing powder makes its way to the Women's Committee food bank.

Scene Fourteen

Cynon Valley Workingmen's Hall

The box of washing powder is centre stage on a table.

Penny *and* **Shaz** *are packing food parcels.*

Penny   We're getting low on dried goods.

Shaz   Tanya said there was a donation coming from Denmark.

Penny   Oooh, Denmark.

Shaz   Should be here tomorrow.

Penny *gets a clipboard and makes a note.*

Stealthily, **WPC Richards** *enters with another* **Officer**.

Shaz   Honestly, I can't stop farting today.

WPC Richards   Girls.

Shaz   Oh! Didn't see you there, Officer.

Penny   Oh! You frightened us.

Shaz   What do you want?

WPC Richards   You having any bother here? Any kids messing about?

Shaz   No, everyone's being respectful.

WPC Richards   I 've seen some kids hanging about here.

Shaz   No, they're fine, thanks.

WPC Richards   Good good. I'm glad everyone's. Good. You getting a lot of stuff?

Shaz   Yeah, people are being very kind.

WPC Richards   It's all food, is it?

Penny   Some cleaning products. Toiletries. Everything you need to run a household.

WPC Richards I 've donated stuff. At the drop off point by the Co-op.

Shaz Well, it's much appreciated.

WPC Richards It's the kids, isn't it? They're the ones caught up in this.

Penny No one wants to strike.

WPC Richards No.

WPC Richards *browses some more parcels.*

Have you been getting anything else other than food?

Shaz Like what?

WPC Richards Money. I'm here to ask about the money. Because if you're getting cash sent through from the NUM, I'd have to take it. Have you been receiving any money?

A tense moment as **Shaz** *and* **Penny** *hold her stare.*

WPC Richards I know you're a support group.

Beat.

But are you working for the NUM as well? Distributing money? You can tell me, it's fine. You won't be in any trouble, I know what Ceri is like. Anything?

Beat.

It's just if you don't tell me, and I then find some, you'd be guilty of conspiracy to launder money which can carry a custodial sentence. Bet Ceri didn't tell you that. So. Is there any money here?

Silence.

Shaz Well …

Penny No. We just have food here. We receive food, household goods and we make up parcels for families. That's it. There's no money here, is there?

Shaz *shakes her head.*

Penny   Just food parcels.

WPC Richards   So if we check through these food parcels. There's not gonna be any money in there, is there?

WPC Richards *stares at* **Shaz**.

All **Shaz** *can do is shake her head.*

Shaz   Um ... well.

Penny   No, nothing.

WPC Richards   OK.

WPC Richards *starts going through boxes/bags.*

Penny *goes to* **Shaz** *and puts her arm around her, for support.*

WPC Richards *and the other* **Officer** *start taking lots of things out and searching.*

WPC Richards *empties things and makes a mess - she shows no respect.*

She opens a pack of biscuits and starts to eat them.

She empties every single parcel.

She gets to the laundry powder box. She shakes it. Something isn't right.

Penny *and* **Shaz** *hold their breath.*

She opens the laundry powder box and pours it on the floor or table.

White powder pours everywhere. And after a while she gives up.

Penny   Are you gonna help us tidy the place up?

WPC Richards   Well, if you just told me where the money is, I wouldn't have to make such a mess.

Penny   There is no money. There's just food and goods to help keep families together. Now, I want your number because I'm going to speak to your superior about this.

We're a support group, we're not criminals. There's plenty of them out there that you seem incapable of catching, why don't you get out there and stop some real crime rather than coming in here and making a mess of everything.

WPC Richards *steps back.*

WPC Richards Be very careful.

WPC Richards *takes her biscuits and walks out.*

Penny *and* **Shaz** *wait until the coast is clear.*

Shaz Jesus Christ. Where did you put it?

Penny *picks up a toilet roll and pulls out £10.*

Penny Everyone gets a note.

Shaz *gets a bottle of something and pours herself a drink.*

Penny We wouldn't go to jail.

Beat.

Shaz. We'd be fine.

Shaz You don't know what you're talking about.

Penny She's trying to scare us.

Shaz I'm not going to prison.

Penny They wouldn't put us in prison for this.

Shaz You have no idea. No idea.

Shaz *walks out.*

Penny Shaz? Shaz!

Penny *is left alone.*

She picks up the phone.

Penny It's me. The police have been sniffing around. No. No. Nothing. Shaz has been spooked though. We're going to have to be more careful.

Beat.

No, I'm fine.

Beat.

It's fine, Ceri.

Penny *looks at her hand - rock solid.*

Honestly. I'll do whatever we need to do.

Beat.

Why? What do you need?

Scene Fifteen

Gwydir Forest

Billy *is covering a hole with a shovel.*

Dai *has marked a tree nearby and then is counting his paces towards the hole.*

O'Donnell *is on the phone in a phone box.*

O'Donnell   Yeah, so Andy's trousers have arrived.

Beat.

But they need taking in. I've marked them. They're.

O'Donnell *leans out to* **Dai**.

Dai   Fifteen.

Dai *gives a thumbs up.*

O'Donnell   Fifteen inches too long. I'd say get him to try them on, with his back to where I've marked. And then measure out fifteen inches and you'll see where they need to be shortened.

Beat.

O'Donnell   Yeah. That's right.

O'Donnell *looks at the boys.*

He takes a moment.

That's really kind of you.

Beat.

But we've got quite a bit of work on at the moment.

Beat.

Yeah. Reckon we won't be back for a few more weeks.

Beat.

Billy Whaaat?

Dai What are you saying?

Billy What the fuck are you saying?

Dai Give me the phone! Give me the phone! Give me the fucking phone and let me talk to him.

Billy Give me the phone.

Dai *and* **Billy** *try and fight for the phone.*

O'Donnell *twists and turns away from them, protecting the phone*

O'Donnell Oh yeah. That sounds interesting.

Beat.

O'Donnell Got it. Thanks, Ceri. Bye! Bye.

O'Donnell *hangs up.*

Dai What the hell / was that? We're meant to be going home.

Billy What did / you say that for?

Dai What was that about?

O'Donnell I, dunno.

Dai What you mean / I dunno, you fucking bell?

Billy Why did you say / we'd do a few weeks more?

O'Donnell I dunno.

Billy I'm not doing anymore. I've had enough. I wanna go home.

Dai Why'd you say that?

O'Donnell I duuno.

Billy I'm ringing him back.

Dai Ring him back, Bill.

Billy *punches some numbers into the payphone.*

O'Donnell *steps away from them.*

O'Donnell He said there's a big picket coming. / All hands on deck.

Billy What's the number? What's the number?

O'Donnell It's a payphone. He's gone.

Dai He told you that *after* you said we could carry on. What was that about?

Silence.

O'Donnell I dunno.

Dai Don't you wanna go home?

O'Donnell Yeah.

Dai What's changed?

O'Donnell I dunno. I just. I wanna go home. But. If the Welsh miners stop, this whole thing falls apart.

Beat.

Billy It's not all on us to win this.

O'Donnell I know.

Billy Others have done less. Are doing less.

O'Donnell I know, you're right.

Dai We've put a shift in.

O'Donnell We have, yeah.

Silence.

Just sort of think Rory would be pushing us to keep going.

Very long silence.

They all take a seat somewhere.

Billy What did he say? Ceri.

O'Donnell About what?

Dai The picket.

O'Donnell It's a big one. All hands.

Dai All hands?

O'Donnell All hands.

Billy Where is it?

O'Donnell Orgreave.

Scene Sixteen

Orgreave

*A **Police Officer** stands on stage in a high visibility jacket. He blows a whistle.*

Officer Here for the Orgreave picket, lads?

O'Donnell Uh, yeah, that's right.

Officer You're in the right place.

Dai Great.

Officer Right this way. Did you park in the lower field?

O'Donnell Yeah, one of your officers directed us there.

Officer   Yeah, that's right - this way now. Follow the crowds. You got water? It's gonna be a hot one.

O'Donnell   Yeah, we're OK. Thank you.

Officer   Follow the road, you'll see a big gate, take a left, past the church, and then you'll see a big field. That's where everyone's gathering. You can't miss it.

O'Donnell   Thank you, officer. We normally get lost at these things, it's always somewhere new.

Officer   I bet. Right down there, you can't miss it.

O'Donnell, **Billy** *and* **Dai** *head off.*

Officer *pulls the numbers off his epaulettes and follows them off.*

Later.

Billy, **Dai** *and* **O'Donnell** *join a group of* **Miners** *standing around with picketing signs.*

Dai   This has to be the best organised picket I've ever been to.

Billy   Yeah, because the NUM aren't doing it.

O'Donnell   Maybe we should ask the police to organise all of our pickets?

Dai   Not a bad idea.

They all laugh.

O'Donnell   Is that? Have they got horses over there?

Dai   What they got horses for?

O'Donnell   Carrying supplies? I dunno.

Sound of horses approaching.

Billy   What are they doing?

Dai   There's loads of them.

Billy   Have they got helmets on?

Pause.

O'Donnell Lads. Get back. Get back.

O'Donnell *pushes everyone behind him.*

Dai What are they wearing? Are they police? Or …

Sound of horses thundering closer gets louder and louder.

O'Donnell GET BACK!

But it's too late as a new degree of violence is licensed by the state on the working class men of the country. It is sustained and terrifying, with the police now armed like the military for the first time in UK history. In the melee a **Police Officer** *batters and throttles* **Dai**.

Scene Seventeen

Orgreave

O'Donnell *and men are sat with their backs to each other.*

A **Mounted Officer** *with a helmet that looks like a single eye circles them.*

O'Donnell *is battered and bruised. All around him,* **Miners** *are bleeding and writhing in pain.*

Billy *holds* **Dai** *in his lap.*

Mounted Officer NOBODY MOVE!

Billy Come on, butt. Come on. Wake up.

Dai *is bleeding badly.*

Billy Jesus Christ, look at him.

Billy *starts cleaning up* **Dai**'s *blood.*

O'Donnell Was that the army?

Miner 1 It's riot gear.

O'Donnell We're not rioting, we're picketing.

Billy John, come and look at him.

O'Donnell I never seen nothing like it. Why are they doing that?

Miner 2 Because we're the enemy now.

Billy John.

Miner 1 Did anyone notice none of them had shoulder numbers?

Billy You've got to / look at him.

Miner 1 Any of them break the law, we can't report them.

Billy John.

O'Donnell Is he breathing?

Billy He needs a doctor. He's not right.

O'Donnell *goes to move.*

Mounted Officer NOBODY MOVE!

Miner 3 No, you'll get arrested. I know lads who got arrested in April for breach of the peace, they're still in jail. And they won't get their jobs back after this. You get arrested, you've lost everything, job, pension, the lot.

O'Donnell *looks to* **Billy**.

Billy But he needs help.

Miner 3 You'll get arrested.

O'Donnell He needs help.

Miner 3 If he arrests you he's gonna arrest the lot of us. I'm not losing my pension because you can't keep your head down.

Billy John …

O'Donnell OK.

Billy John, he needs to go hospital.

O'Donnell OK. Let me. Let me. Let me. OK. I'm gonna distract him, I want you guys to get Dai out of here, OK?

Miner 2 No, don't!

But **O'Donnell** *is gone, he engages with the* **Mounted Officer**.

O'Donnell What force you from then?

Mounted Officer Shut up!

O'Donnell Yorkshire? No.

Wiltshire? No. The Met.

Mounted Officer *begrudgingly smiles.*

O'Donnell The Met. Why were you sent up here then?

Mounted Officer That's operationally sensitive information.

O'Donnell What's that mean?

Mounted Officer Above my payscale. Long as I get paid, I don't really think about it.

O'Donnell That's all I want to do. Get paid to do my job.

Mounted Officer Don't seem like that.

O'Donnell Why's that?

Mounted Officer Who are you?

O'Donnell I'm nobody.

Mounted Officer What's your name?

O'Donnell What's your number?

Beat.

You know, if they said they were shutting down twenty police forces, and you lot went on strike, we'd support you.

Mounted Officer We're not allowed to strike.

O'Donnell If you did. We'd support you.

Mounted Officer We're not allowed to strike. We have to suck up whatever they throw at us. Longer hours, less pay, no training. More risk. Going to shouts on our own. We have to suck everything up. We've got no way of fighting back. We just have to get on with it. Maybe you should too.

O'Donnell But if they cut your pensions just like that. / Can't afford them.

Mounted Officer Look.

O'Donnell Not economically viable. So they cut them all by half.

O'Donnell *sees that* **Billy**, **Dai** *and the* **Miners** *have escaped.*

Mounted Officer Look, you want to go on strike, go on strike, but don't stop other people from working, that's my thing. You don't know what some people are having to deal with and they might need to work. I don't mind you striking, that's your right. Be my guest. But the bloody picketing. The picketing. Trying to shut down places. Have your argument with the Coal Board but leave everyone else out of it. You're bullies.

O'Donnell *could run but he chooses not to.*

O'Donnell You're the bullies. One of your lot beat my mate nearly to death!

Mounted Officer It's time someone stood up to you. / I'm glad someone finally is.

O'Donnell By beating us / unconscious?

Mounted Officer You've held the country / to ransome for a decade.

O'Donnell Charging us with horses? / Beating us to a pulp?

Mounted Officer We didn't vote for you! We *can't* get rid of you. / So you need bringing down a peg or two.

O'Donnell You're not a police force, you're a gang of / criminals.

Mounted Officer Outside of your bubble, everyone hates the fucking miners.

O'Donnell *grabs a placard and strikes him with the stick right in the face.* **Mounted Officer** *falls off the horse.*

Billy *returns.*

With the **Mounted Officer** *on the floor* **O'Donnell** *raises the stick above his head and drives it into the prone* **Mounted Officer** *repeatedly.*

Billy Jesus Christ! What have you done?

O'Donnell *drops the stick.*

End of Act One.

Act Two

Scene Eighteen

Doncaster Gate Hospital

Bandaged and plastered, **O'Donnell** *sits on a row of plastic chairs.*

Miners *come and go in various states of injury.*

Bleeding and on a crutch, **Ceri** *enters.*

Ceri   Is it true?

Beat.

You beat up a police officer?

Beat.

Self defence. It was an organised bloodbath.

Beat.

A mass assault on the working people of this country, by the State, that's what it was.

Beat.

You did nothing wrong, you hear me. Nothing. Don't go getting all … guilty about it. You did nothing wrong.

Beat.

Was he … was he moving? When you left him?

Beat.

Did nothing wrong.

Ceri *hands* **O'Donnell** *a flask of whisky.* **O'Donnell** *drinks from it.*

O'Donnell   He said we're the bullies.

Ceri Was he on a fucking big horse when he said that?

O'Donnell They think *they're* the underdogs and *we're* the bullies.

Beat.

Someone's going to get killed.

Ceri I wonder if we'll ever trust them again or if they'll ever trust us.

Beat.

Dai *and* **Billy** *appear.*

O'Donnell You're alright!

O'Donnell *rushes to hug* **Dai**.

Dai Concussion. I'm alright.

Billy He'll survive, nothing a few weeks in his own bed won't fix.

O'Donnell *and* **Ceri** *share a look.*

Ceri Yeah, yeah. I can see that. But … after today's events

Beat.

I think it's best if you all get back on the road.

Dai I'm concussed.

Ceri Yeah, yeah. You're concussed. So rest up. And then get back on the road.

Billy Ceri.

Dai I wanna go home.

Ceri Yeah, yeah but for the time being it's best you boys stay out of South Wales.

Billy Why?

Ceri They had photographers there today. So let's just stay out of South Wales while things calm down.

Dai Please, Ceri.

Billy He wants to go home.

Ceri It's safer for everyone this way.

Billy He needs to rest.

Beat.

He needs Cathy.

O'Donnell *looks to* **Ceri**.

Ceri He's concussed, he's not dying. He can rest, but if he goes back there's a good chance he'll get arrested and he'll never get his job back or his pension. They'll get all our names … it's too risky.

Dai *sits down.*

Dai They was charging us on horseback. I seen men trampled on. Guys on the floor and coppers just whacking them with truncheons over and over again.

Beat.

And then I got whacked with a truncheon but that wasn't the worst of it. I was in this crowd of miners trying to get out of the way and this copper - he put his hands on me and started strangling me. Looking me dead in the eyes. I thought he was going to kill me. I think he was trying to kill me. And he was in a uniform.

Beat.

It's politics for Scargill and Thatcher. All fun and games. But for me it means someone in a uniform trying to strangle me to death.

Beat.

Billy *and* **O'Donnell** *look to each other.*

Dai How the fuck have we got into this?

O'Donnell I know But. I don't think it's safe for us to go home now.

Billy What?

O'Donnell I don't want them knowing who we are, where we live, or who our families are. We can't trust them.

Billy So, what then?

O'Donnell Ceri?

Ceri Well. The international fundraising committee need men.

Billy Abroad? Where?

Dai No!

Ceri Countries sympathetic to our cause. Places where people want us to win.

Billy Ceri.

Ceri We can't beat them on British fundraising alone.

Dai No way, I'm not going.

O'Donnell I don't think we've got a choice.

Beat.

Dai Does anyone, on either side, give a shit about me?

Billy and **O'Donnell** *look to each other.*

Scene Nineteen
Penrikyber Canteen

Anxiously, **Simon Billsborrow** *sits and waits.*

In a hairnet and uniform, **Penny** *enters.*

Penny Oh, hiya.

Simon Alright?

Penny You on your own?

Simon Yeah.

Penny What's your name?

Simon Simon.

Penny Simon what?

Simon Simon Billsborrow.

Penny *writes it down.*

Penny No one with you?

Simon They told me to wait here. Been here two hours, like.

Penny How'd you get in?

Simon Through the front.

Penny How was that?

Pause.

Simon I had to, walk, to the police station in Nelson. And then, they like put me in the back of a police car, and then they like put a blanket over my 'ead. And then, they had a police escort, and drove me through the gates. They was chucking bricks and bottles at the car.

Penny Anyone see your face?

Simon Don' think so, like.

Penny Did anyone see your face?

Simon *shakes his head.*

Simon I was down in the footwell the whole time.

Beat.

I been told to wait here, like, and no one's come.

Penny I don't think anyone's coming for you.

Simon Are you on double time an' all?

Simon *unfolds a letter.*

Simon It says by here I'll get double time like. But I haven' done nothing since I been here.

Penny There's no safety-men, you can't go down the pit. You can't operate the machinery on your own.

Simon What am I supposed to do 'en? Not going through all that to not get paid.

Penny Oh, they'll pay you. You'll just have to sit here all day.

Simon Wha'? An' do nothing?

Penny Yeah. Can't mine on your own.

Simon I'll clean the toilets if they want. I don't care. If that's what I need to do look after my kids.

Penny *stops in her tracks.*

Penny You've got kids?

Simon *nods.*

Penny How many?

Simon Two.

Penny Me too.

Simon *hangs his head.*

Very long silence.

Simon They don' deserve none of this. They don'.

Beat.

I sold the piano my daughter got off Father Christmas. Try explaining that. She cried for days. And then. She drew keys on the window sill. And sits playing them. Tapping away. Just tapping.

He taps the table.

I can't take it anymore. I can live without the telly and the car.

Beat.

It's the tapping.

Simon *hangs his head in shame.*

Penny *goes to him.*

Simon Are they paying you double?

Penny *stops herself.*

Penny *(beat)* Uh. Um … uh they're - um they're no. They're not.

Simon Why not?

Penny I uh. I well.

Swallows hard.

I uh-actually I - uh well, I don't actually, uh work, here.

Simon I don't get it. I thought you …

Penny I don't work here.

Simon But you're in uniform. You must work here.

Pause.

Penny The NUM sent me.

Simon *springs to his feet and scans the room in fear, maybe he picks up a chair.*

Simon Who sent you? Ceri? Is he with you?

Penny I'm on my own, I'm on / my own, it's just me.

Simon Why did they send you? / What's going on? WHAT'S GOING ON?

Penny They. Shhh. They wanted, they asked me, to get your name.

Simon You're fucking spying for them? HELP! She's a fucking spy! / The NUM. They're in here! They're in here!

Penny Shhh, shut the fuck up.

Simon She's a fucking spy! How'd you get in here?

Penny Will you keep / your voice down, please?

Simon You fucking cow. You tricked me. You tricked me into giving you - you fucking got a uniform / and you tricked me, you're a fucking sly bitch ... This is my fucking life. My family. It's not a fucking game.

Penny OK! OK, just stop! Stop. OK. Listen What if, what if I don't tell them?

Simon *What*?

Penny What if I don't tell them your name? I don't have to tell them your name. / I don't have to do anything.

Simon What the fuck are you talking about?

Penny *gets the paper with his name written on - and rips it up.*

Penny Ceri just wants you to stop coming. So stop coming!

Simon You're gonna tell them anyway.

Penny I won't! I'll keep it a secret.

Simon You're a fucking spy. I don't trust you.

Penny I'll keep it a secret!

Simon Why should I trust you, you've been lying to me since you came in here?

Penny I'm pregnant!

Beat.

I'm pregnant. There I said it. I haven't said it out loud before. I'm pregnant. I didn't know if I wanted it. I don't know if I want it. Of course I want it. I just. I don't know if it's good to have another one or if it's unfair to have another baby when I can barely feed my other two. I haven't even told my husband. Because I don't want it to be true. I know that makes me a terrible mother.

Beat.

Simon You can feel all those things and still be a good mother.

Penny Thank you.

Beat.

So now you know my secret.

Beat.

We can keep our secrets from everyone. Walk out the back door. Go back on strike. And no-one will ever know.

Beat.

Simon I can't.

You can. What if I talk to the NUM and get them to buy the piano back?

Simon Fucking hell.

Penny I reckon we can get one.

Penny *gets her notebook out. She writes 'piano' on it.*

Simon It's not about the piano.

Penny What is it about?

Simon Everything. I've had enough.

Penny What else do you need?

Simon Everything!

Penny Food? Do you need food? I can get a food parcel to you every week. We can get it delivered to your house if you can't make it to the club.

Simon *stares at her.*

Simon It's not about this stuff.

Penny Well, let's sort this stuff out first. Would a food parcel help?

Simon Yeah.

Penny Is there anything else you need? Anything. It can be anything.

Simon Doors.

Penny Doors? Where've your doors gone?

Simon I cut them up for firewood.

Penny (*writing*) Doors. I can get doors. How many?

Simon *re- imagines his house.*

Simon Three.

Penny *adds that number to her book.*

Penny I'll add a bag of coal, too.

Simon I get bits off the tip.

Penny There's teams pinching from the stockpiles, I'll get you some coal. Is there anything else? Let's get it on the list. Anything to help? I'm trying to help.

Simon My daughter, she's … Y'know. She's a teenager. She's - y'know

Penny I'll make sure everything she needs is in the food parcel.

Simon Thank you.

Simon *is not fine.*

Penny You had a wobble.

Beat.

No one needs to know.

Beat.

You're not the first and you won't be the last.

Silence.

We need to be sympathetic to each other. Not smashing each other's windows in and intimidating each other. You've done nothing wrong.

Simon That's not true.

Penny It is.

Simon I've let my kids down, and my friends.

Penny You've done nothing of the sort. You're a good dad. And a good friend.

Simon I'm not, I'm not, I know I'm not.

Penny You sold your daughter's piano for your friends, and you crossed a picket line for your daughter. You're amazing. You're amazing.

Simon *puts his head in his hands.*

Penny *puts her arms around him.*

Scene Twenty

O'Donnell's home

Penny *is at home - she watches a TV screen.*

News Reporter (*off- stage*) Violence broke out between striking miners and police at the Harworth Colliery in Nottingham. Officers faced violence and brutality from picketing miners in an increasingly dangerous industrial dispute. Seventy-one picketers were charged with riot offences and twenty-four with violent disorder as police officers tried to defend themselves, the colliery and those trying to get to work.

As the newsreader speaks - **Miners** *and* **Police Officers** *fill the space.*

Penny *feels pain in her stomach and doubles up. She grips the chair/table in pain -*

As **Penny** *writhes in pain so do the* **Miners** *and* **Police Officers** *as they clash all around her.*

As **Penny** *holds herself she finds she is bleeding.*

At the same time, the **Miners** *bleed - she is losing this life, and so are the* **Miners**.

Scene Twenty-One

Australia /Afghanistan/Italy/Norway/Spain/France/ Germany/ Ukraine

Billy, **Dai** *and* **O'Donnell** *enter.*

Billy Is this what jet-lag feels like?

O'Donnell I think so.

Dai My ears still haven't popped.

Billy Are we sure this is right?

O'Donnell I think so, I dunno. I'm exhausted.

Dai Hey, we've flown half way around the world, and it's the same old shit wandering around trying to find an address.

Billy They're not gonna have a clue about our situation. I dunno why Ceri has sent us here.

Reveal - a large crowd of **Australian Miners** *- an Australian Miners' Federation banner!*

Barry You must be John, Billy and Dai? Welcome, welcome to the Australian Miners' Federation.

Your suffering is our suffering. Your struggle is our struggle. So we'd like to give to you, 30,000 British Pounds. We've shut down exports of Queensland coal to the UK in solidarity with your struggle. We estimate that over six thousand men have been laid off as a result of their boycotting actions in support of your strike in the UK.

Silence.

O'Donnell I'm sorry … did you say six thousand men?

Barry Yeah, six thousand men.

O'Donnell Laid off work.

Barry Yeah.

O'Donnell For supporting our strike?

Barry That's right. Australia is right behind you fellas.

Cheers.

O'Donnell We, had no idea … that anyone cared about us …

Barry You're going to win this. And you're going to win this for all of us. There's someone over here who wants to meet you.

Sound swirl.

Nadia (*in Darsi*) Khoshamadin rafiki as Afghanistan, ini fund-raiser bara Afghanistan ast.

Translator Welcome to the Friends of Afghanistan fundraiser.

Nadia Council as Afghanistan da azur bara NUM mita ziad kishmish mita bara family British.

Translator The Central Council of Afghanistan Trade Unions has raised ten thousand British pounds for the NUM and a gift of ten tons of raisins is being sent over to feed your families.

Lars Velkommen til Arbeidstakerforbundet I Norge

Translator Welcome to the General Workers Union of Norway, who have raised twenty two thousand pounds.

Mathilde   Bienvenidos a la Comisión Obrera Controlada por los Communistas de España.

Translator   Welcome to the Communist Controlled Workers' Commission of Spain, who have raised three thousand pounds.

Arnaud   Bienvenue à la Confédération générale du travail de France

Translator   Welcome to the General Confederation of Labour in France, who have raised eight thousand pounds.

Dieter   BegruBen Sie die Sozialistische Arbeitergruppe Deutschland.

Translator   Welcome to the Socialist Workers Group of Germany, who have raised twenty-seven thousand points.

Artem   My, Shaktari Donbas, vitayemo vas v Urayni

Translator   We the miners of Donbas welcome you to Ulkraine - who have raised seventy-five thousand pounds.

O'Donnell   (*in unison*) The miners united will never be defeated!

Barry   (*in unison*) The miners united will never be defeated!

Artem   (*in unison*) Mayners Yunayted nikoly ne zaznaye porazky!

Mathilde   (*in unison*) Los Mineros Unidos nunca seran derrotados!

Les Miners United ne seront jamais

Die Miners United werden niemals

I minatori uniti non saranno mai

Lars   (*in unison*) Gruvearbeiderne forent vil aldri bli beseirere!
The boys are swept up with the global solidarity.

Scene Twenty-Two

Libya

A **Libyan Revolutionary Nun** *with an Ak47 approaches* **O'Donnell**.

Rania   This way please.

Rania *takes* **O'Donnell** *into a tent.*

Colonel Gadaffi *enters.*

Colonel Gadaffi   As-salam-alikum.

Rania   Wa-alikum-salaam.

Colonel Gadaffi   Salaam.

O'Donnell   Salaam.

Rania   Marhaben ajoohal haqid hadtha John O'Donnell min National Union of Miners South Wales District.

(*trans. Colonel, this is John O'Donnell from the National Union of Miners South Wales District.*)

Colonel Gaddafi   Mr O'Donnell. Please take a seat. Take some tea.

Gaddafi *pours him some tea.*

O'Donnell   Thank you.

Colonel Gaddafi   Here. This will guide you in your struggle.

Gaddafi *holds out a Green Book to* **O'Donnell**.

Colonel Gaddafi   All revolutionaries should study this book.

O'Donnell   What is it?

Colonel Gaddafi   The Green Book. My political philosophy. Mao has the Red Book. I have the Green Book.

O'Donnell   Thank you. I'll read it.

Colonel Gaddafi Please.

Gaddafi *encourages* **O'Donnell** *to drink his tea.*

O'Donnell *drinks his tea.*

Colonel Gaddafi How can Libya help your struggle?

O'Donnell Thank you. And thank you for finding the time to meet us. We really appreciate it. I won't waste your time as

I know you're a very busy man. We are fighting the British Government on a number of fronts. The streets, the boardroom and the courts. The easiest and fastest way to support all those fronts is money. We need money.

Colonel Gaddafi Libya can support you with money.

O'Donnell Thank you. Thank you.

Colonel Gaddafi But for a revolution, you need guns.

O'Donnell Uh …

Colonel Gaddafi I support IRA this way.

O'Donnell I see.

Colonel Gaddafi I support you this way.

O'Donnell Well.

Colonel Gaddafi For your revolution.

O'Donnell *looks to* **Gaddafi**. *To* **Rania**. *To* **Gaddafi**.

O'Donnell I'm - well. That's very kind of you. Thank you. I'm not sure. We. Y'know. It's not that kind of.

Colonel Gaddafi If you want a revolution you need guns.

O'Donnell I'm … well. I'm not sure. I'm not sure. If we want a revolution.

Gaddafi *laughs.*

O'Donnell *laughs.*

Rania *joins in.*

It goes on longer than expected.

Colonel Gaddafi You don't want guns!

O'Donnell No!

More laughter.

O'Donnell We just want our jobs.

More laughter.

Colonel Gaddafi Thatcher has guns.

Everyone stops laughing.

Colonel Gaddafi You want guns.

Beat.

O'Donnell I'm not a leader.

Colonel Gaddafi Leaders don't have guns.

O'Donnell I'm sorry. I don't want to offend. But we just need money.

Colonel Gaddafi Read my book and then you will see. You need guns. Now. Please. Drink.

O'Donnell *drinks his tea.*

O'Donnell Thank you.

Scene Twenty-Three

O'Donnell's home

Shaz *and* **Penny** *sit together.*

Shaz The kids are asleep.

Beat.

There's a shepherd's pie in the fridge and I've put a wash on.

Beat.

Drink this.

Shaz *helps* **Penny** *drink.*

Shaz I lost my first. No one ever really talks about how brutal it is. But it is. Have some more.

Penny *drinks.*

Shaz Little bit?

Penny *drinks again.*

Shaz You'd think they'd have come up with a better way of doing things by now. But no.

Shaz *strokes* **Penny**'s *hair.*

Shaz Just brutality for us.

Beat.

And all we want to do is look after someone.

Beat.

They have no idea what we go through just to look after someone.

Beat.

Penny I feel old.

Shaz I feel old.

Penny Empty.

Shaz *comforts* **Penny**.

Penny Tired.

Shaz I'm tired.

Penny Guilty.

Shaz Oh God, yes. Yes, I'll have that one. Guilty.

Beat.

Neglected.

Penny Oh.

Shaz Annoyed.

Penny Numb.

Shaz Yeah.

Penny I'm numb.

Beat.

Shaz But I feel proud as well.

Beat.

Come on.

Penny Not feeling that at the moment.

Shaz No.

Beat.

But you've only got space for a few feelings at a time. Let yourself feel these ones. And in time, you'll make a little bit of space for new ones.

Penny You promise?

Shaz   I promise.

Penny   Thank you.

Silence.

Penny   Sorry.

Shaz   What for?

Penny   Making you lie. The other day.

Shaz   Oh don't be daft. / You got nothing to be sorry for.

Penny   I'm sorry for making you lie to the police.

Shaz   That wasn't / your fault, that was my own

Penny   I shouldn't have put you in that / position.

Shaz   Issues. Honestly, I just get a bit / wrongfooted.

Penny   I should have known.

Shaz   You weren't to / know.

Penny   No, I shouldn't / have presumed …

Shaz   Look, it's nothing to do with you. I'm, terrified of prison. Terrified.

Beat.

Penny   Of course, it's fine.

Shaz   No. My dad went. To prison.

Penny   OK.

Shaz   He'd had a stroke so he couldn't work, and he must have been trying to save us money, fiddling the electric. I was only little. His solicitor said he'd get community service because it was his first offence but they made an example of him. And. He was never the same after that.

Beat.

I don't trust them. I don't trust those in power to be fair.

Beat.

I can't. And it wasn't only me who thought it wasn't fair. Everyone did. His solicitor couldn't believe it. He came to Dad's funeral he felt so bad about it.

Silence.

Penny The funeral.

Beat.

I can't afford a funeral.

Shaz *takes a moment.*

Penny *shakes her head.*

Penny How am I going to pay for it?

Shaz OK. Don't you worry about that.

Penny I don't have any money.

Shaz We'll figure something out.

Penny What am I going to do?

Shaz We'll figure something out. I don't know right now but trust me, we will come up with a solution so, so your baby can have a proper funeral.

Penny How am I going to do that?

Scene Twenty-Four

Polish Mines

With headlamps on, **O'Donnell**, **Billy** *and* **Dai** *walk through the mines.* **O'Donnell** *holds a hold-all.*

O'Donnell This way. The map Jerzy's given us says it's this road.

Dai What was Jerzy's surname?

O'Donnell Pietroviwz. Why?

Billy What the hell are we doing? What was wrong with the car?

O'Donnell They're checking at the border. Jerzy said we can't risk it.

Dai Why don't we just wire the money and then get a train across?

O'Donnell The Government have intercepted our last three transfers. We can't wire any more money. It's gotta be cash in hand, all the way back to Wales.

Beat.

This mine, takes us across the border to Germany where we can drop it off to a miners federation agent who's going to Kent for a meeting. He can get it to Wales for us.

Billy But if we get lost …

Dai We're fucked.

O'Donnell Just stick to the map.

They walk some distance.

Billy Hey, look at this.

They shine a light and they see a coal seam.

Dai It's the seam.

All three of them rush to it and put their hands on it.

They admire it.

Billy Look at the size of that.

Dai Wow.

Beat.

It's like being back home.

O'Donnell Looks good quality.

Dai Yeah. Oh, I've missed this.

Billy Could cut this right now.

Dai She'll be shipping this back home.

Billy They've tripled their exports to us.

O'Donnell Yeah.

Billy This seam here is gonna ruin the strike for us.

Dai Aye. They'll raise money for us but they won't stop shipping it back home for us. Not like the Ozzies.

O'Donnell I don't think they have a choice. Couple of copper miners went on strike a few years back and they shot them dead.

Beat.

We're not the only ones being screwed over by this seam. Come on.

O'Donnell *and* **Dai** *leave but* **Billy** *stays.*

Dai Bill.

Billy *runs his hand across the seam.*

Dai What you doing?

O'Donnell *and* **Dai** *stop.*

Billy It's crazy, in't it? Like. What is it what we want to do? We want to come down to places like this and fetch this stuff up and give it to other people. That's all we wanna do. That's all my father did. And his father. Find this stuff. Fetch it up and give it to people so they can stay warm. How did it get all so complicated?

O'Donnell I dunno.

Dai I dunno.

Billy We're in a mine in Poland with a couple of grand in a hold-all.

O'Donnell We're running the batteries down.

Billy And I just wanna do this. I'm good at it.

O'Donnell I get it, look -

Dai What was that?

O'Donnell What?

Dai Did you see something then?

Billy I didn't see nothing.

Dai I'm sure I saw something move.

O'Donnell Nothing's moving down here.

Beat.

Billy Hang on. What was that?

O'Donnell Don't you fucking start.

Billy I saw something. Over there I definitely saw something.

O'Donnell I'm not in the mood to be wound up by you two.

Dai I definitely saw something, I'm not shitting you.

Billy I saw something over there. I don't feel right.

Dai I don't feel right, like I'm gonna be sick.

Billy Is that stink damp?

Dai It's / stink damp.

O'Donnell It's not.

Dai It's stink damp.

O'Donnell It's not. I've smelt that before.

Billy The hairs on the back of my neck … are … Is that black damp?

SFX Sound!

Billy I don't like it.

Dai I don't like it.

Beat.

Billy I don't feel right, John.

Dai I'm scared.

Billy Me too.

O'Donnell We've got to keep going forward.

Dai I dun … really wanna go any further.

Billy Me neither.

O'Donnell We can't split up!

Billy I don't think this is safe.

O'Donnell What are you talking about? / It's fine.

Dai I don't want to die. / We don't know these mines, John.

O'Donnell We're not gonna die.

Dai How do you know?

O'Donnell Fucking hell! We haven't come all this way, to fucking die doing the one thing, the one thing! We actually know what we're doing, which is going through a fucking mine. It's just not going to happen. It's not!

Billy I'm not going any further!

O'Donnell We need to get this money home!

Billy That money is not going to beat this coal!

O'Donnell What are you saying?

Billy The strike's collapsing! Thatcher's paying more for this stuff than she'd ever pay me and you. We can't beat her with this. We can't turn the lights off, with tonnes of this arriving every week. We can't nationalise all the coal on the planet. We can't even unite the miners in our country. Half of Yorkshire have gone back to work. No-one's coming to our rescue. The TUC ain't coming. The Labour

Party ain't coming. We are on our own and you need to understand that.

O'Donnell Well, what do you want us to do? Give up!

Billy Maybe yeah! I dunno.

O'Donnell Ah, fuck that.

O'Donnell *turns his back and leaves* **Billy** *and* **Dai**.

Billy John. John. JOHN!

Dai John! Come back!

But **O'Donnell** *has gone.*

We see images of what's racing through **O'Donnell**'s *mind.*

The police.

Penny *and the kids but he can't get to them.* **Penny** *and a third child ...*

Bars - jails ...

O'Donnell *goes ahead, alone. He travels for some time he crosses some astral planes ... Is he in another dimension? Another time, another place, is he becoming something else?*

Exhausted, **O'Donnell** *lies down.*

He buries his head in his hands, **Penny** *is waving goodbye to him.*

And then **O'Donnell** *stirs and there before him is the ghost of* **Rory**.

O'Donnell Rory?

Rory John.

O'Donnell You're dead.

Rory You're lost ...

O'Donnell You died. Underground.

Rory Come with me.

O'Donnell I uh I-I-I-

Rory Come with me.

O'Donnell I-I-I-I should get back to the boys.

Rory I'll take you to them. This way.

O'Donnell *is unsure.*

Rory Come on, butt.

Slowly **O'Donnell** *goes with* **Rory**.

The ghosts of **David Jones** *and* **Joe Green** *appear.*

O'Donnell I don't think this is the way I came.

Rory Here's who you're looking for.

O'Donnell Who are you? You speak English?

David I'm David Jones.

O'Donnell Where's your lamps?

Silence.

You look …

Beat.

Am I dreaming?

Beat.

David No, you're seeing clearly.

Rory To see us. You need to see clearly.

O'Donnell What is this place, Rory? Am I dead?

Rory Not yet.

O'Donnell Can you get me out of here?

David You need to promise us something first.

O'Donnell Anything.

David I need you to tell me girls I weren't scared when I died. I were at peace. I were at peace with it. I don't want them worrying that I were scared. I weren't scared. Not at the end.

O'Donnell What happened?

David I were mining at Wakefield. And we come out, and, we picketed all round by ours. Soon enough everyone were out. So, then all focus shift to Nottingham, don't it? So, we get there. It were carnage, fights breaking out. Like it weren't like a picket. It were a battle.

Beat.

People just fighting in the streets. And I seen some lads kicking a car window in. And I were about to go over and say, hey what you doing? When something hit me right in the chest and it were that heavy I hit the floor. I couldn't

breathe. I thought I'd been shot. I thought someone had brought a gun and shot me.

Beat.

The pain. It were like chains around me body. Squeezing me. I couldn't breathe or owt.

Beat.

I asked if I'd been shot. And someone said it were a house brick. One of the scabs had thrown a house brick at us.

Beat.

Ambulance came. And the doctors tried. I were in pain but I kept thinking 'I'll see my girls in a minute. They'll come in and somehow, I'll figure out how to breathe again. Like it weren't the broken ribs or punctured lung that were strangling me, it were the idea of not seeing me girls. And if I could just see them. I'd breathe again. They'd walk in, and I'd just …

David *takes a deep breath.*

Beat.

But they never come.

Beat.

And I never got that breath.

Beat.

So. I need you to go tell them. I were OK. And that I weren't scared. Or sad. Or in pain. I want you to tell them. I were alright at the end, even if I weren't. I want you to tell them. 'Cause I'm their dad. So can you do that for me?

O'Donnell   I can do that for you.

Joe   I'm Joe Green.

O'Donnell   What's your story?

Joe   Thirty years underground. Retired three years ago.

Beat.

When Fife shut down, came down to Yorkshire. Picketed in '72 and '74. When this strike was called I'd been out three years. But still. Wanted to do my bit. Ferrybridge Power Station's near me. So. Every day, I'd take a loaf of bread and use it all up to make sandwiches, and I'd take two bottles of pop and I'd join the pickets outside. Every day for months.

Beat.

Lorries would come in and out and we'd try and flag them down and try to speak to the drivers. If we could stop the lorries moving the stockpiled coal into the power stations, we might get the lights off.

Beat.

And then one day. This lorry. Was going too fast. Came too close to where we were standing. All happened so fast. I was holding a cup of tea and I saw this lorry coming. I'd turned to talk to one of the lads, one of the lads had called my name.

Beat.

and then I went under one of the wheels.

Beat.

O'Donnell What can I do for you?

Joe I don't have family. But. I'd like to be remembered. That's all.

O'Donnell I can do that for you.

Rory There's someone else.

Sat on his own ... is **David Wilkie**.

O'Donnell Who are you?

David Wilkie Who are you?

O'Donnell I'm John O'Donnell.

Beat.

What happened to you?

Joe *and* **David Jones** *look at each other.* **O'Donnell** Is there something I can do?

David Wilkie What do you want?

O'Donnell I want to get home.

David Wilkie We all want to get home.

O'Donnell Can I help you?

David Wilkie Should be a man's right. To get home safely.

O'Donnell Maybe I can help.

David Wilkie How are you not dead?

O'Donnell I don't know.

David Wilkie Why am I dead? And why are you still alive?

O'Donnell I don't know. Luck, I guess.

David Wilkie Luck, is it?

O'Donnell I don't know.

David Wilkie Maybe everyone you love has died while you're away. Maybe that's how things balance out.

O'Donnell I don't know why you're so angry but if you don't want help, then that's fine.

David Wilkie *springs out of his seat and grabs* **O'Donnell** *and pins him to the floor throttling him.*

David Wilkie How does your luck feel now?

Rory David ...

David Wilkie Has your luck changed? Or is it the same? Shall we a toss a coin whether you live or die here?

Rory That's enough.

David Wilkie What do you say? Heads or tails? Heads you live, tails you die, shall we play that? Shall we?

David Wilkie *continues to strangle* **O'Donnell**.

Rory Knock it off.

David Wilkie *throttles* **O'Donnell** *a little longer before finally releasing him.*

Coughing, **O'Donnell** *staggers to safety.*

Joe Green *and* **David Jones** *tend to him.*

O'Donnell I don't understand.

Rory David was a cab driver. One day, he had a fare to drive a scab in and out of Merthyr Vale Colliery with a police escort. Two police cars and a police motorbike, just to get a scab in.

Beat.

On the heads of the valleys road, two striking miners dropped a concrete block from a bridge above and it smashed through his windscreen killing him instantly.

Rory He's got four kids. One of them was born after he died. He never met them.

O'Donnell What does he want from me?

David Wilkie I want you to pay for what happened to me.

O'Donnell How?

David Wilkie I want to take your faith.

O'Donnell I don't believe in God.

David Wilkie In people.

Silence.

O'Donnell People from around the world are helping me.

David Wilkie And someone close to you is betraying you.

O'Donnell *looks to the others.*

O'Donnell *looks to* **Rory**.

David Wilkie Thank you. It's that way …

A path opens up.

O'Donnell *walks, he nods goodbye to* **Rory**.

Penny (*O/S*) Miss Molly had a dolly who was sick, sick, sick

O'Donnell Penny?

Penny (*O/S*) So she called for the doctor to come quick, quick, quick

The doctor came with his bag and his hat

O'Donnell Penny? Where are you?

Penny (*O/S*) And he knocked on the door with a rat-a-tat- tat

He looked at the dolly and he shook his head

O'Donnell Penny!

Penny (*O/S*) And he said, Miss Molly, put her straight to bed

He wrote on the paper for a pill, pill, pill

I'll be back in the morning with the bill, bill, bill.

The ghosts disappear and **Billy** *and* **Dai** *appear.*

O'Donnell Dai, Billy, there / you are!

Dai Jesus Christ, / he's here!

Billy Where the / hell did you go?

Dai What are you / playing at?

Billy You can't do that again, / you hear me! I don't care what's happened between us, we stick together! Understood?

O'Donnell Yeah. Sorry.

Billy You're a fucking twat.

O'Donnell Sorry.

Billy We stick together. Am I being understood?

O'Donnell Yes.

Dai Yeah.

Billy Fucking hell.

Beat.

Right, it's this fucking way and don't you dare wander off or I'll fucking leave you this time.

Billy *leads the way.* **Dai** *and* **O'Donnell** *follow,* **O'Donnell** *looking over his shoulder.*

Scene Twenty-Five

Aberdare Park

Penny Thank you for meeting me.

Huw It's fine.

Penny It's very kind of you.

Huw It's fine.

Penny So.

Huw Uh, Andrew the, uh, undertaker, explained your situation. I'm so sorry for your loss.

Penny Thank you. It's very sad.

Huw Yes.

Penny And I'm sorry for you. Was it your father?

Huw Yes uh, my dad. He hadn't, uh he hadn't been, uh well for a, a, a long time.

Penny I'm sorry.

Beat.

So.

Beat.

Did Andrew explain, that I can't afford a funeral or burial, for my baby?

Huw Yes, he did.

Penny And he suggested. That someone. Kind. Might. They might let my baby be buried alongside their loved one. In the same coffin.

Huw He said, yeah.

Penny And he said, you might be open to that.

Huw *nods.*

Penny Thank you.

Huw No, it's fine.

Penny Thank you.

Huw It's no problem.

Penny I - uh ... don't know ... what to

Huw We spoke about it, uh, and, uh we all felt. Y'know.

Well. It came down to. What dad would have done. And he, he would have. Sorry. I still get a bit, when I talk about him. Ah. He would have liked the chance to help. He'd help anyone. 'Give without remembering and receive without forgetting.' He used to say. So ... we'd be honoured to bury dad, with your baby. Did your baby have a name?

Penny Rhiannon.

Huw Rhiannon. Lovely.

Beat.

Penny What was your father's name?

Huw Elfed.

Penny That's a nice name.

Huw Yes. Yes.

Silence.

Penny Can you tell me about him?

Huw He was. Well. He was amazing really.

Beat.

He was gentle. Gentle soul. Mam is the opposite. She's great, but Dad would say she's hot-blooded, if you know what I mean. He sort of balanced her out.

Beat.

She'd scream and shout and then he'd come in and we'd be upset and he'd say, 'Kids she can't help it, she's from Bridgend.'

Beat.

Penny He sounds very special.

Huw He was.

Penny I won't forget this.

Huw Um ... At the service. If you um, want to. We thought maybe you uh, might ... might want to uh, choose a hymn.

Penny Oh, uh.

Huw You are coming. You are planning to come?

Penny I don't want to impose.

Huw You won't.

Penny I don't want to distract.

Huw He'd want you there. I think he'd be proud of us. For finding a solution.

Beat.

Makes the whole thing more *Dad.*

Scene Twenty-Six

Poland

A row of phone boxes. **Billy** *and* **Dai** *are in phone boxes.*

O'Donnell *paces back and forth, listening.*

Dai Yeah, that's / great.

Billy Thanks, yeah. / I'll have a think about that.

Dai Thanks, yeah. / That's great.

Billy Fucking hell. / That's great.

Billy OK yeah, well, let me have a think about. / We'll be back soon. Hey … I'd better go but thanks for that, yeah. I'll be in touch.

Dai Better go, yeah. Yeah, thanks. That's great. I'll call you as soon we get to where we're going.

Dai *and* **Billy** *step out.*

O'Donnell *steps out.*

O'Donnell All OK?

Billy Yeah.

Dai Yeah.

O'Donnell What's the news?

Dai They're dribbling back to work all over.

Billy Everywhere except South Wales it's falling apart.

Dai Some people are heading to Nottingham, taking shifts there. Triple pay.

Billy Yeah, the colliery's open twenty-four hours, seven days a week in Nottingham.

Dai I heard that.

Billy *Triple* wages.

Dai And the NUM's cut the strike pay.

Billy *exhales.*

Dai It's hard to judge. When it's like that.

Billy After ten months, yeah.

O'Donnell Ceri wants us to go Moscow after this.

Dai There isn't a donation big enough that can turn this around.

O'Donnell It's not a donation. It's. To go to college.

Billy What?

O'Donell Revolutionary college.

Dai I'm done.

Billy I think I am too.

Dai I want to go home.

O'Donnell And what? Picket outside Merthyr Vale.

Dai Pff ... I'm not picketing anymore.

O'Donnell So what? You're gonna cross a line.

Dai No. But.

O'Donnell Tell me you're not thinking about going back to work.

Dai It's been ten months. I told Cathy it would be six weeks. I've done my shift. No one can call me a scab. I don't go back now, I won't have a wife.

O'Donnell Oh come on, Dai.

Dai We've gone without food, without sleep, without washing, we've been chased, beaten, we've broken the law. There isn't anything that's been asked of us that we haven't done. And still Scargill can't win this thing for us - maybe he doesn't deserve our support no more.

Beat.

O'Donnell Have you already got work lined up?

Beat.

You've got work lined up.

Beat.

What are you doing? Labouring? Taxis?

Dai No.

O'Donnell What are you doing? You're not going back underground.

Beat.

You been offered something? What have you been offered?

Dai Nothing.

O'Donnell If you've got something lined up then just say it.

Dai I haven't.

O'Donnell YOU HAVE! Where is it? Where is it? You're going to tell me right now. Right now. Where are you going? Where are you going? WHERE ARE / YOU GOING?

Dai Cotgrave. I'm going to Cotgrave.

Silence.

O'Donnell *goes weak at the knees, nearly falls over.*

O'Donnell Nottingham.

Beat.

And you?

Billy *hangs his head. He can't even say it.*

O'Donnell Bill. Bill?

Billy I'm tempted!

O'Donnell Bill.

Billy What? What else can we do?

O'Donnell Nottingham.

Silence.

Billy I'm not a scab.

O'Donnell *can't look at them.*

Billy This is different.

O'Donnell Are you sure?

Dai Be careful, John.

Billy I've been on strike ten months, no one can call me a scab.

O'Donnell If we win, no one will ever work with you ever again.

Billy Will you?

Silence.

O'Donnell No.

Silence.

Dai It doesn't matter because we're not gonna win.

O'Donnell How do you know?

Dai We're not gonna win.

Beat.

It's just a matter of when we give up. And it has been for a while.

Beat.

We're not gonna win.

O'Donnell Then we'll all be on the dole. Ready for that, are you? Because I'm not.

Beat.

What's the offer? Hmm? Nottingham. What's the offer?

Billy I dunno, Dai put me in touch.

O'Donnell *looks to* **Dai**.

O'Donnell Come on, then. What is it?

Dai Triple pay / and accommodation. Night shifts.

Billy *hangs his head.*

O'Donnell And what did you say?

Dai Said I'm interested. That I wanna speak to my wife.

O'Donnell And you?

Billy Said I'll think about it.

SFX - Phone ringing.

SFX - Second phone ringing.

Dai That's them. They said they'd call back to see what we say.

O'Donnell What we say?

Dai They asked me to talk to you.

Dai *goes to answer,* **O'Donnell** *beats him to it and hangs it up.*

Dai They're expecting us.

The phone starts ringing again.

O'Donnell So?

Dai We should answer.

O'Donnell No we shouldn't.

Dai Why don't you speak to them?

O'Donnell I'm not speaking to them.

Dai Speak to them.

O'Donnell I'm not speaking to them.

Billy Fucking hell.

Dai Just hear them out.

Billy This is so depressing.

Dai Just listen to what they have to say.

O'Donnell No.

Dai No one's gonna judge you at this point.

Billy Don't be fucking stupid, Dai, everyone's going to judge, most of all ourselves.

Dai Are we trying to do what's right or are we trying to win?

The phones continue to ring.

Dai You haven't got to agree to anything.

Billy Just listen to them? Just listen to what they have to say?

O'Donnell *doesn't move.*

The phone continues to ring.

O'Donnell *goes to the phone. He stares at it, eventually he picks up the phone.*

O'Donnell Hello? John. O'Donnell … Dai. Electrician.

Yeah. Yeah. Thank you. OK. How much a shift?

O'Donnell *hangs his head.*

Billy *goes over to him and puts a comforting hand on* **O'Donnell**'s *shoulder.* **Dai** *has his head in his hands. This is agony for all of them.*

O'Donnell (*voice cracking*) Yeah.

(*Clearing throat.*) Thank you.

Beat.

Thank you.

O'Donnell *hangs up.*

O'Donnell *returns to the boys and wipes tears from his eyes.*

Billy *wipes tears from his eyes.*

Billy Fuck's sake.

Dai So. What do you think?

Silence.

O'Donnell I think.

Beat.

You've been informing on us.

Dai What?

Billy   What you on about?

O'Donnell   Dai.

Dai   What?

O'Donnell   He's been informing on us.

Dai   I dunno what you're talking about.

O'Donnell   How long?

Dai   You've gone mad.

O'Donnell   How did Cotgrave get hold of you?

Dai   Cathy. She had a letter. Told me to give them a call.

O'Donnell   If I rung Cathy right now she'd say that, would she?

Pause.

Dai   Yeah.

O'Donnell   Ring her then, and give me the phone.

Dai   She goes to, uh, she goes to the club on Thursdays.

O'Donnell   That's fine, it's Wednesday.

Beat.

Dai   She probably won't remember.

Billy *swaps sides and joins* **O'Donnell**'s *side.*

Billy   Dai.

O'Donnell   Let's try shall we?

Dai *doesn't move.*

O'Donnell   You don't want to call her because you're lying. The Australian money got intercepted. The Canadian money didn't make it home either. The strike's grinding to a halt because the NUM haven't got any money. The money we're raising isn't getting back.

Because somehow they know everytime we try and send money back.

Dai You're paranoid.

Billy Yeah, steady on John.

O'Donnell Why did you want Jerzy's last name?

Billy *looks to* **Dai**.

Dai Being polite.

O'Donnell You wrote it down.

Dai It's hard to remember.

O'Donnell What do you need to remember for?

Dai I dunno.

O'Donnell Is the job offer a thank you?

Dai No!

O'Donnell And it coming to Billy and me gives you cover.

The phone rings, **Dai** *goes for it.*

O'Donnell No.

Dai I don't know what you're talking about.

O'Donnell How much are they paying you?

Billy Dai.

O'Donnell How much are they paying you?

Dai They're not paying me!

O'Donnell When did it start? Have you been informing since the start? Or did something flip a switch for you?

Silence.

Please, Dai.

Beat.

Bring it to an end now.

Beat.

It must be killing you.

Beat.

O'Donnell *hugs him.*

Silence.

Dai I was concussed. Nobody gave a shit.

Billy What you on about? I don't get it, what are you on about?

O'Donnell You've been informing since Orgreave.

Billy What?

Dai I'm sorry, John.

O'Donnell How much are they paying you?

Dai Twenty-five quid a tip off.

Billy YOU'RE A POLICE INFORMANT?

Dai I only give them / bits, I don't give them the whole picture.

Billy What the - what the fuck is going on? What are you saying? You're a fucking police informant?

Dai No!

Billy Well, what are you?

Dai I'm not a police informant. Every now and again. I'll give them bits of information. I'm not *informing* on you. I don't give them the whole picture. / Just little bits of detail. I've got two kids.

Billy WHOA WHOA WHOA. / What the fuck are you talking about?

O'Donnell You know this is over now.

Dai It was just bits of detail, nothing big, / I didn't give them anything big!

O'Donnell You're a police / informant!

Dai No I'm not! / I'm not some fucking spy.

Billy EVERYONE FUCKING SHUT UP! SHUT UP! You shut up! And you better fucking explain what is going on or I am going to fucking lose my shit. Talk.

Silence.

Dai Since Orgreave. I've been giving. Well. I've been giving the police … tip offs. Bits of information. Nothing massive. Just names of people. Times of meetings. That kind of thing. And they drop cash off at the house for Cathy and the kids.

Billy You've been working with the police behind our backs?

Pause.

Dai Yeah.

Billy You fucking two-faced lying fucking !

Billy *rushes to* **Dai** *to swing for him.*

O'Donnell *gets between them.*

Dai Whoa! / Back off! Calm down!

Billy I'll fucking kill / you! How could you do that to me?

Dai I was concussed! No one gave a shit.

Billy I carried you off the field! I held your hand / in hospital, you fucking twat.

Dai No one high up! Ceri! Kim! HQ, no one gives a shit.

Oh, you're concussed, are you? - Fuck off to Australia. They don't give a shit. Thatcher doesn't give a shit about us. And Scargill doesn't give a shit about us either. And if you can't see that then you're fucking mugs.

Silence.

Bill.

Silence.

It was only bits. I promise.

Billy I don't know / what to say.

Dai It wasn't that bad. Bill. Please. I still want us to win. But we're not gonna win.

Billy I'm done. Don't speak to me. Don't speak to my family. Don't come near me. Or my family.

Dai Bill. Bill!

Billy The best slave, is the slave who beats himself.

Dai Bill.

Billy I only want to hear your name if you're dead.

Billy (*to* **O'Donnell**) I'm done.

Billy *tuns and walks away from* **Dai** *and* **O'Donnell**.

Dai Billy!

Beat.

John?

Beat.

It was just a couple of tip offs. You know what I've done for the cause.

O'Donnell *turns his back and walks off in the opposite direction.*

Dai *is left on his own.*

Scene Twenty-Seven

Graveyard

Penny *watches as a coffin is lowered into the ground.*

Next to her stands **Huw Smith**.

A song is sung as **Huw**'s *family drop earth onto the coffin. Once they have all done.* **Huw** *turns to* **Penny**.

With all eyes on **Penny**, *she finds it within herself to walk to the grave, take some earth in her hands and drop it on the coffin she couldn't provide for her baby.*

Huw joins Penny, and they interlock arms, creating a new bond in grief. When they are both ready, they leave the graveside together.

Scene Twenty-Eight

Russia

Yura *has a a chalkboard which is written on it:*

'How to precipitate the context necessary to bring about the conditions suitable for revolutionary change'

Yura The proletarian class needs a vanguard group to lead the revolution.

The vanguard needs to raise the consciousness of the proletarian class to consolidate the revolution.

The wealthy and privileged class will not give up their advantages through democratic means. They will try to keep existing power structures that work to their advantage.

O'Donnell *enters.*

O'Donnell Sorry I'm late.

Yura Take a seat.

O'Donnell *takes a seat.*

Yura Dismantling power structures will only come about through a violent confrontation with the state.

The proletarian class need to match the state's level of preparedness for violence. The state is always prepared for violence.

The proletarian class needs to match and then outstrip the privileged class's willingness to inflict violence.

O'Donnell What if you can't do that? What if all you have is protest?

Yura Everything you hold dear. Every right. Whether it's your democratic right to vote. Or your weekend. Has come out of violent struggle with your oppressors. Violence is part of your history and culture. You cannot protest your way to liberty.

Beat.

Your only hope is the revolutionary brotherhood. Turn to the comrade beside you - introduce yourself. Tell them about your struggle … because they will win your war for you.

O'Donnell *turns to a fellow student and shakes his hand.*

Scene Twenty-Nine

IRA hideout

We're back with the IRA. Now they are all sat around, comfortably, maybe even at **O'Donnell***'s feet.*

O'Donnell And I met one of your colleagues - Liam. And that's how I ended up washed up here.

McGinty   Jesus Christ.

Con   That's one hell of a story.

O'Donnell   So, fellas. I hope you can see now that I'm not a spy. I'm not an informant. I've come to collect something Liam said you could help me with.

Beat.

And I'm happy to pay for it.

Beat.

Open my bag.

McGinty *opens a bag.*

Packets of money fall out.

O'Donnell   You know my story.

Beat.

You know I have the money.

Beat.

Now.

Beat.

Give me a gun.

Lights down.

Scene Thirty

Penrhiwceiber Police Station

An anxious **O'Donnell** *approaches.*

He paces back and forth with his hand in his pocket concealing a weapon.

Out steps a police officer, **PC Roger Hopkins***, to smoke, he doesn't see* **O'Donnell**.

O'Donnell *girds himself, trying to find the courage.*

He charges towards **PC Hopkins**, *who turns.*

PC Hopkins   John?

O'Donnell *freezes.*

PC Hopkins   It's Roger.

Beat.

Roger Hopkins.

Beat.

Hoppy. We were in school together.

O'Donnell   Hoppy?

PC Hopkins   How's it going?

O'Donnell   Uh …

PC Hopkins   You going in for something?

O'Donnell   No, no, I was just passing.

PC Hopkins   You still striking?

O'Donnell *nods.*

PC Hopkins   Fucking unbelievable what they're doing, innit?

Beat.

Breaks my heart.

Beat.

All you boys.

Beat.

I see Penny now and again at the school gates. When I'm on nights. I pick them up before coming in and see her then, I always ask about you. You still up by Haulwen?

O'Donnell   Still up there.

PC Hopkins My mam's still up there. Number 82. She's got a dog in a wheelchair.

O'Donnell I know.

PC Hopkins Pushes him around.

O'Donnell I've seen her pushing him around.

PC Hopkins How much longer you reckon you'll stay out for?

O'Donnell Dunno.

Beat.

Till it's over.

PC Hopkins Gutted for you being caught up in all this. You know the Government are arseholes but the NUM are arseholes as well. It's like our lives are turned upside down because they can't do their jobs. It'd all be sorted by tea time if you took them out and stuck a couple of our Mams in there.

Beat.

I'm telling you.

Beat.

Instead we've got all this.

Beat.

And what the fuck have we got if we haven't got the pits?

O'Donnell Dunno.

PC Hopkins Fag?

O'Donnell *nods.*

PC Hopkins Remember we found a pack of fags in Porthcawl once?

O'Donnell Oh yeah. Trecco Bay.

PC Hopkins Trecco Bay. Fucking brilliant. I used to love Miners' Fortnight. The whole village would all go down the same caravan site for a fortnight. Same families, same kids from school but we'd be playing on sand dunes rather than slag heaps. It was brilliant, wasn't it?

Beat.

Remember all the deck chairs we used to have to carry down?

O'Donnell Fucking hell, I remember them. They were so heavy. And getting your finger caught in them.

PC Hopkins I cut my foot on glass once and this miner found me and carried me all the way across the beach, across the front, up to the caravan site until we found my mam.

Beat.

Didn't put me down once.

Beat.

Cheering me up the whole time, telling me I'll be alright. That I'm brave. He carried me all the way.

Beat.

Who's gonna carry that kid now? When all this is gone.

PC Hopkins *puts his fag on the floor and stamps it out.*

PC Hopkins Good to see you John, butt. Give Penny my love.

PC Hopkins *shakes* **O'Donnell**'s *hand.*

O'Donnell *doesn't want to let go.*

Somehow **O'Donnell** *pulls* **PC Hopkins** *in for a hug.* **PC Hopkins** *is caught by surprise.*

Eventually **PC Hopkins** *reciprocates the hug.*

O'Donnell *lets him go.*

PC Hopkins *heads in.* **O'Donnell** *approaches a bin.*

He pulls out a gun takes one final look at it and throws it in the bin.

Scene Thirty-One

Cynon Valley Workingmen's Hall

Penny *is preparing boxes for the community.*

Community Members *come in and out, drink tea and seek sympathy.*

O'Donnell *enters.*

He watches **Penny** *working.*

He approaches.

Penny   Anything special you need in the box?

O'Donnell   No.

Penny *puts some final items in and hands it over to* **O'Donnell**. *When she finds him, their eyes meet. Both of them have their hands on the box but they both drop it.*

They hug.

And then she starts hitting him.

Penny   Why don't you pick up the phone?

O'Donnell   They're tapping our phones!

Penny   Just pick up the phone! I thought you were dead!

O'Donnell   I'm back. I'm back.

Beat.

I'm not going anywhere ever again.

Beat.

I'm home. I'm home.

Beat.

Come here.

He hugs her again.

Penny You hurt me.

O'Donnell I know. I'm sorry. I'm not going anywhere. I'm not going to leave your side.

Penny You don't know me anymore.

Pause.

O'Donnell Pen.

Penny I'm not who you left behind.

O'Donell Pen. I'm sorry. I'll do whatever you want to make it up to you.

Penny 'Make it up to me'?

O'Donnell What do you mean?

Penny You have no idea.

O'Donnell Penny.

Penny I have work to do.

Beat.

O'Donnell Pen, I've been half way around the world, I've been arrested, chased, kidnapped, beaten, robbed, I've been followed by spies. The one thing that has kept me going is thinking of you and the kids.

Penny We are not a prize for bravery.

Silence.

O'Donnell I know.

Penny You taught us how to live without you. It's been the hardest lesson, especially the kids. We didn't want to learn it, but we did.

O'Donnell I'm back now.

Penny And you might be off / tomorrow.

O'Donnell It's over.

Beat.

It's over. We're not going to win.

Very long silence as **Penny** *looks at all of her hard work. Everything she's created and how* **O'Donnell** *is taking it all away.*

O'Donnell Come on. Let's go home.

Penny *hangs her head.*

Penny You're going back to work?

O'Donnell I dunno. But I'm not doing this anymore, come on.

Penny But.

O'Donnell The strike's collapsing. Any day now, we'll all be going back. So you might as well give up as well.

Penny *stops.*

Penny People still need help.

O'Donnell Come on.

Beat.

Because it's done. It's over.

Penny Says who?

O'Donnell Says me.

Penny You don't get to say it's over.

O'Donnell OK then, Scargill will say it's over in a matter of days.

Penny He doesn't get to say either.

O'Donnell What are you talking about?

Penny You don't tell me what to do.

O'Donnell NO. *THEY* DO.

Penny *THEY* DON'T TELL ME WHAT TO DO EITHER.

O'Donnell You have no idea what I've been through.

Penny And you have *no* idea what I've been through. And I will never forgive you for that.

A stand off.

O'Donnell Penny.

Penny No.

Penny *reverts to packing another box.*

O'Donnell I've been back five minutes, can't you just …

Beat.

You can't beat them with food parcels.

Penny Maybe I'm not trying to beat them! Maybe I'm not trying to win. Maybe I know that it's not a game. That it's bigger than that. Maybe it's not all about pickets and fights and coppers and guns and men chasing each other with sticks.

Maybe it's more than that. Just because you've stopped running around chasing each other doesn't mean that it's over.

O'Donnell What the hell can you do with a few tins of soup?

Penny Fuck you, John.

O'Donnell I'm sorry. I'm sorry. I'm sorry.

Penny Fuck you.

O'Donnell I'm sorry. I'm sorry.

Penny Go and see if there's some coppers to wrestle with. I've got work to do. People who need me. People who respect me. People who pick up the phone.

O'Donnell Fine. I'm going … I'll see you at home.

Penny Get back here.

O'Donnell I am this close.

Penny Get back here NOW.

The volume and force shocks everyone, even **Penny**.

O'Donnell *stops.*

Slowly he returns to her.

Penny *gathers herself and hands him a box.*

Penny Soup, bread, veg, sanitary products and cereal. Pack it.

O'Donnell I'm not packing boxes.

Penny You're packing boxes.

O'Donnell Why?

Penny Because this isn't about you. Or your ego. And if you haven't learned that yet, you're going to learn it now. It's not about you or them or the NUM. It's about the person standing next to you and the person standing next to you needs a box. And if we can provide that, then as far as I'm concerned. That's a win.

Beat.

Maybe you're right, maybe I can't change them. But they won't change me.

Shaz *enters with a box.*

Shaz Christine's bringing the van around in a minute, these shoes are doing my fucking - oh. Hello, John.

O'Donnell Shaz.

Shaz Haven't seen you for a long while.

O'Donnell *smiles.*

Shaz (*discreet*) You OK?

Penny (*discreet*) Yeah.

Shaz Been too long. Gonna take some adjusting.

O'Donnell I'll wait.

Shaz For *you*. I'll get the door.

Shaz *leaves.*

Penny We're opening now. I'll be serving people for however long there's a queue.

Mike *enters.* **O'Donnell** *sits down.*

Penny Hiya, Mike, how's your mother?

Mike Not too good.

Penny There's some painkillers in there for her.

Mike Thank you, Penny.

O'Donnell (*discreet*) I'll see you back at the house.

Penny (*cheerfully*) No.

O'Donnell (*discreet*) I don't want to hang around here with all these people.

Penny *hands him a box.*

Penny Soup, bread, veg, sanitary products and cereal. Hiya, Lisa! How's the kids?

Lisa Eating me out of house and home. Matthew got a merit in his art this week.

Penny Did he?

O'Donnell What you want me to do?

Penny (*to* **O'Donnell**) Pack it. (*To* **Lisa**.) Bring it in, we'll stick it on the wall here.

Lisa I will!

O'Donnell (*discreet*) I'm not packing boxes.

Penny See you next week.

Penny *smiles at* **Lisa**, *then glowers at* **O'Donnell**, *who slowly starts to pack.*

Liam *enters.*

Liam Have you got any tinned ham?

Penny I'll just check.

Penny *turns to* **O'Donnell**. **Penny** *indicates for him to go and check the stores.* **O'Donnell** *silently communicates his bemusement,* **Penny** *silently tells him to move his fucking arse.*

O'Donnell *heads to the stores and starts searching.*

Penny No JPR today, Liam?

Liam He's at the vet's, he's got a perineal abscess.

Penny Oh, poor JPR.

O'Donnell I found it! I found it!

O'Donnell *rushes over and puts tinned ham in the box.*

O'Donnell Tinned ham.

O'Donnell *taps it with pride.*

Liam Thank you, butt.

O'Donnell Welcome.

Penny *looks to* **O'Donnell**. *His shame lifting ...*

Penny *slides another empty box over.*

Penny   Soup, bread, veg, / sanitary products and cereal.

O'Donnell   Sanitary products, cereal.

O'Donnell *knows what he's doing now.*

Sara *enters.*

Penny   Here you go, love.

Sara   Oh thanks, Penny.

Penny   How are you bearing up?

Sara   Day at a time.

Penny *goes around the table and hugs* **Sara**. *She holds onto her tight.*

At first **O'Donnell** *doesn't know where to look, he feels embarrassed.*

Eventually, **O'Donnell** *stops trying to distract himself and he takes in what* **Penny** *is doing.*

Helen *enters.*

Helen   Alright, love.

O'Donnell   Oh, here you go.

Helen   Have you got any toilet paper?

O'Donnell   Let me check.

O'Donnell *goes to the stores.*

Toilet paper, toilet paper, toilet paper!

He adds it to the box.

Helen   You're a star, thank you. I don't know what I'd do without you.

Helen leaves.

Penny *disengages from* **Sara**.

Sara I'll see you soon.

Penny Pop in any time now, any time.

Vinny *comes in.* **O'Donnell** *hands him a box.*

Vinny Thank you, butt.

O'Donnell No problem.

Vinny Not picketing?

O'Donnell Uh no, not any more. I don't think.

Vinny *reaches over and pats* **O'Donnell** *on the shoulder.*

A break in demand.

O'Donnell How long have you been doing this?

Penny Months. And I'm going to keep doing it for as long as people need it.

O'Donnell *gets a box out and starts packing it.*

Penny *smiles and joins him.*

O'Donnell *and* **Penny** *pack boxes and* **Community Members** *keep coming in, for parcels ... They are packing boxes and as* **Community Members** *stream in, they turn behind* **Penny** *and* **O'Donnell** *and change the scene from 1984 to 2024. The Mining Family Relief Centre has become a foodbank/warm bank. The* **Community Members** *hold mobile phones rather than newspapers. Cups of tea are served, support is given, hugs are shared, no judgement is offered, no shame is cast, the struggle continues.*

A moment between them - a glimmer of hope for repair.

Penny reaches out her hand and John takes it, they hold hands.

The End.

Nye

Thanks

Rufus Norris, Kate Varah and all at the National Theatre. Ben Power, Sarah Clarke, Sarah Corke, Nina Steiger, Stewart Pringle and all at the NT Studio. Graeme Farrow and all at the Wales Millennium Centre, Pádraig Cusack, Michael Sheen, Roger Evans, Remy Beasley, Sharon Small, Lee Mengo, Dan Hawksford, Matt Bulgo, Francesca Goodridge, Jess Williams, Steven Hogget, Paule Constable, Vicki Mortimer, Will Stuart, Donato Wharton, Kinnetia Isidore, Patricia Logue, Meredydd Barker, Hamish Pirie, Mawgaine Tarrant-Cornish, Dr Matt Morgan, Dr Lara McMillan, The King of the North, Cathy King and all at 42, Big Pit, Neil Kinnock, The South Wales Miners' Museum, Councillor Alyson Tippings and all at Tredegar Town Council, Phil, Menna, Matthew, Maryline, Joseph and Sophia Price, Franklin Moss Price, Martha Moss Price, Chloë Moss, Gary Marsh, Mark Jefferies.

Author's Note

This play took over ten years to write, and I was lucky enough to make it with actors who I have worked with for over twenty years. It is a great comfort to look at the cast list and see decades-long friendships. During the writing of this play we lost a friend, one of the finest actors Wales has produced. While he had nothing to do with the show, if he was still with us there is no doubt he would have been in the room and on the stage beside us. His name isn't in the cast list but it feels right that his name is in this book because whatever we do, he is still very much with us and always will be – Alex Beckett.

Nye was first performed at the Olivier Theatre, London, on 6 March 2024, before transferring to Wales Millennium Centre, Cardiff, from 18 May to 1 June 2024.

Cast

Nye Bevan, *various ages, Welsh*
Jennie Lee, *various ages, Scottish*
Nurse Ellie/Arianwen, *twenties*
Dr Dain/Winston Churchill, *forties/eighties*
David Bevan, *various ages, Welsh*
Neville Chamberlain/Dr Frankel, *forties, English*
Archie Lush, *various ages, Welsh*
Clement Attlee/Matron, *fifties, English*
Patient 1/Herbert Morrison MP, *fifties, English*
Lucy Prichard, *nine and twenty-one, Welsh*
Alun Jones, *nine, Welsh*
Owen Thomas, *nine, Welsh*
Luke Williams, *nine, Welsh*
Mark Smith, *nine, Welsh*
Sarah Roberts, *nine, Welsh*
William Jones, *nine, Welsh*
Ross Evans, *nine, Welsh*
Dyfan Williams, *nine, Welsh*

Jack Stockton, *twenty-one, Welsh*
Gwen Davies, *various ages, Welsh*
Neil Jones, *various ages, Welsh*
Councillor Jones, *Tredegar Iron and Coal Company (any)*
Councillor Hopkins, *Tredegar Iron and Coal Company (any)*
Councillor Williams, *Tredegar Iron and Coal Company (any)*
Clerk, *any*
Tory MPs 1–5, *MPs, any*
Patients 1–20
The Cleaner
Speaker
Mr Howells *any, Welsh*
Mrs Jones *any, Welsh*
Mr Hill *any, Welsh*
Mr Llywelyn *any, Welsh*
Mr Fury *any, Welsh*
Mrs Lewis *any, Welsh*

Mr Leslie, *any Welsh*
Mr Francis, *any, Welsh*
Civil Servants 1–10 *any*
Doctor Voiceover

Author's note

/ *indicates when the next line should start being spoken.*

... *indicates the trailing off of a thought.*

– *indicates an interruption of thought.*

() *means a word that Nye was trying to say but gives up and switches to another.*

Bold *words mean the word could be treated by sound design.*

On stuttering

Like all stutters, Nye's changed and evolved throughout his life; as he gained more control with age, new sounds became more difficult. The text suggests where stuttering is likely to have occurred and when, but it is also for the performer to find where these might occur. Plosive sounds, alevolar consonants, the voiceless alevolar sibilant at the start of words.

Prologue

NHS Royal Free Hospital 1960

Fantasia – sound design swell.

In his pyjamas, **Nye** *stands.*

Death's *arms engulf* **Nye**.

Nye   ARIANWEEEEN! HELP!

Nye *screams, terrified.*

Lights down.

Scene One

NHS Royal Free Hospital Hampstead 1960

A busy NHS Ward with 8 beds in curtains around their bays. Doctors and Nurses attend to various Patients.

Upstage sits **Matron** *at a desk with a lamp.*

Archie *and* **Jennie** *pace back and forth.*

A patient nearby behind curtains struggles to breathe and wheezes in an oxygen mask.

A patient struggles to walk with a cane.

Another patient sits reading a newspaper.

A manual buzzer sounds as patients call for a nurse.

On the radio somewhere, 'Get Happy' plays.

Matron Yes, he's just out of theatre. Nurse, straighten your apron. Chaps, patient incoming.

Being pushed by a porter – **Nye** *is wheeled onto the ward. His arrival is noted by patients and nurses – a pause as he is taken to his bay. As* **Nye** *is settled into his bay:*

Archie   OK. (*Discreet.*) Are you OK?

Jennie (*discreet*)   I'm OK.

Archie *gives* **Jennie** *an awkward hug.*

Archie (*discreet*)   Gonna be OK. We'll do it together.

Nye *is grimacing.*

Nye   Hmmmaaw . . .

Jennie   He's coming round. He's coming round.

Nye   Hmammma . . .

Long silence.

Nye blinks awake.

Archie   Here he is. Hello.

Nye   Jennie.

Jennie   Here I am. I'm here.

Nye *puts his arms out to her, they hug. He kisses her.*

Nye   Archie?

Archie   Alright butt?

Jennie   How are you feeling?

Nye   Awful.

Nye *is grimacing.*

Jennie   Nye, try and lie still, you've just had an operation.

Nye *shifts again wincing.*

Nye   Where am I?

Jennie   The recovery ward.

Archie   You had an operation. The ulcer?

Jennie   You're in hospital.

Archie   Remember?

Jennie The nurses have been *wonderful*. They've been coming to check on you. Making sure everything's OK.

Nye It hurts.

Jennie You've had an operation. You're in a hospital.

Archie Hospital you built. Look.

This lands with **Nye**.

He blinks.

Nye Look.

Slowly, he becomes more conscious of his surroundings, he sits up, and takes in the surrounding ward.

He sees socialised medicine in action:

1) A Patient passing in a wheelchair.

2) A Nurse putting flowers into a vase for a patient.

3) A Librarian pushing a trolley of books.

4) A Patient wearing an oxygen mask, doctors listening to his chest.

5) Nurses helping a Patient learn to walk with a with a crutch.

6) A curtain animating as a Nurse finds her way out.

Nye *turns to* **Jennie** *with the biggest broadest smile –* **Jennie** *has to hide her heart breaking.*

Archie I'll, uh. I'll see if the Doctor is free.

Nye So nice. Seeing it. Without everyone . . . standing to attention. Isn't it?

Jennie Nye.

Nye Look at what we did.

Jennie Darling, / there's something . . .

Nye And there's more to do.

(Off Jennie.)

I'm fine. I'm not going anywhere. Except maybe Number 10.

Dr Dain *appears.*

Jennie has to gather herself, she looks for Archie but there's no sign

Dr Dain   Mr Bevan. Good to see you're awake. How are you feeling?

Nye   Bit rough.

Dr Dain   It'll take some time for the effects of the anaesthetic to wear off. Are you comfortable? Would you like me to come back later?

Jennie   Yes, maybe later.

Nye   No no, it's fine. Go ahead.

Dr Dain   Are you sure?

Nye   Yes yes.

Dr Dain   OK. Mind if I examine you?

Nye   Go ahead.

Dr Dain   Deep breath for me. One more, good.

Dr Dain *checks* **Nye**'s *pulse. He shines a torch in* **Nye**'s *eye. He examines* **Nye**'s *surgical wound.*

Dr Dain   All looking as it should. Mr Bevan, I need to talk you through some things with the operation. It was meant to be a two-hour procedure, but in the end, we kept you under for six hours continuous.

Nye   Why so long? You got the ulcer, didn't you?

Dr Dain   So.

Jennie   Yes! Yes, they got it. All went fine.

A moment between **Jennie** *and* **Dr Dain**.

Scene One 143

Jennie It was fine. Wasn't it? You just need to be careful. And get plenty of rest. Doctor, you can you tell him, can't you? Everything went fine. Didn't it?

Jennie *is imploring.*

Dr Dain Yes. I performed a, a laparotomy. And I found a large, duodenal, ulcer. About an inch and a quarter by an inch. Then we used an omentum patch, some fatty tissue, to patch over the top. There were no complications, beyond finding such a big ulcer, which is why it took so long. So, bed rest for three weeks.

Nye When can I leave?

Dr Dain Let's focus on getting better, shall we?

Nye I want to get back to work.

Nye *grimaces in pain.*

Jennie You'll be back to work soon. Won't he, Doctor?

Beat.

Dr Dain I can't see why you can't be back at work. Soon. We tell people, no lifting for at least three months.

Nye Can I – AAAHhh . . .

Nye *writhes in pain.*

Jennie What is it? Doctor! What's wrong?

Dr Dain Try not to move too much, Mr Bevan . . . it will subside.

Jennie What's happening, Doctor?

Dr Dain *presses a buzzer – 'Buzzer!'*

Matron *approaches.*

Dr Dain Matron, a fifth of a grain of morphine please.

Matron *leaves.*

Nye HELP! AAhhhh

Jennie What is going on? Is this . . . the operation or . . .

Dr Dain Mr Bevan, deep breaths if you can . . .

Nye *writhes in pain before eventually collapsing back in his bed exhausted.*

Dr Dain Can we move Mr Bevan to bay seven?

Porters appear and start to move **Nye**. **Dr Dain** *walks with him.*

Jennie Where are you taking him?

Dr Dain Just somewhere with a little more privacy.

Nye AHH, JESUS CHRIST!

Nye *tries to grab something.*

Matron Mr Dain, some pentobarbital maybe?

Dr Dain Yes. Two grains please.

Matron This will make things more comfortable, Mr Bevan.

Nurse Ellie *fits the drip to* **Nye**'s *hand.*

Jennie He's in a lot of pain.

Nye Please can you do something?

Nurse Ellie This will take care of it, Mr Bevan, just a few minutes and you'll start to feel the difference.

Jennie Is this . . . uh, *normal*?

Matron *helps* **Nurse Ellie** *with the drugs.*

Dr Dain Could I speak to you outside?

Jennie Uh. Yes. Yes of course.

Jennie *stands up, she doesn't want to leave* **Nye**.

She kisses **Nye** *and eventually follows* **Dr Dain** *out.*

Nye Can I have a drink?

Nurse Ellie Some water?

Nye A drink drink.

Beat.

Whiskey.

Nurse Ellie You can't get whiskey on the NHS, Mr Bevan.

Nye Well, that's a bloody oversight.

Nurse Ellie This shouldn't take too long before you start to feel more comfortable.

Nye *groans.*

Nye Talk to me. Distract me.

Nurse Ellie I can't tell you the number of girls I've had offering to swap shifts with me.

Nye What for?

Nurse Ellie Everyone wants to look after you.

Nye Does everyone know I'm here?

Nurse Ellie Well. Not officially, no. But, we're *nurses*.

Nye Oh God. Everyone knows. Be in the bloody *Daily Mail* tomorrow.

Nurse Ellie No, they just want to know what you're like. One girl wanted to know what you're reading? What colour your pyjamas are?

The pain begins to subside.

Nye I hope you said I'm the best dressed patient you've ever had.

Nurse Ellie Absolutely, I can't lie about that. Feeling anything now?

Nye Hmm . . . not sure. Still a bit . . .

Nurse Ellie Can you try counting back from ten for me?

Nye Ten . . . Nine . . .

Nurse Ellie That's right . . .

Nye Eight . . .

Nurse Ellie It's funny being this close to you.

Nye Seven . . .

Nurse Ellie I went to see you speak once.

Nye Six . . .

Nurse Ellie My sister and I came down from Nottingham. Keep counting . . .

Nye Five . . .

Nurse Ellie I was already signed up for nursing, and she was doing a secretarial course . . .

Nye Four.

Nurse Ellie But after seeing you speak she switched to nursing like me.

Nye Three

Nurse Ellie She's at Bart's now. We could barely see you and now look, I'm tucking you in.

Nye Two . . .

Nurse Ellie Making sure you're comfortable. I'm going to look after you, I promise. And then, I'm gonna tell my sister.

Scene Two

Family home 1925

Nye Sister.

Arianwen You're late.

Nye *turns and he sees his sister* **Arianwen** *who is also, somehow,* **Nurse Ellie**.

Nye I'm uh . . .

Arianwen You're late, Nye.

Nye I was just . . .

Arianwen How come you're so late? What happened?

Nye I dunno. Archie was there.

Arianwen Going over the cases for tomorrow.

Nye Yeah, I think so.

Arianwen Did they give you a room in the club?

Nye I can't remember.

Arianwen Have you eaten?

Nye *feels his stomach, it's sore.*

Nye Um . . . I'll be OK.

Arianwen You need to eat, there's soup.

Nye It's fine.

Arianwen *hands him some soup.*

Nye I'm fine.

Arianwen No, you need to eat, you probably haven't eaten all day. You can't be a miner's agent if you're fainting at tribunals.

Eventually **Nye** *concedes and eats the soup.*

Arianwen How did you get home?

Nye Www-walked.

Arianwen Why didn't you get the bus?

Nye I fancied a ww-walk.

Arianwen With all your papers?

Nye I fancied the walk.

Arianwen Up the hill with your papers? Were the buses running?

Nye Yeah mh-but it's ff-fine.

Arianwen *goes to a purse and puts a coin on his soup tray.*

Nye *stares at it.*

Arianwen Mrs Richards Garw Nant, paid for her curtains in advance.

Nye I don't mind walking.

Arianwen I don't want you coming home exhausted and falling asleep in the chair.

Arianwen *pushes the coin towards him.*

Nye *takes it.*

Nye I'll pay you bbmh-back. That was d-d (delicious) tasty, thank you.

Nye *gets up to leave.*

Arianwen Get the bus tomorrow.

Nye Yeah, I'll try.

Arianwen No.

Beat.

Get the bus. Get home a bit earlier.

Nye I've got a lot on / with all the cases.

Arianwen I know.

Nye I've got three hearings / this w-week.

Arianwen I'm not saying you're not busy. Just get home a bit earlier.

Nye If I can't get men bbmh-back into w-work then they're destitute / Arianwen.

Arianwen I know.

Nye I've got whole fff-families relying on me.

Arianwen So this family can't rely on you?

Nye What do you ww-want from me? You've been on pins since I got in.

Arianwen I want you to come home on time.

Nye Fine. I'll come home on time.

Arianwen And then when you come home on time, I want you to sit with Dad, someone needs to sit with him all the time now and if you start doing your bit then it means Mam and I can have a rest.

Nye Do you have any *idea* how much reading I've got to do?

Arianwen Do you have any idea what I've got on? I've got my sewing work. I'm caring for Dad. / I'm doing housework for Mam. I'm getting medicines. Shopping. Cooking your tea. And it seems all you do, is your Union work which doesn't pay enough even for a bus fare.

Nye OK OK.

Arianwen I'm sorry. But. It's Dad! You've always put him on a pedestal. Why don't you care?

Nye I do cc-care.

Arianwen Then show it.

Nye You're better at looking after him than me.

Arianwen I'm better than you at everything. / Doesn't mean I should do everything.

Nye Right, I'm done here.

Nye *turns and leaves.*

Arianwen He asked after you.

Nye *stops in his tracks . . .*

Nye What, what did he say?

Arianwen 'Where's Nye?'

Nye That's all?

Arianwen Well, that nearly killed him. And if he has to ask again, it might kill him.

Nye That's all he said?

Arianwen That's all he could say.

Nye Has the doctor been?

Arianwen He's been.

Nye What did he ss-say?

Arianwen What he always says, steam and tonic, steam and tonic. Up and down the valley.

Nye That's why we need to try and a-get compensation / we need to

Arianwen Dad doesn't want compensation.

Nye He bloody should, we need to / take the case to the

Arianwen Dad doesn't want money.

Nye It's not about the money, it's about natural justice, it's about somebody seeing / what he's going through.

Arianwen Dad doesn't want anyone to see what he's going through, / he wants privacy and his family.

Nye No-one's looking at our lives and thinking it's not fair that men are dying in their fifties. Or that children have got rickets. Or that women are dying of childbed fever. No-one's thinking about us. So we have to mhp-p (push) fight for every grain of justice or fairness. And this is not fair. And if no-one will speak for us then I will.

Arianwen The thing that you're not hearing is, no-one is asking you to.

Pause.

Nye Mh mh-but . . . I cc-can. I can get justice

Arianwen No-one is asking you to do this though, Nye.

Nye I can fix things / I can mh-p-p (put) make things right.

Arianwen No-one wants you to fix things. No-one expects you to fix things. Dad doesn't want you to fix things. He just wants to see you before he dies.

Arianwen *leaves . . .*

Nye *turns to his father's bed.*

Filled with fear, he pulls a curtain . . .

Scene Three

Sirhowy Elementary School 1908

*To reveal his childhood classmates (***Neil Jones**, **Gwen Davies**, **Owen Thomas**, **William Jones**, **Luke Williams**, **Sarah Roberts**, **Ross Doherty**, **Lucy Pritchard**, **Mark Smith**, **Archie Lush***) all singing. They are also patients and staff from the ward.* **Mr Orchard** *is somehow monstrous.*

Part 1 – The Caning

Schoolkids 'I hear thy welcome voice, That calls me, Lord, to thee; For cleansing in thy precious blood, That flow'd on Calvary. I am coming, Lord! / Coming –'

Mr Orchard *sees* **Nye**.

Mr Orchard Bevan! Where do you think you're going? Trying to escape. Stand up! Don't slouch. Straight, I said . . . Your sister Arianwen is a star pupil yet you seem to want to get out of every class.

Nye Sssssssssssssorry . . . ssssssir

Mr Orchard Seats.

The school children run to their seats.

Mr Orchard Page one. Together.

Schoolkids I wandered lonely as a cloud that floats on high o'er vales / and hills

Mr Orchard Jones, Neil, take over. Loud and clear, enunciate every word, please.

Neil When all at once I saw a crowd

Mr Orchard Jones, William take over.

William A host, of golden daffodils.

Mr Orchard Pritchard!

Lucy Beside the lake, beneath the trees

Mr Orchard Bevan!

Nye Fffffl . . . Fluttttring and d-d-ddd dd.

Mr Orchard Dancing!

Nye Ddddd d ddd

Mr Orchard Everyone is waiting, Bevan.

Beat.

Fluttering and dancing in the breeze. Next line.

Nye C-c-ccc-c-ccc-ccc

Mr Orchard ENUNCIATE! CONTINUOUS! Spit, it, out, boy! Continuous! Enunciate!

Nye C-c-coontt -tttt-tt t–

Mr Orchard Continuous! Don't look down! What are you looking at your shoes for? Continuous as the stars that shine

Beat.

Don't shake your head at me. You will say continuous, or I will cane you.

Silence.

Nye Cc cc . . .

Mr Orchard Continuous.

Nye Cc-ccc-ccc . . .

Mr Orchard Continuous.

Nye Tsssss.

Mr Orchard CONTINUOUS CONTINUOUS /CONTINUOUS!

Nye I CAN'T!

Archie He's gorra a stutter, sir, why don' you ask one of us to read?

Mr Orchard Because, Lush, you all need to learn self-reliance! No-one is going to look after you when you leave school. Bevan, give me your hand. Hand, Bevan.

Nye I-III . . .

Mr Orchard HAND, BEVAN, NOW!

Silence.

Say continuous.

Nye C-cccc

Mr Orchard *canes* **Nye***'s hand.*

Nye AAAoooww!!

Mr Orchard Continuous!

Nye Ccc-ccc-c-ccc

Mr Orchard *canes* **Nye***'s hand.*

Nye Awwwoooo.

Mr Orchard Continuous.

Mr Orchard *prepares to swipe.*

Archie Continuous.

Nye Continuous.

Mr Orchard *has to stop himself.*

Mr Orchard Lush! Stay out of this. Continuous as the stars that shine

Nye As the sssssss-sss-ssss-ss

Archie Stars!

Nye Stars

Archie That

Nye That

Archie Shine

Nye Shine

Mr Orchard *has to drop his cane.*

Mr Orchard One more word out of you, Lush, and I swear I will cane you too! Continuous as the stars that shine.

Nye C-cc-cccc

Archie Continuous.

Nye Continuous . . .

Mr Orchard Lush, step forward.

Nye Nnno no nnnnno nnnooo. NNnnnnnooo s sssssssssir he was just he was jus' 'elping ssssssss. Ssssssss. Sssssss ir.

Mr Orchard Hand.

Nye NNNnnnnoo nnnnno nnnnnnoo sssssssir ah he ah sssssssiii nnnnnnoo he was jus' he was 'elping . . .

Mr Orchard Hand out, Lush.

Archie *puts his hand out.*

Mr Orchard *is about to swipe when* **Nye** *puts his hand on top of* **Archie***'s.*

A moment.

Mr Orchard Move. Move your hand, Bevan, or you will get ten strokes for disobedience.

Nye *doesn't move.*

Nye Nnnnooo, sir.

Mr Orchard Fine. I will cane you until you move your hand.

Mr Orchard *raises his hand to swipe . . .*

And then **Lucy** *runs and puts her hand on* **Nye***'s.*

Mr Orchard What are you doing?

And **Neil** *and* **Owen** *and* **Gwen**.

Mr Orchard What are you doing? Sit down!

Lucy No / sir.

Neil We're not sitting down, sir.

Owen Nor / us, sir.

Gwen Not fair, sir / and you know it.

William We're not sitting down until you stop caning them, sir.

And **William**, **Mark**, **Ross**, **Sarah**, *everyone else except* **Luke** *has their hands on* **Archie'***s.*

Mr Orchard SIT DOWN NOW! THE LOT OF YOU!

Mr Orchard *swipes his cane, the children pull their hands away.*

Part 2 – The Fightback

Nye *steps towards* **Mr Orchard**.

Nye Not until you sssssstop ttt-t-trying to hit everyone.

156 Nye

Mr Orchard *swings his cane to strike* **Nye**, *the children rush* **Mr Orchard** *and bundle him.*

Neil Stop it, sir! / You can't be trying to hit everyone.

Gwen Get him! / Put him over there.

Owen You can't / do this, sir.

Mr Orchard WHAT THE HELL DO YOU THINK YOU'RE DOING? PUT ME DOWN IMMEDIATELY!

Mr Orchard *swipes for the children.*

Nye Sir! You're out of c-c-c-c-control, sir!

Mr Orchard's *attention is drawn to* **Nye**; *he approaches him.*

Mr Orchard I'll show you control! I have never heard so much insolence in all of my days.

Mr Orchard *goes to attack* **Nye** *again; the class swarm* **Mr Orchard** *again.*

Part 3 – The Bundle

Neil Pin him down! Hold him down!

Ross Hold him / down, Hold him down!

Sarah Please, sir / we're trying to help!

Mark Get his / cane off him!

Lucy Grab his cane!

Mr Orchard *breaks free and points a cane at* **Lucy**.

Lucy Stop / it, sir!

William Leave her, sir.

Mr Orchard In your / seat, Pritchard.

Lucy No, sir!

Archie You can't do this, / sir!

Nye You're gonna g-g-g-get sssssacked, sir!

Mr Orchard I will make sure that every single one of you is expelled.

Luke I'd like it known that I have had nothing to do with this.

Neil When I tell Mr Hopkins he's gonna sack you.

Mr Orchard *lunges for* **Neil**.

Mr Orchard Don't threaten me, Jones!

Mr Orchard *lunges at the group.*

Part 4 – Orchard Fights Back

Archie I'm telling!

Archie *exits.*

Nye You need to calm down.

Mr Orchard *turns towards* **Nye**.

Mr Orchard You, Bevan! You started this insurrection. I'll make sure Mr Hopkins holds you down / himself while I –

The children protect **Nye**.

The children behind **Mr Orchard** *grab him.*

Ross Grab / him! Put him over there!

Sarah You'll make it worse.

Neil Put / him in the bin!

Gwen You / have to stop, sir!

Owen Grab / his cane!

Mr Orchard Put me down! How dare you put your hands on me? / Put me down immediately.

Mark If you want us to listen to you, you'd better start treating us with some respect!

Mr Orchard Shut your mouth, Smith.

Mr Orchard *traps* **Mark**.

Part 5 – The Final Battle

Nye You shut up, sir! You're a ffff-fucking mmhm a-bully! And everyone knows it!

Mark *escapes and* **Mr Orchard** *swipes towards* **Nye**.

Lucy You're gonna get sacked, sir!

Mr Orchard *swipes for* **Lucy**.

Neil What's he doing?

Gwen He's gone mad!

Mr Orchard *swipes again.*

Mr Orchard Shut your mouths!

William PLEASE, SIR!

Neil My dad said you were prick, sir!

Mr Orchard *lunges for* **Neil** *and strikes* **Luke** *by accident.*

The children circle **Mr Orchard**, *and* **Mr Orchard** *swipes for every one of them in every direction.*

Mr Orchard ALL OF YOU WILL RECEIVE FIFTY CANES EACH.

Mr Orchard *is about to strike* **Ross**.

Ross We ain't done nothing, sir!

Nye I'm the one you want!

Mr Orchard *chases* **Nye** *around the chair, all the children run and hide.*

Nye *is left on his own . . .* **Mr Orchard** *towers over* **Nye** *with his cane.*

Sarah Quick, / get Mr Hopkins!

William Go / go go!

Mark Run / run, get Mr Hopkins!!

Gwen Stop blaming Nye!

Neil You're just picking on him because you're a bully!

Mr Orchard If you won't learn through instruction then you will learn through / pain.

Scene Four

NHS Royal Free Hospital Hampstead 1960

Archie Here you are. I can't find a doctor anywhere.

Jennie Sh...He's just been.

Jennie Sh ... He's just been.

Archie Oh, did I miss him?

Jennie Nye was in a lot of pain so they sedated him.

Archie *looks to* **Nye**.

Archie Is he?

Jennie He's sleeping.

Archie I wanted to be here. Bloody hell, / I wanted to be here.

Jennie Shh...

Archie Is he? Was? How was he with the news?

Jennie Oh. We didn't . . .

Archie Oh? Oh OK.

Jennie Wasn't really / . . . the time

Archie No Ok. Makes sense yeah.

Silence.

Archie *escorts* **Jennie** *out of* **Nye***'s earshot.*

Archie How did the Doctor…(put it)

Jennie He just said. You know, he told Nye…everything went fine.

Archie And Nye didn't. *(hushed)* He didn't cotton on to anything?

Jennie No I don't think so.

Archie Ok. So when he wakes up, we'll…he'll be more rested, the pain will be under control, it makes more sense. We'll tell him together and he'll be able to absorb it. It's better this way.

Jennie Yes. I suppose.

Archie He will, he'll be fine.

Jennie Yes, well, we'll see.

Archie He will. We'll all be here, we'll do it together.

Jennie I just don't want to worry him unnecessarily.

Archie You won't you won't I promise. It'll be hard. And sad./ But (once we've)

Jennie That's why I thought maybe. Actually. It's best we don't tell him.

Beat.

Is it that bad?

Archie He would want to know.

Jennie Yes he would. But. Is it kinder to not tell him?

Archie No.

Jennie We didn't tell my mother/ and she's-

Archie He would want to know.

Pause.

Archie What brought this on? Hey.

Jennie I don't know.

Archie What happened?

Jennie He. He woke up.

Archie Yeah I was there.

Jennie He saw the ward. He saw all this.

Beat.

And.

Beat.

He had.

Beat.

He had a twinkle in his eye. And I know what that means.

Archie What does that mean?

Jennie It means he's-

Beat.

It means he's planning, he's dreaming for the future for all of us and I don't want to be the one who takes that away from him.

Beat.

Archie I don't think it's a good idea.

Jennie Ok.

Archie Ok, you'll tell him or…

Jennie Ok, you don't agree. It's fine.

Archie Shouldn't we try to find consensus?

Jennie This isn't a party conference.

Archie We need to find a way to deal with this.

Jennie This is next of kin stuff Archie.

Archie Look, if you're scared / you know I'll be

Jennie   I'm not scared. I'm not scared.

Archie   But, if you are. Y'know. I'll be there. I'll be there and it won't be as scary as you think it is. I break bad news to people all the time. One of the privileges of being Nye's man in the valley, he breaks the good news I break the bad. People think he's a God and that he can fix everything. But he can't and it's me who has to tell them and it's hard. But it's the right thing to do. Telling him, is the right thing to do.

Jennie   But my main purpose in life is to protect him.

Archie   You can't protect him from this.

Jennie   Then what has it all been for? Really?

Archie *gives a philosophical shrug - this is life.*

Jennie   If I can't protect him from this then what is the point? In anything? I might as well go with him.

Archie   Don't say that.

Jennie   Why not say that? Why not? It's how I feel. My whole existence has become about him.

Beat.

If you'd told me in my twenties I'd spend a large part of my life in domestic servitude to a bloody man I would have laughed and then slapped you, but it is just bloody typical that I end up with the one man who's been the best chance socialism has ever had in this country.

Beat.

This is just another one of those inconvenient life details, that I will keep to myself so he can be happy for however long he's got. We'll be fine.

Archie   Jennie.

Jennie   No, we'll be fine.

Beat.

Jennie I don't want to talk about this anymore. You don't have to stay.

Archie I know.

Jennie That was a polite way of asking you to leave.

Archie And that was a polite way of saying I'm not going anywhere.

Scene Five

Tredegar Workingman's Library 1908

Nye Where am I?

Archie Shh. Look at this. Look at this, this is my favourite place in all of Tredegar. I've never brought no-one else here and you can't bring no-one else 'ere, right. Promise?

Nye Promise.

Archie Shh. I'm serious, Nye! D'you promise?

Nye I promise, on my life.

Archie Swear on your mam and your dad's life.

Nye I ss-swear on my mam and d-dad's life I won' bring no-one else.

Archie Wha' you think 'en?

Nye It's nice.

Archie It's not nice, Nye, it's fucking / brilliant.

Nye It's ffffff-fucking brilliant.

Archie That's right, it is, it's fucking brilliant. Look at it, mun. My dad brought me 'ere once, and now I come an' read the comics an' stuff. And you can just sit 'ere and read wha'ever you wan', and no-one tells you you can't. It's called a library. You jus' 'ave to put the book back tidy like after.

Nye And we c-c-can jusssst. Read 'em? For free, like?

Archie Yeah. The miners paid for them all. An' we can read 'em. We just got to put 'em back tidy like. An' then someone else can read it then after, that's how it works. And the best thing is. They get new ones every week. I've seen 'em bringing them in, in the boxes.

Nye There must be thousands 'ere.

Archie Yeah. Get one down. Choose one.

Nye I carn.

Archie Yeah, you can. Watch me.

Archie *takes a book out, flicks through it and puts it back.* **Nye** *is looking for an adult to unleash consequences.*

Nothing.

Nye No-one's gonna say nothing?

Archie No-one's gonna say nothing. Look.

Showing off, **Archie** *takes another book out looks at it and puts it back.*

Archie Go on, give it a go, mun.

With tremendous apprehension **Nye** *finally chooses one. He takes a book off a shelf. He checks all around him to see if he's in trouble.*

Then being very careful, he opens the book and looks all around him again to see if he's in trouble.

Nothing.

Nye I jus', I can jus' / read it?

Archie Shh. Yeah. You can jus' read it.

Nye Why'd you keep going 'sh'.

Archie I dunno it's how you talk in a library.

Nye *turns the pages, reading.*

Archie Is it good?

Nye Yeah. No.

Beat.

Have I got to read it all, now like?

Archie No, if you don' like it. You jus' put it back. Tidy like.

Nye *thinks about it. He puts it back.*

Nye How many goes do you get?

Archie You can have as many goes as you want. You can just keep trying them all. Get another one.

Nye I can have another one?

Archie Yeah. Sh. No-one says nothing. Look.

Archie *shows him. He gets two books out. Puts them back.*

Nye So it's not like a shop. Or school.

Archie No. And if you can't finish it, you can borrow it and take it 'ome and read it there and bring it back when you finished. For free.

Nye *takes one book down. Then another. Then another.*

Before long he has a stack he can barely manage.

Nye I can't believe this, Arch, look at all these books for free!

Archie I know!

Nye I can't believe it. I'm gonna come here every day, and I'm gonna read this whole pile, and then when I've finished this pile, I'm gonna make another one and read that one and then / when I've finished that one . . .

Archie You know. When it's just me and you. You don' stutter.

Long silence.

Nye Dun really like tt-t-t-talking about it.

Archie Sorry. It's just. Sometimes it totally goes. Like you don' 'ave one. So like. You *can talk*. You *can* do it. Why d'you think it is, though?

Nye I dunno.

Archie Why'd you think though?

Nye I dunno, Arch! Fuck off, will you?

Archie You fuck off. I'm only saying.

Nye You fuck off. I said I don't want to talk about it and you're still going on about it.

Long silence.

Archie You can tell me to fuck off alright. That comes out, no problem.

Nye Well, it hasn't got a 'ssss' in it, has it?

Pause.

Anything with a sssss is a fucking nightmare.

Archie It's mad how some words are fine and others aren't.

Nye Well, welcome to my fucking life, Arch.

Beat.

I can . . . ssss-see them. C-c-ccc-coming. Like roadblocks in mmmy in my, in my sssss ssss-sen-tence . . . there's all these roadblocksss a-up. Ahead. I c-c-c-ccc-can sss sss sss-see them coming. I just can't a-get 'round them. And then I ww-wwww-worry about it, I think oh shit sssssss-see has a s at the ssss-start of it. I'm I'm a-gonna sssss-stutter on tha' and then, ww-when I get to it. It's even worse 'cause I've been www-worrying about it the whole time.

Silence.

Archie Is that why you do that weird thing with your neck?

Nye Sometimes I pull a muscle and I can't turn my head. And then I have to lie to my mam and tell her I've got a bad tummy so I don't have to go to school and I then, I just lie in bed not moving and not talking. It's a nightmare. That's when I think, you know . . .

Archie Y'need help.

Nye That I shouldn't exist.

Pause.

Archie No. You just need to stop saying see.

Nye How the fuck can I do that, / Arch?

Archie I dunno. If you can see it coming just dodge it. / You know it's coming.

Nye I fucking do but it's hard to think of another word to switch it with. That's how I get by most of the time. Tricks and switching words but it's hard to think of them.

Archie Arianwen knows loads of words.

Nye Yeah 'cause she's always got her head in a bloody book.

Slowly they look to each other – having the same thought.

Nye Ssss-see if you can find another word for ssssssssseee.

They run to the bookcases, pulling books out, flicking pages, swapping books.

Archie Vis-u-a-lise? Vis-ualise. Visualise. You could say that instead of see?

Nye Visualise. I can't visualise that happening. Visualise. Visualise.

Archie I can visualise the words coming like.

Nye I can visualise them coming. I can visualise them coming. I can sssss ssssss find another word for sssssss-say.

They pull books out, flick pages. Reach for more and pore over pages.

Nye It's hard to find one. Enunciate? Enunciate. I can ssss-asay that. I can't ssssaasay sssssaay. But I can. Enunciate, enunciate. *Enunciate.*

Archie You can enunciate.

Nye I can visualise the words coming. And I can enunciate them.

Archie What, what just happened?

Nye I can visualise the words coming. And I can enunciate them.

Archie You can talk.

Archie *and* **Nye** *grab each other and jump with excitement!*

Nye I can talk.

Archie You can bloody talk, Nye! You're not stuttering.

Nye I can visualise and enunciate!

Archie And you sound posh as well, like. Clever.

Nye I can't wait to tttt. I can't wait to ttt . . . Oh . . . bloody hell.

Nye *grabs another book, he flicks pages.*

Nye No. No. Hang on.

Beat.

Yeah. I can't wait to *inform* my dad I've been here.

More delight.

Archie It's working.

Nye And now I ccca –

He gets another book and flicks the pages.

I can now *articulate* my words. These books.

Archie They can't hurt you now, butt.

Nye If I can't say a word, I'll just come 'ere and find another one. I'll find a way around *every single roadblock*. I'll just come 'ere and I'll read 'em all. I'll read poetry. Philosophy. The classics. I'll learn about science! History. Economics. Politics. Marx. Engels. Dialectical materialism. Socialism. Class struggle! Ideological control! Freedom of association! Collective bargaining! Blacklisting!

Scene Six

Upstairs – Tredegar Workingman's Library 1921–29

The Query Club: **Archie Lush, Gwen Davies, Jack Stockton, Neil Jones** *and* **Nye**.

Jack *holds some paper in front of them all.*

Jack Read this. We're all on it. They denied it but we've got proof – they're running a blacklist. We are never gonna get work in South Wales again.

Archie Is that true?

Jack Look who else is on it, they're all out of work. Nye, you got us into this mess, you gotta get us out of it. How long you been out of work, Arch?

Gwen It's not Nye's fault, this is the Tredegar Iron and Coal Company.

Jack How long?

Archie Nine months.

Jack How long's Dai been out?

Gwen Fifteen months.

Jack Neil?

Neil Eight months, three weeks and two days.

Jack How long have you been out?

Nye Three years.

Jack Three years your sister and her sewing has kept a roof over your head and food in your stomach. It's done. It's over.

Gwen Alright, Jack.

Neil Shall we start talking about this week's book?

Jack Fuck the book. Fuck this reading club and fuck Marxist syncladism or whatever the fuck we're supposed to be.

Gwen Stop blaming Nye / for what happened.

Jack Why? It's his fault!

Gwen We all wanted better conditions. We all took issues to the foremen ourselves.

Jack And look where it's got us, out of a job and on a fucking blacklist.

Nye Look. It's hard.

Beat.

We need a wholesale bb-breakdown in industrial relations before things can change.

Jack It's too late.

Gwen It does feel like we're sitting around reading books, waiting for the revolution and the revolution's not happening.

Neil Speaking of revolutions, this week's book was *The Civil War in France* / by Karl Marx, shall we talk about that?

Gwen Oh, / Neil, knock it off.

Archie For / fuck's sake, Neil.

Jack Shut up, Neil, fucking / hell.

Nye We need a collective action / before we can . . .

Gwen The strike's not / gonna happen, Nye.

Nye When the t- uh conditions / are right –

Jack The strike's not gonna / happen!

Nye No no no, not a strike. Not a strike. The working classes will c-uh unite around an event.

Gwen A strike?

Nye An industrial confrontation.

Gwen Like a strike.

Nye An event that disrupts relations.

Gwen A strike. Just say a strike. It's a strike.

Nye OK, a strike.

Jack The strike's not going / to happen!

Gwen It's not gonna happen after this (blacklist). We need a plan.

Neil You know who had a plan? The French / after the civil war.

Jack Shut / up, Neil.

Archie Oh / Neil.

Gwen Neil! Nye. When my mother taught me how to sew. First, she explained it all, the different threads, the different materials, the different stitches. She explained it all. But I didn't learn how to sew until I *did* it. We need to stop reading all these books and try something new. /

Jack You're all mad.

Gwen How do people get power without confrontation? Without violence? How do the coal owners hold onto power?

Neil Well, after the French / civil war.

Collective groan.

Archie Alright, Neil, you read this week's book, well done, but we're actually trying to talk about stuff here.

Neil This is the first one I've actually read. I finally bloody read a book and no-one wants to talk about it! Put tabs / on the good bits and everything.

Nye Hang on, hang on, hang on. Gwen's right.

Gwen I am? I am. / I am.

Nye How does the Tredegar Iron and Coal Company hold onto power?

Jack They own all seven pits and they won't let me work in any of them.

Archie They've bought up all the land to stop other companies sinking pits.

Gwen They own all the houses we rent.

Archie Most of the shops too.

Nye And what are the checks and balances on that power?

Pause.

Neil Until we talk about this week's book I'm not joining in.

Gwen The county council?

Nye The county council. What else?

Archie Chamber of Trade?

Nye Chamber of Trade.

Gwen Medical Aid?

Nye Medical Aid Society. Working Men's Institute. Justices of the Peace. Hospitals' committee. The Tredegar Iron and Coal Company have a man on every board and committee, and they make sure none of those institutions challenge the company's interests but protect them. That's how they get away with all they're doing. Longer shifts, less rescue teams, blacklisting. So, if we can't take them on with a strike, maybe we take them on in the boardroom and get these institutions to protect *us* not *them*.

Jack It's too late for us, mun!

Nye If they've got a man on every committee then we need at least a man / on every

Gwen Or woman.

Nye Or woman on every committee.

Jack What's the point if we can't get work? If I don't get a job soon my dad says I've gotta go to Australia, he can't keep me no more.

Beat.

Gwen Did he say that?

Jack I've got till the end of the month.

The group are devastated at this news.

Nye Some of these committees are paid jobs.

Jack They're not gonna accept workers on these committees.

Nye They might?

Jack We're miners, coal-loaders, timbermen. No-one's going to elect us.

Nye Why not?

Jack We haven't got any experience in running things, we're all workers. They're all managers. We don't actually know how to run anything. We got no right to be on the boards or councils. We won't know what we're doing. I'm sorry, Nye. It's not gonna work.

Long silence.

I'm sorry. I can't do this anymore.

Jack *starts to exit.*

Neil OK, I'm just gonna say this and then I've said it. But there were a *lot* of committees in the Paris Commune.

Gwen Oh my / God, Neil.

Jack Fuck's / sake, Neil.

Archie Change / the record, Neil.

Neil No, hear me out. Hear me out. The whole place was run by committees. Loads of them. And they were all run by workers. No bosses or managers anywhere. And they ran Paris. Why can't we run Tredegar?

Nye Neil's right!

Neil I'm telling you, it's a good book.

Nye Why can't we run Tredegar? Miners, timbermen, why can't we? Why can't we? Jack. Hear me out. We are going to read constitutions, / articles of association and when we know how every one of them works, we're going to get elected, because what's the one thing we've got that they haven't?

Beat.

Jack Black lung.

Gwen People.

Archie Books.

Neil Time.

Nye Time. We've got time. We'll be more knowledgeable, better prepared and more capable than anyone else on these boards. And once we're on, we'll slow them down with pedantry, and scrutiny, and we'll keep getting working people elected, until *we* have the majority. And then.

Beat.

Then, we'll run this town.

Councillors Hopkins, Williams and Morgan enter.

Quiz Part 1

Clerk Welcome to our new town councillors, councillors Bevan, Davies, Jones, Lush and Stockton, welcome to Tredegar Town Council! I'm the town clerk and, if you're not familiar with proceedings, Mr Williams will carry on in the post of chairman on grounds of seniority; as long as there's no objection, he'll go first . . .

Buzzer!

Nye *accidentally knocks a buzzer.*

Nye *is startled and looks to his team. And then his button. And then his team again.*

Clerk Councillor Bevan? Everyone's waiting, Councillor Bevan.

Nye No no. I'm just . . . trying to figure out how this all works . . .

Clerk Let's move on, shall we?

Nye No, no hang on. Um . . . So . . . you know . . . I suppose . . . what uh . . . well . . .

Clerk Going to have to push you.

Buzzer.

Councillor Davies.

Gwen How long has the principle of rotation been in operation?

Clerk Well –

Gwen And for how long has it been shelved?

Clerk Um . . . well . . . this is not something we normally discuss. Do we need a formal motion? I don't really know.

Councillor Williams We don't need a formal motion because we all agree with the principle of seniority.

Buzzer!

Nye Who agrees that the election of the role of chairman is not the concern of councillors?

Clerk Well, we all agree that . . .

Buzzer!

Gwen I don't.

Buzzer!

Archie Me neither.

Buzzer!

Jack Nor me.

Buzzer!

Neil Nor me.

Buzzer!

Nye How long has the role of chairman been decided by the Tredegar Iron and Coal Company and not the councillors?

Buzzer!

Councillor Williams Every member here has been elected by their wards, and to suggest otherwise is un . . .

Councillor Hopkins Unparliamentary . . .

Councillor Williams Uh, unparliamentary language.

Buzzer!

Nye That's fine, we're not in Parliament. And which part of my question was a suggestion?

Buzzer!

Gwen No part.

Buzzer!

Nye Excellent, so as per the constitution of the council we will go through a nn-nomination and election p-process for the post of chairman.

Archie I nominate Councillor Bevan.

Gwen Seconded.

Buzzer!

Clerk If we can stick to the agenda and submit nominations for the chairman role into *next week's* agenda / that would help us keep control of . . .

Nye All those in favour of Mr Williams continuing as chair say 'aye'?

Councillor Hopkins A/ye.

Councillor Williams A/ye.

Councillor Morgan Aye.

Nye All those in favour of me taking the role of chair say 'aye'.

Nye/Archie/Gwen/Jack/Neil Aye.

Nye Motion carried, I will assume the role of chair for the rest of the term.

Councillor Williams This is not on the agenda for today's meeting, it is vital that council meetings are conducted in a professional manner.

Councillor Morgan Is this even in the constitution?

Jack Article 14.3. On the selection and appointment of chairs.

Councillor Hopkins In the middle of a meeting?

Archie Article 33.5 – emergency submissions to an agenda.

Councillor Williams Even so, you can't change chairs in the middle of a meeting.

Neil Article 9 – assuming the role of chair.

Nye It's all there, I recommend you read it!

Quiz Part 2

Clerk Very well, chairman Bevan.

Nye Right, as chair, I propose we scrap today's agenda.

Councillor Hopkins You can't do that, how can we consult anyone if we don't know what the agenda is?

Archie Article 33.6 – resubmitting agendas.

Nye I open the floor to councillors to raise any mm-matters of their concern. All those in favour say 'aye'.

Nye/Archie/Gwen/Jack/Neil Aye.

Nye Motion carried.

Buzzer!

Councillor Davies?

Gwen Why have the Tredegar Guardians not lobbied for special measures for the valley?

Nye Councillor Hopkins? This is your area of expertise as one of the Guardians.

Councillor Hopkins Um. Uh . . . well . . . now then . . . The Tredegar Guardians have written to / the County council . . .

Nye Maybe we need fresh blood on the Tredegar Guardians board? Do I have a volunteer councillor?

Archie *and* **Gwen** *raise hands.*

Gwen Me!

Nye Excellent, Councillor Davies, you can join Councillor Hopkins on the Tredegar Guardians' board.

Buzzer!

Nye Councillor Stockton.

Jack Why has the Medical Aid Society not provided relief from premiums for those suffering unemployment?

Buzzer!

Nye Councillor Williams?

Councillor Williams The board of the Medical Aid Society decided that it cannot offer relief for those suffering unemployment / whilst maintaining its commitment to

Jack How many trustees made that decision?

Councillor Williams The board.

Jack The minutes say there were six in attendance, in the articles of association you need eight to be quorate.

Nye Do I have a volunteer to join Councillor Williams as the council representative on the Medical Aid Society?

Archie *and* **Jack** *put their hands up.*

Jack Me.

Nye Excellent. Councillor Stockton will join the board of the Medical Aid Society.

Councillor Williams This is infiltration! / This is – you are – this is some kind of political trojan horse!

Councillor Morgan Infiltration by Marxists!

Buzzer!

Neil Why has the Working Men's Institute not ringfenced a budget for the purchasing of books?

Councillor Hopkins The Working Men's Institute has a limited budget . . .

Nye Councillor Jones will be joining the Working Men's Institute board with special oversight of the library.

Buzzer.

Mrs Pritchard?

Quiz Part 3

Lucy Pritchard Why do I have to go begging to the Tredegar Guardians, writing letters from my sick bed? How can I get better if I'm worried my children will be starving or in the workhouse just because I got sick?

Councillor Hopkins She's not even a councillor, what is going on here?

Nye It's our responsibility as councillors to take representations from the community, I invite anyone to the chamber to question our representatives.

Buzzer!

Mr Llywelyn?

Mr Llywelyn Why can't there be more nurses on the ward?

Buzzer!

Nye Mr Leslie?

Mr Leslie Why are overnight stays so expensive?

Buzzer!

Nye Mrs Jones?

Mrs Jones Why have the Tredegar Guardians not rejected the Government's cuts to poor relief?

Buzzer!

Nye Mr Fury?

Mr Fury Why are there so many paths in the park?

Buzzer!

Nye Mr Howells?

Mr Howells Why are our rates going up?

Buzzer!

Nye Mrs Lewis?

Scene Six   181

Mrs Lewis   Why can't we build another hospital for the women?

Buzzer!

Nye   Mr Francis?

Mr Francis   Why do the drains get blocked every time it rains?

Buzzer!

Nye   Mr Hill?

Mr Hill   Why can't we get buses to the top of the valley?

Buzzer!

Nye   Councillor Lush?

Archie   Why haven't I been picked for any committees?

Ensemble   Why? Why? Why? Why? Why? Why? Why? / Why? Why? Why? Why?

Clerk   Enough! Enough! Councillor Bevan! You have now been elected *chairman* of the Justice of the Peace, the miners combined lodge, the Labour Party, the town guardians, the Medical Aid Society, the hospital trust and the Working Men's Institute, as well as *Member of Parliament for Ebbw Vale!*

The band strikes up! **Nye** *grabs the mic and sings 'Get Happy' with the cast.*

As the song finishes, the ensemble vanish.

Dr Dain (*God voice*)   **How is he?**

Matron (*God voice*)   **No signs of discomfort.**

Jennie (*God voice*)   **His breathing seems erratic.**

Dr Dain (*God voice*)   **That will stabilise, the morphine will do its work.**

Jennie (*God voice*)   **Thank you, doctor. Thank you.**

Scene Seven

Houses of Parliament 1929

The House of Commons.

Speaker Thank you to the Honourable Member for Worcester for his supportive contributions. Next we have the maiden speech from the Member for North Lanarkshire . . .

Jennie I must confess that this dying House is not exactly a place of inspiration, and I look upon myself more as a chip of the next Parliament, which has made a rather precipitate arrival than as one really belonging to the present House. And I say to Honourable Members opposite that there is only one explanation for this Budget, and that explanation is that, in the eyes of the Chancellor of the Exchequer, the people of this country are made up in this way – the great majority of them are fools, and the remaining minority knaves. That is the only possible explanation of such a Budget as has been put before us, and I can only describe it, as a mixture of cant, corruption and incompetence.

Nye Hear hear!

Neville Chamberlain I thank the Honourable Member for North Lanarkshire for her full-throated scrutiny of the Budget. One of the functions of Government is to try to keep the House, and the country, from getting into hot water – and sometimes, it has to put cold in for the purpose. And so the question of balancing the Budget is one which seems to offer numerous illustrations of the old saying that 'a little learning is a dangerous thing'.

Beat.

I have been astonished since I undertook my present office by the extraordinary number of correspondents who write to me with some infallible plan for solving all the problems of the economy. These ideas. I notice that they generally embody their ideas in a pamphlet or some such thing. When I hand them out to my experienced staff, they are always received with a weary sigh, because really, the only practical solution is a significant reduction in unemployment benefits.

Nye D-d-d-does the . . . Honourable Member know that winter is approaching?

Neville Chamberlain I thank the Right Honourable Gentleman for his interjection, and I can assure him that I am fully au fait with the concept of seasons.

Much convivial laughter.

Nye Is he . . . Is he ff-familiar, with the nnn- concept, that half my a-constituency are unemployed and a further three million in the country are (out) without work?

Neville Chamberlain I am afraid I cannot offer any hope that the Government have discovered a plan by which they can avoid or postpone the approach of *winter*.

Much widespread uproarious laughter.

You see, human nature being what it is, to show people that they can be maintained by somebody else in idleness, at the same standard of living as those who are doing an honest full week's work, is something which might undermine and weaken the fibre and character of the people. How many of the workers are wastrels?

Winston Churchill Hear / hear!

MPs Hear hear! Hear hear! Hear hear!

Nye You know, Mr Chamberlain, the worst thing I can ss – observe about democracy, is that it has tolerated you for four and a half years.

Winston Churchill That's / downright offensive. I demand the Honourable Gentleman withdraw!

Ad lib MPs' outrage.

Nye I shan't withdraw a word!

Tory MPs Withdraw! Withdraw! Withdraw! Withdraw! Withdraw! Withdraw! Withdraw! Withdraw! Withdraw! Withdraw!

Speaker Order! I ask the Honourable Gentleman to return to his bench and reflect on his shameful remarks.

Nye The shame is on you [Speaker] for presiding over this! No, no, when the banks were in d-difficulties, loans were voted for their ss-salvation, and we bailed them out in a *matter of hours*. They put the *whole* resources of the State behind the shareholders and the rich when they get into difficulties, nationalising debt for the privileged. Christ drove the moneychangers out of the temple, but you inscribe the title deeds on the altar cloth.

Tory MPs Shame. Shame. Shame.

Clement Attlee For the record, this is not the Labour Party's view.

Speaker I thank the Honourable / Member for Ebbw Vale . . .

Nye I look around and I ssss – can see men raised by nannies! Sent away to board! Educated in Oxford and Cambridge! Cocooned in privilege from birth! Have any of *you* been means tested? Have you? Hands up who's been means tested. Who here has been means tested?

Not a single hand.

Nye *raises his own hand.*

Nye I was uu-uuh I was without work for three years. Am I a wastrel? Am I? You want to cut my benefits. For people just like me? How can you uu-u – a – comprehend the devastation reducing m-benefits will have on people like me if you have *never lived on them yourself*?

Neville Chamberlain The burden cannot fall entirely / on the State.

Nye Neither can it fall ss(solely) – entirely on families, goddamit!

Clement Attlee Nye.

Nye A fluctuation in the price of coal means thousands of men are ss- laid off across South Wales. Nothing to do with the qu-quality of their work, or their a-a-ability to work, but entirely to do with the p-p- capricious nature of capital and financial markets. You worry about weakening the fibre of the character of the people by helping them. Without m-benefits, people cannot afford food and they cannot afford doctors and medicine when they are sick. I say the State weakens the fibre of, of society by *not* helping.

Winston Churchill *mutters to* **Neville Chamberlain** *and they both laugh.*

Nye I don't want to threaten the noble lord. But if we were not in this place, I would wipe / that grin off your face.

Nye *scrambles over the benches.*

Ad lib outrage – MPs start to leave.

Speaker ORDER! / ORDER!

Herbert Morrison Nye!

Clement Attlee Nye, get back here / at once, this is ridiculous!

Herbert Morrison What the hell are you doing?

MPs WITHDRAW! / WITHDRAW!

Nye YOU AND YOUR FAMILY HAVE THRIVED ON THE PROCEEDS OF BANDITRY AND SLAVERY / FOR CENTURIES.

Speaker The Honourable Gentleman will withdraw his remark!

Nye You're a collection of political gangsters! You use the sacred emblems of patriotism to further the racket of protecting profits. You come here for the purpose of rescuing this country from the evils which afflict it, but *you* are the authors of our troubles!

Members leave.

Nye *realises he is now on his own.*

Scene Eight

House of Commons Stranger's Bar 1929

A convivial House of Commons bar.

Nye *sees a young* **Jennie** *on her own at the bar.*

Nye We haven't met, but I wanted to say, I enjoyed your maiden speech, Jennie Lee.

Jennie Thank you. Aneurin Bevan.

Nye You know who I am?

Jennie Everyone knows who you are. Charging around the place like a rutting stag.

Nye C-can I buy you a drink?

Jennie No. Thank you. I'm waiting for a friend.

Nye Ww-would that be the Honourable Member f-for Leicester East?

Jennie It was really nice to meet you.

Nye *is hurt.*

Is he going to try again?

No.

Is he?

No.

He'll just play it cool.

He's not cool.

Nye What's a guy like Ff-frank Wise got that I haven't?

Jennie *is shocked and impressed by his provocation.*

Jennie   A decent suit.

Nye *looks at his suit and then to* **Jennie***. And then to his suit.*

Nye   My mam helped me choose this.

Jennie   Your mam needs to find a better tailor.

Nye   Lost all my confidence now.

Nye *sits down next to her.* **Jennie** *did not want this.*

Nye (*to bartender*)   Gin and tonic, please. Double.

Nye *looks to* **Jennie** *and points to the bartenders.*

Jennie   Fine. Gin and tonic.

Nye (*to bartender*)   Two gin and tonics, please. Doubles. Can I ask you a question? When you look around a room like this and you see all the men this place attracts, do you feel like an imposter?

Jennie   I think they're the imposters.

Nye   I know that, but how many women MPs are there? Four, five?

Jennie   There's five of us.

Nye   Because I ff-feel like an imposter and I'm a man.

Jennie   To them we're both imposters, that's why this place needs us.

Drinks clink.

Can I give you some advice?

Nye   Please.

Jennie   You're quite charming. You don't need to steamroller everyone all the time.

Pause.

Nye   I am quite charming, aren't I?

Jennie *nearly spits her drink out.*

Nye What's your office like?

Jennie Cold, damp and really far away.

Nye Sounds like North Lanarkshire.

Jennie Or Ebbw Vale. And I have to share it with the four other women MPs. None of whom are in my party.

Nye Well mine hasn't got a ww-window.

Jennie Mine hasn't got a toilet.

Nye We should complain.

They laugh.

Jennie I dare you.

Nye If I could only find out who's in ch-a-charge of stamps and stationery I'd ww-write a letter.

Jennie No-one knows, the whole place is a mystery.

Nye Tomorrow I'm going to the tailors to put mmm (money) a pound down on a suit that could impress a pacifist Independent Labour Party Scot.

Jennie Don't take your mother.

Nye I won't. I'll take you instead.

Jennie No chance.

Nye I'm serious. (*Off* **Jennie**.) I'm serious. Come on. Help me choose a suit.

Jennie I am not going suit shopping / with you.

Nye Why not? What else are you doing? What are you doing tomorrow?

Jennie Well I . . . uh / . . . I've made plans.

Nye No you haven't, come into town with me. We'll make a day of it. Lunch. Gin and tonics, cartwheels in the park and some overpriced suits. How about it?

Jennie I'm washing my hair.

Nye No you're not.

Jennie Yes I am.

Nye Why are you ILPers so stubborn?

Jennie Maybe because we have principles?

Nye Join the Labour Party.

Jennie I'm a socialist. Join the ILP.

Nye I'm a m-pragmatist.

Jennie That's just another word for collaborator. Anyway, it was nice meeting you, Aneurin Bevan.

Nye Nye.

Jennie It was nice meeting you, Nye.

Nye You're going?

Jennie Yes.

Nye Frank stood you up?

Jennie I don't ask you about your private life, don't ask me about mine.

Nye I'm sorry.

Jennie I know what gossip is like in this place.

Nye I'm sorry.

Jennie And I won't stand for it.

Nye I'm sorry.

Jennie Not from you, not from anyone.

Nye Look, look, I'm lowering my antlers. I'm lowering my antlers. They are low, / down on the a-ground

Jennie What are you doing?

Nye in a mm-public / display of submission and humility.

Jennie Get up.

Nye I am ssss-sniffing around on the ground and the shame I feel is so powerful my antlers are now dd-drooping. Look at me. Pathetic. And subservient.

Jennie Get up, Nye.

Nye And now I'm dd a-delicately, quietly, trotting my hooves around the room, like a downy fawn, so as not to cause offence to the *ss-supremely* dominant Alpha, but also hoping to catch the Alpha's eye, to ask if I may be granted the honour of walking her home.

Jennie You're an idiot.

Nye Nevertheless, can I walk you home?

Beat.

Jennie Come on then.

Nye Having said that, we've done gin and tonics, I think it would be naïve not to do dinner.

Jennie No.

Nye And then cocktails.

Jennie No.

Nye And dance late into the night.

Jennie No.

Nye Carouse with each other into the small hours.

Jennie No.

Nye And realise we're not drunk but actually intoxicated with each other.

Jennie No thank you.

Nye And the only cure is to wrap our bodies around each other.

Jennie Dear God.

Nye Until there are no secrets between us.

Jennie No chance.

Nye Our love will grow like a beautiful garden.

Jennie No it won't.

Nye And it'll be so good we'll simply have to get married.

Jennie **I am never getting married.**

Scene Nine

NHS Royal Free Hospital 1960

Jennie *enters with a vase of daffodils.*

Jennie We don't have a normal marriage.

Archie OK.

Jennie We're not like everyone else.

Archie OK.

Jennie I've had affairs. He's had affairs.

Beat.

You know he has, Archie.

Archie I uh . . . well . . .

Jennie You don't have to cover for him. Really. I hope he's had a lovely time. I know I've tried to.

Archie I don't know what to say.

Jennie You don't have to say anything, it's fine. I'm sure he's put you in a number of uncomfortable situations having to cover for his dalliances. It's fine, Archie. I'm not angry.

Archie I never approved of any of that stuff. And I told him.

Jennie It's fine. We don't have a normal marriage.

Beat.

We don't share everything. We don't do those. Chats. Politics, yes. The messy complicated affairs of the heart. No. We have, and have always had, private lives. When we first got together, we were seeing other people. And. We. Never really stopped. We've never been ones for bourgeois convention. I know Tredegar has a special place in damnation for me, but Nye was a full-blooded participant, as I'm sure you know.

Archie Hmmm . . . Well. Y'know I . . . turned a blind eye to . . . anything I . . . why . . . why are you telling me this?

Jennie Because keeping things from each other, hasn't harmed our marriage. It strengthens it. I didn't even love him when we got married. We got married for our careers- my career we were trying to save my seat and he was in love with me and he pushed and pushed, so I agreed to a marriage of convenience for political expedience.

Beat.

On our wedding day I told him that I would never love him. And that's how it was for a long time. A long time.

Beat.

And one day he walked down the stairs and my stomach fluttered. I remember him standing there in his pyjamas and all I could say was `I appear to be madly in love with you' and he yawned and said `About bloody time.'

Beat.

Ours wasn't a hot blooded romance. Ours was more of a slow-burn. He planted love all around me, and that love flowered and bloomed like a garden. That's the only way I can describe it.

Beat.

That's how we talked about our relationship. He'd call from London or Washington, or Delhi and he'd say `I can't wait to get back to the garden.' I'd write to him and say `come home to the garden'.

Beat.

Archie He loves coming home.

Jennie Yes. he does.

Beat.

We didn't have children, so I gave him myself instead. I don't know if I was ever enough. He's from a big family and I know he wanted a whole litter.

Beat.

But. I couldn't. We never really talked about that either. Not to each other nor anyone else.

Pause.

Archie He talked about it to me.

Pause.

Jennie He talked to you about-

Archie Yes.

Jennie What did he say?

Archie Well.

Beat.

I know you lost a baby.

Nye *twitches.*

Jennie He told you that?

Archie Yes.

Jennie He told you? When?

Archie At the time.

Jennie What did he say?

Archie Just that it had happened. And that you were sad. That you both were sad. I remember him crying quite a bit.

Jennie He didn't cry in front of me. I didn't think he wanted to talk about it. I didn't think-What did he say to you?

Archie I can't remember.

Jennie What did he-how did he-how did it/-how did it it

Archie I don't remember it was a long time ago.

Jennie Was he angry, with me? Do you remember if he was angry?

Archie No he wasn't angry.

Jennie How did he- what did he say? Please.

Archie I remember he said it wasn't fair.

Jennie Did he blame me? Archie?

Medical equipment beeps...bongs.

Archie What's going on?

Archie *goes to a curtain.*

Archie Nurse?

Jennie What does this mean? What's happening?

Nurse Ellie *enters.*

She checks his vitals.

Archie What's going on?

Nurse Ellie I think his oxygen levels are low.

Nurse Ellie *checks* **Nye**'s *pulse with her fob watch, and checks his dressing for blood.*

Nurse Elle *buzzes the buzzer three times.*

Nurse Ellie He is struggling to breathe deeply, his blood pressure could be dropping. His heart rate has increased.

Jennie Why's this happening?

Nurse Ellie It could be from the operation.

She puts on the sphygmomanometer (*a blood pressure pump*) *on* **Nye**'s *arm.*

Jennie Is he going to be OK?

Nurse Ellie We'll give him all the support he needs.

Doctor Frankel *enters.*

Dr Frankel Hello, I'm Mr Frankel. Nurse, what were his observations?

Nurse *reads obs.*

Nurse Ellie Observations were normal, Mr Frankel. Heart rate seventy. Blood pressure one twenty over eighty. Temperature thirty-seven.

Dr Frankel Blood pressure dropped seventy-five systolic, fifty-five diastolic.

Nurse Ellie *notes these down.*

Dr Frankel *starts to examine* **Nye**.

Dr Frankel (*to outside*) Porter? Urine output?

Nurse Ellie Maintained.

Dr Frankel Signs of bleeding?

Nurse Ellie None noted.

Dr Frankel Bring the oxygen cylinder, increase the rate of fluids.

Nurse Ellie *raises the fluid bag higher.*

Dr Frankel And we're going to move Mr Bevan to the high dependency ward for further support.

Jennie Is he going to be OK?

Nurse Ellie He's very sick, but we'll give him all the help he needs.

Nurse Ellie *leaves.*

Jennie Is he going to wake up? What if he never wakes up?

Sound design swells.

Scene Ten

House of Commons 1938–1942

Boom!

Neville Chamberlain *at the despatch box as dust falls and the building shakes.*

Neville Chamberlain My good friends, for the second time in our history, a British Prime Minister has returned from Germany, bringing peace with honour. I believe it is peace for our time . . . Go home and get a nice quiet sleep.

BOOM! War sounds! The room shakes.

Nye WHAT THE HELL ARE YOU WAITING FOR?

Tory MP One Don't undermine the Government when we're at war!

Tory MP Two Support our troops!

Tory MP Three Show some loyalty to your country!

Tory MP Four We're at war! You need to support our Government!

Neville Chamberlain Um . . . Uh . . . steel production for the first quarter of the year has been increased to a figure of . . .

Nye WHAT THE HELL ARE YOU DOING? WE'RE AT WAR.

Tory MP Five You can't criticise the Government during a war!

Nye WE NEED TO D-DO SOMETHING!

Clement Attlee Observe the truce. We have men fighting, no-one wants to hear the Government is failing.

Nye This is Parliament! This is w-where their voices should be heard! How many thousands of lives have to be lost before you Tories can be moved? Is that what you're waiting for? A national tragedy?

Death *nears . . .*

Boom! War sounds, distorted.

Everyone hits the floor. Dust! People cough and are dazed.

Everyone looks to **Neville Chamberlain**.

Neville Chamberlain *gathers himself before . . .*

Neville Chamberlain As I was saying, steel production has been increased . . .

BOOM! War sounds, distorted further.

Everyone staggers again.

Nye Tonight, we have *empty* benches here. Is it necessary to have a ttt-terrible calamity before we get these bbb-benches filled and Honourable Members doing their job?

Clement Attlee I'm sorry, I can't defend the Honourable / Gentleman's position.

Nye The job has to be done! It is a bad business, I tell you. We need leadership!

BIG BOOM! War sounds, mixed with hospital sounds.

This is the closest one yet, everyone is knocked over and dazed.

Nye What the hell are you doing? This can't continue! We need leadership! What is your policy on leadership?

BOOM, BOOM. Beat. BOOM.

Winston Churchill *appears.*

Winston Churchill You ask, what is our policy? I can say: it is to wage war, by sea, land and air, with all our might and with all the strength that God can give us; to wage war against a monstrous tyranny, never surpassed in the dark, lamentable catalogue of human crime. That is our policy. You ask, what is our aim? I can answer in one word: it is victory, victory at all costs, victory in spite of all terror, victory, however long and hard the road may be; for without victory, there is no survival.

BOOM! BOOM! BOOM!

Everyone has to hide. The room shakes. People fall over.

Nye You're worse than Chamberlain! We're losing every battle! Men are dying because of *your* incompetence! Ww-we're going to lose the whole war if something isn't done about it. No-one dares say anything because everyone worships you like a god.

Clement Attlee I beg to remind the Honourable Gentleman that in the national interest we need to support the Prime Minister, not / criticise him.

Nye I propose the motion that says: This House, has no confidence in the general direction of the war.

Silence – gasps and shock.

Arianwen Nye, stop!

Winston Churchill This motion undermines the morale of British troops fighting for our liberty.

Nye It's not speeches in Parliament that undermine their morale, it is what they are experiencing in battle.

Arianwen Nye, stop!

Winston Churchill Criticising the Government in the midst of a battle . . .

Nye We're at war! We're always going to be in a battle somewhere.

Arianwen Nye!

Winston Churchill Criticising the Government in this House breaks the parliamentary truce . . .

Nye Events are criticising the Government! Events.

Arianwen Nye!

Nye You win every debate and lose every battle.

Arianwen Stop it!

Nye You plan nothing and improvise everything.

Arianwen Nye!

Nye You are little more than a synthetic military glamour boy.

Arianwen Nye!

Nye And this country deserves more!

Scene Eleven

Family home 1925

Arianwen Stop!

Nye Stop what? What now?

Arianwen All of this. / Just stop it.

Nye I'm trying to help.

Arianwen Mam and I have tried everything.

Nye Bath salts, have we tried bath salts?

Arianwen We've tried bath salts.

Nye What about lemon juice / in water then?

Arianwen We've *tried* lemon juice in water.

Nye Mullein leaf / extract then?

Arianwen Oh my God! We've tried everything. Everything.

Nye Maybe we need another doctor then.

Arianwen Nothing is going to work.

Nye Have you *tried* another doctor?

Arianwen Have you asked *Dad* if he wants another doctor?

Nye Oh, he hasn't got a clue what's going on, he can't say anything / (*Off* **Arianwen***'s hard stare.*) I mean, I'm just saying, we shouldn't be asking him.

Arianwen He can make it known what he wants. He can communicate.

Nye But / when it comes

Arianwen You just have to spend time with him. Learn what he's trying to say.

Nye I'm trying to get us some more time.

Arianwen We can't get him more time!

Nye OK, well bloody make him / more comfortable!

Arianwen We can't make him more comfortable!

Nye Well, he's not fucking comfortable, Arianwen! He's not. / I'm not judging. But he's not. And someone needs to do it for him!

Arianwen Well, the bucket's there if you want to give him a bed bath! Or if you want – to try and lift –

Nye Don't be pathetic / Arianwen, honestly.

Arianwen You're pathetic! You avoid any kind of care and then when I ask you to go and see him, all you can manage is to *look* at him like he's a specimen. I need you to *be* with him. Spend time with him, reassure him.

Beat.

Nye I'm not going to just sit there when I can be reading / and trying to find out . . .

Arianwen That's what nursing him is!

Nye It's not! There's more important, / more useful things I can do.

Arianwen There's nothing more / important!

Nye I might find something that can help!

Arianwen A cure? Don't worry everyone, Nye's worked out how to fix black lung.

Nye Oh piss off, Arianwen / I'm not talking to you when you're like this . . .

Nye *goes to leave.*

Arianwen No, no! Nye! / Stop! No. *No*

Nye Let me / . . . out of the way . . .

Arianwen No! You are not going anywhere. You're not. You're not. You are staying put. I'm not lying anymore! When he asked for you, I told him you were busy. I told him you *want* to sit with him. But you're very busy at the moment.

Beat.

I told him, sometimes there's even lawyers coming up from Cardiff to argue with you in tribunals. I told him you're out early and back late. That you sleep in the chair sometimes and sometimes you don't have time to eat.

Beat.

I lied for you. And I lie for Will. And sometimes even Blod. Myfi's here every day. But I cover for *everyone else*. He's worrying about us. He can't breathe and he's still worrying about everyone, so I cover. Because that's my job, isn't it? Protecting you, protecting him. Making sure *everyone* feels loved but never *accountable*.

Nye OK. OK!

Arianwen *Everyone* gets your time and attention except us. You see a gap in this town and you shove yourself into it without thinking about the gap in this family.

Nye It's not that . . .

Arianwen You've made me a tool to avoid this. You turn a blind eye to every / inconvenient truth.

Nye I'm scared, OK?

Arianwen I'm scared! But you exploit me. You are no better than every mine owner in this town, Aneurin Bevan.

Arianwen *leaves.*

With a mix of shame and courage **Nye** *pulls the curtains apart.*

Sound design swells.

David Bevan *lies on a bed fighting for every breath.*

Scene Twelve

Family home 1925

Nye (*to offstage*) ARIANWEEEEN! HELP! HE'S –

David Bevan *gasps for breath.*

Nye It's OK, Dad, it's OK Dad. Oh God oh God. PLEASE! ARIANWEN!

Scene Twelve 203

Not knowing what to do, **Nye** *tries to get up but* **David Bevan** *grips* **Nye** *in mortal terror.*

Nye Dad, I think I need help. I think I need help.

He climbs in and holds his father.

David Bevan's *arms flail and grip* **Nye** *in fear.*

The hands of **Death** *are the hands of his father.*

Nye Oh OK. OK. It's OK. I'm not. I won't go. I won't go. I'm not going anywhere.

David Bevan *relaxes as much as he can, frightened.*

Nye *looks around . . . there's no help coming. He looks at his dad, who is terrified.*

Nye They'll be back soon. Mam and Arianwen. Maybe Myfi will come with them too. Blod will come see you soon too. And Will. Will, will come round. And we'll all be together. Mam will cook something and we'll have to take turns around the table.

Beat.

Nye *looks around – no-one is coming.*

Terrified he might not live to see this, **David Bevan** *fights for breath again.*

Nye No no no. Dad. Dad. Look. Just . . . Let's look . . .

They lock eyes. **David Bevan** *stops panicking and takes comfort from* **Nye**'s *voice.*

Nye *watches him. He can't take much more. He makes the hardest decision of his life.*

Nye Try. Try not to fight it, Dad. Don't fight anymore. Don't. Just . . . let's . . . look.

He strokes his father's face.

I'll look after you and don't you worry. I'm gonna look after everyone for you. I'm gonna look after everyone.

Nye *is totally alone with this suffering.*

His father dies in his arms.

Jennie (*God voice*) **Will he wake up?**

What if he never wakes up?

Nye *startles – he looks up.*

Nye Jennie? Where am I? What's happening to me?

Interval.

Scene Thirteen

Ty Trist mine 1907

Nye *stands in the dark . . .*

David Bevan *appears . . .*

Nye Dad? Dad?

David Bevan I want to show you something. Come this way.

Nye *follows* **David Bevan**.

Nye Dad? Where are you taking me? It's so dark down here. I don't want to go down here.

David Bevan This way.

Nye It's so dark.

David Bevan Follow me.

Nye It's too dark.

David Bevan Just . . . let's . . . look.

Father and son lock eyes.

Nye *is reassured.*

David Bevan Hold my hand. Only in the dark can you see what your life is really about.

Nye How much further?

David Bevan Little bit further.

Nye How much further?

David Bevan Little bit further.

Nye I'm scared.

David Bevan Don't be scared.

Nye How much further?

David Bevan This is what I've been wanting to show you.

David *raises his miner's lamp and reveals an enormous, regal, seam of coal.*

David Bevan Touch it.

Beat.

Go on, touch it.

Beat.

Nye It's so cold.

Beat.

David Bevan It's so pure.

Beat.

Give me your hand. See. Feel the seam. See. Feel the seam. Cuts the earth. Like a tree root. See how she moves? Full of power. Like a horse. You ever felt a horse's neck? The power. Feel it. Go on. Feel it. Come on! Feel it. How can you mine it, if you don't feel it? Now. See how she twists and turns? See? This is all we have to look at. So look. Other jobs. You can read the paper. Look out the window, watch the world go by. All we've got is the seam. Show it respect. Tell the truth and the seam will give you everything. But if you get it wrong, you're scratching around on your hands and knees for days, wondering what you've done wrong. Now. Feel this. Go on. Feel it.

Beat.

Now, the bad miner just hacks away at this all day, and it's splitting and you have to climb up in there on your hands and knees. But the true miner, the learned miner, gets to know it. And finds the point where one true blow will bring it tumbling.

Beat.

Take your time.

Beat.

Study.

Beat.

Study what you're up against. Don't fear it. Don't flinch. Don't doubt yourself. Because one true blow can last a lifetime.

Nye *starts to follow the seam . . .*

He approaches the seam; he holds his lamp up to admire its beauty. He feels the seam this time, not minding the cold. He runs his hand along it and begins to understand better.

He runs his hands all along the seam, getting to know every part of it. He sees how delicate it is.

Scene Fourteen

Houses of Parliament tearooms 1941

Winston Churchill *approaches holding a cup and saucer.*

He offers **Nye** *a cup of tea.*

Winston Churchill   And here he is, the noisy member for Ebbw Vale.

Nye   Prime Minister. Why are we . . . why are we in the tearooms? You never come in the tearooms.

Winston Churchill I visit the tearooms.

Nye You never visit the tearooms.

Winston Churchill I visit the tearooms. I like tea. Also, I like to give them something to gossip about, seeing us together. Biscuit?

Nye No, thank you.

Winston Churchill So. Aneurin. You have been my chief critic throughout the war.

Nye I have been your *only* critic / throughout the war.

Winston Churchill And it has cost you dearly. Ostracised by your parliamentary party, your constituency party is furious. / You are entirely isolated.

Nye My criticism has been entirely justified, I am perfectly sure of that.

Winston Churchill You are a merchant of discourtesy.

Nye And you are a wholesaler of disaster.

Winston Churchill Let's see if the rest of the country agrees with what you have to say, shall we?

Winston Churchill *produces some newspapers from a tea trolley.*

Winston Churchill (*one paper*) 'Bevan the traitor.' (*Another paper.*) 'Bevan the squalid nuisance.' I like that picture of you. 'Traitor.' 'Traitor.' 'Treasonous Bevan strikes again.' 'Welsh windbag strikes again.'

Nye You printed your own newspaper in the General Strike, you might as well be doing the same now.

Winston Churchill Whatever reputation you had before the war as a principled agitator, you've destroyed it. And now, you're the most hated man in Britain. Aren't you? Excrement in the mail. Death threats. You're assaulted in the street, the security services tell me, I know. You are *universally* despised. After Hitler, the next person the country hates / is you.

Nye Everyone else is too scared. You have the whole House eating out of the palm of your hand.

Winston Churchill We're at war.

Nye I am protecting the principles of the House.

Winston Churchill If I don't win, there is / *no House*.

Nye I won't defeat one dictator by creating another!

Winston Churchill I'm the best chance / we have of defeating Fascism.

Nye A vote for you is a vote for the very conditions that have *led* to the rise of Fascism! You conscript men to mine coal underground, and then you allow the coal owners to *sell* that coal to our navy for a *profit*! A navy trying to defend the realm! This crisis is a privateering racket with your friends lining their pockets.

Winston Churchill I am the only chance we have.

Nye It's a privateering *racket*!

Winston Churchill I am the only chance we have.

Nye The Labour Party has never been able to unite the working class. We've spent decades trying to educate through speeches, libraries, colleges, all trying to raise the consciousness of our class, and we've *failed*. The working class has never been united in my lifetime. Until you came along.

Beat.

With your statesmanship and your cigars and your (*impression*) *'our finest hour'*. You did it in a matter of weeks.

Beat.

Because the moment the ruling class is under threat, you *need* a united working class. You *need* a united country to defend your privilege. So, you declare a ceasefire on us. No more blaming minorities, or benefits claimants, or the Irish or the poor, or the workless, for the harm *your class* is inflicting on us – no, it's all

Blitz spirit and 'White Cliffs of Dover' because now you're under seige as well! So, you use all your tricks, all your apparatus, your newspapers and your emergency powers, and you've united the working class! At last. Thank you. You've done my job for me. Once Hitler has been defeated, the next enemy *is you*.

Beat.

Biscuit.

Winston Churchill *hands him a biscuit.*

Winston Churchill I asked you here because I have a request. I've called for a vote of confidence in my leadership. And I want your support.

Nye You want *me* to vote for *you* in a vote of confidence?

Winston Churchill Yes.

Nye I'm an opposition backbencher.

Winston Churchill Yes.

Nye I broke the parliamentary truce.

Winston Churchill Yes.

Nye I literally tabled a motion of no confidence in your leadership.

Winston Churchill Yes, I remember.

Nye I have no confidence / in you.

Winston Churchill Still. I'd rather like your vote.

Nye Oh? We're going to do this / are we?

Winston Churchill We're going to / do this.

Nye OK. You've lost Norway, Malaya, Crete, thousands of men have died, we've had ships sunk in the Pacific, you've lost more battles than you've won. You have no plan. You have no industrial strategy. I could go on. You're a great speaker, Wins – Prime Minister, but you are a *terrible* military leader.

Silence.

Winston Churchill Fuck off.

Nye You fuck off. I can't support someone who can't / – canvass opinion.

Winston Churchill Can't what?

Nye Can't canvass opinion. Or seek advice. Or evaluate. Or re-evaluate.

Winston Churchill Like you, you mean? Have you ever compromised *your* position on anything, / ever?

Nye I've certainly made / adjustments to . . . to my . . .

Winston Churchill Here lies Aneurin Bevan who never learned anything because he was born with divine / intuition

Nye I have / learned everything

Winston Churchill Giving him sole right to be my chief critic throughout.

Nye I have learned everything I need to learn about *you*.

Winston Churchill You've learned nothing because you're a petulant child.

Nye Well, this has been lovely; we should do it more often.

Winston Churchill I can't defeat Hitler without American help.

Nye Agreed.

Winston Churchill I need to convince our American friends it is in their interests to defeat Fascism. That time is now.

Nye Agreed.

Winston Churchill Universal approval at home would make my dealings with our American friends more . . . presentable.

Nye *I* make *you* look bad?

Winston Churchill No. But you could make me look better. So, it falls on you to do your bit for the war effort, and vote for me. The stakes couldn't be higher.

Beat.

You seek power, but you're afraid of it. You demand to govern, yet insist on being ungovernable. You demand solidarity, but don't vote with your own whips. You are a born contrarian. The educated miner, the stuttering orator. The bed-hopping husband. What you need to learn about power, Aneurin, is this: compromise *everything* to get it. Because once you have it, you no longer have to compromise. That is the privilege of power. Compromise. Vote for me. Leave the activist behind. Become a politician.

Nye *faces two doors, one with 'No', one with 'Aye'.*

He weighs up what he has to do.

Finally he heads to Aye, and steps through . . .

Scene Fifteen

10 Downing Street 1942–1945

A convivial ensemble meets him.

Civil Servant One Good news about the Americans, Mr Bevan.

Civil Servant Two Very good news, Mr Bevan!

Civil Servant Three Not long now, Mr Bevan!

Civil Servant Four Victory in Europe, Mr Bevan!

Civil Servant Five Tide turning, Mr Bevan.

Civil Servant Six Victory in Japan, Mr Bevan!

Civil Servant Seven The troops are coming home, Mr Bevan!

Civil Servant Eight Churchill defeated, Mr Bevan!

Nye What?

Civil Servant Nine Landslide Labour victory, Mr Bevan!

Civil Servant Ten We'll take that, Mr Bevan.

Civil Servant Eleven Just this way, Mr Bevan.

Behind a desk sits **Clement Attlee**.

Clement Attlee Ah Nye. Good to see you.

Nye Clem?

Clement Attlee Prime Minister, actually.

Nye *takes this in.*

Clement Attlee I suppose you're wondering what you're doing here. Shall I put you out of your misery?

Nye I uh . . .

Clement Attlee I brought you here today to invite you to join the Cabinet. I'd like to offer you the job of Minister for Health and Housing.

Nye Health?

Clement Attlee And Housing. I thought it might be a good fit.

Silence.

Nye This is some kind of joke.

Clement Attlee No.

Nye *You*, want *me*, in the Cabinet. I've never been a minister before, I've never even been a shadow minister.

Clement Attlee Well, / I thought

Nye I've never even chaired a select committee.

Clement Attlee Maybe with some / support you could

Nye You kicked me out of the party once! We don't really speak. Why would you possibly want me in your Cabinet, Clem?

Clement Attlee Prime Minister. I sensed a maturing in your approach.

Long silence . . . is **Winston Churchill** *still there?*

Clement Attlee Health and Housing.

Nye What's your game?

Clement Attlee There is no game.

Nye Health and Housing?

Clement Attlee It's a big brief.

Nye You know I have a thing for Health, you know it.

Clement Attlee Indeed.

Nye And you are exploiting that, to what?

Clement Attlee Nothing of the sort.

Nye To . . . to to over-promote me? Is that it?

Beat.

So I, what? So I fail? Is that what you're doing? Making it so I expend my political capital with the left of the party. Is this a set-up?

Clement Attlee Factional paranoia. I brought you in here / with the expressed

Nye Addison's reputation was ruined when he couldn't deliver on Health and that was the end of him. This isn't a brief, it's a trap. You've got your feet under the desk at Number 10, with a massive majority, and you've calculated that the one person who could derail everything now is me.

Silence.

I'm the one who could split the party. You know, I can consolidate the left and hold you to ransom. So, you want to muzzle me with either failure or collective responsibility or both. You say factional paranoia, I say political chicanery, Clem.

Clement Attlee Prime Minister.

The great disruptor and the great diplomat size each other up.

There's some merit to your analysis. Having you in Cabinet mitigates the risk of a split.

Nye Thank you.

Clement Attlee But. Have you considered that I may want to unite the party rather than merely avoid a split?

Nye How?

Clement Attlee By *delivering* for the left, rather than humiliating it.

Nye ...

Beat.

Nye ...

Clement Attlee A united Labour Party, right and left in Cabinet together. Bevan and Bevin. Putting their names to the same policies. United. For the good of the party. The good of the country. The good of the people. The right aren't the enemy, Nye. They're just politicians you haven't worked with yet. And maybe you should try working with them.

Nye As Minister for Health.

Clement Attlee And Housing.

Nye If I deliver you win. If I fail you win.

Clement Attlee Welcome to Number 10.

He places a ministerial briefcase on the desk.

Nye You think I can do this?

Clement Attlee I don't think anyone else can.

Nye That's not what I asked.

Beat.

I need to know; you think I can do this?

Another very long silence.

Clement Attlee I think. What do I think?

Beat.

I think, if anyone can do this, it's you.

Clement Attlee *holds out the ministerial briefcase.*

Nye *stares at the ministerial briefcase. Eventually he reaches a hand out.*

He puts his hand on the case.

Nye Thank you.

Attlee *keeps his hand on the briefcase.*

Nye Prime Minister.

Clement Attlee *takes his hand on off the briefcase.*

He carries it in front of himself. He savours the moment holding his Holy Grail.

As **Nye** *lifts the briefcase his father's presence is felt.*

His father's love and pride is so present and so absent for **Nye** *that he can barely tolerate it. In this moment he is a minister for once, and a son once again.*

The ministerial briefcase twitches.

Nye*'s eyes are drawn to it.*

It moves again, violently.

Nye *opens the briefcase and is confronted with a sea of souls drowning in need.*

Patient One Minister?

Nye Yes, how can I help?

Patient One You have to help, St Hilda's won't take my son because he's got polio and they only do acute medicine!

Nye Your nearest council hospital will deal with infectious diseases.

Patient One But he's got kidney failure as well, so St James' say he's got to go to St Hilda's, but St Hilda's say he's got to go to St James' – neither hospital will admit him! He's going to die!

Nye But what if . . .

Patient Two There's a diptheria outbreak in the schools, people are dying waiting to be tested.

Nye Can't the doctors just prescribe the antitoxin without a positive test?

Patient Two They're rationing the medicine! They won't prescribe it without a positive test! You have to help, my wife is being strangled to death by this disease.

Nye Let me, let me see if I can get another centrifuge moved to your town to help with the

Patient Three Help us, minister, my baby has TB, but they forgot to put the legs of her cot in tins of oil to stop the cockroaches climbing up. A cockroach got into my baby's cot, and now my baby's deaf.

Nye Cockroaches? What hospital is this?

Patient Three I don't trust them to look after my baby anymore but they won't let me take her to another hospital.

Nye Give me the name of the doctor in charge of your baby's care.

Patient Four Minister, my daughter has TB. And we've been waiting for a month to get admitted to St Mark's.

Scene Fifteen 217

Nye Wait!

Patient Four She needs to get away from the dust, she needs fresh air.

Patient Five Please Minister, I don't know who else to turn to, I broke my wrist, and the doctor can repair it but I can't afford the anaesthetic for the operation.

Nye You can't have surgery without anaesthetic.

Patient Five I have to work! But I can't because of the pain.

Patient Six We need more ambulances in our town.

Nye Which town?

Patient Seven My husband broke his leg in the pit and he had to walk three miles home on it.

Nye Which pit?

Patient Eight They judge me, because of how I make a living. Don't I deserve care? Don't I deserve medicine?

Nye Everyone deserves

Patient Eight Where do people like me go when we're sick? I work on the streets and I'll die on the streets unless you do something about it.

Patient Nine Please, Mr Aneurin Bevan.

Nye Yes?

Patient Ten They say you're a good man.

Nye Good.

Patient Nine They say you care.

Nye I do.

Patient Ten There's no beds in King Edward's.

Patient Nine Minister, the maternity ward was overcrowded and there was a rubella outbreak. All the babies were born deaf or blind or with cataracts.

Patient Ten So I had to put my eldest in the coal shed to keep here, away from the babies, because she's got measles.

Nye If you can just

Jennie Nye…Can you hear me?

Nye What?

Patient Eleven You're the only person who can help.

Patient Twelve Please help me.

Patient Eleven There's no cancer specialist in my town so I have to travel five hours for an appointment.

Patient Eight Please help me.

Patient Eleven I can't afford the travel anymore, I don't know what to do. Please help me.

Jennie Can you hear me my love?

Nye Who is that?

Patient Twelve There are no ambulances so the doctor had to reset his leg on the kitchen table, the children had to hold him down.

Jennie Show me a sign eh? Show me you can hear.

Nye Jennie?

Patient Thirteen I want justice. Or compensation. Or just someone to acknowledge that what happened to me wasn't right.

Jennie Nye I'm so scared I don't know what to do.

Patient Fourteen The consultant let six different medical students examine me and I started bleeding and lost the baby.

Jennie I wish I could talk this through with you.

Scene Fifteen   219

Nye Jennie! I can hear you but I don't- I don't know/ Where are you!

Patient Fifteen They won't take any responsibility!

Jennie I'm so scared.

Patient Sixteen Who is meant to help me?

Jennie Can you wake up now?

Patient Seventeen Please, Minister. The almoner says I have to pay two shillings for my radium, but I don't have that money; if I don't pay she's going to stop my treatment.

Jennie Nye?

Nye Jennie?

Patient Eighteen My wife's mother can get penicillin in Newcastle but we can't get it here!

Jennie Wake up now my love.

Patient Eighteen Can you help get supplies to Worthing?

Patient Eight Please?

Jennie Please!

Patient Nineteen I don't know who else to turn to.

Patient One Please!

Patient Nineteen Our GP looks after 18,000 patients. How are we meant to get an appointment?

Jennie Nye? Love, come on. it's Jennie.

Patient 2 Help me!

Jennie Come on, love.

Patient 19 Please help me

Patient 20 Minister!

Patient 19 I need help!

Jennie Wake up now Nye please.

Patient 20 Please help!

Jennie Wake up!

Scene Sixteen

NHS Royal Free Hospital 1960

Nye *has a black oxygen mask on.*

Jennie Wake up Nye! Come on wake up

Beat.

I need to talk to you.

Beat.

Please. Come on Nye. Please. Wake up!

Jennie *starts to shake Nye. Archie enters.*

Archie What are you doing?

Jennie Nothing.

Archie *enters.*

Archie What are you doing?

Jennie Nothing.

Archie What are you doing? He's sleeping.

Jennie I just thought. You know. He should. He should wake up now.

Archie Leave him be.

Jennie *tries.*

She returns to **Nye**.

Jennie Nye.

Scene Sixteen   221

Archie   Leave him.

Jennie   Can you get the doctor, please?

Archie   What for?

Jennie   Just get the doctor.

Archie   Has he stopped breathing?

Archie *springs to* **Nye***'s bedside.*

Jennie   Just get the bloody doctor, Archie.

Archie   What am I asking him to come for? He's drugged up to the eyeballs.

Jennie   Because I need to speak to him, just do as you're told.

Archie   I'm not getting the doctor.

Jennie   Please.

Archie   No, I'm not.

Jennie   What is your problem?

Archie   I don't trust you! You're trying to wake him up against the Doctors advice, you want to wake him up, but you don't want to tell him what's going on.

Jennie   I *do* want to tell him what's going on. If I want to speak to my husband I'll bloody speak to him it's none of / your business.

Archie   You should have told him before.

Jennie   I'm trying to do it now.

Archie   Putting yourself first and it's not the first time you've done that either.

Jennie   What the hell does that mean?

Archie   I've had to pick up the pieces of your meddling, for for-!/ Well this time I'm saying no. You're not doing it. You're not. You've done enough.

Jennie   Who do you think you are? Really?

Archie Dripping poison in his ear for years! You never forgave him.

Jennie For what?

Archie For being more successful than you, and every stupid self-sabotaging/ decision he's made you're behind him, rubbing your hands with glee at the carnage he's created for himself

Jennie O here comes the King of the village. You're nothing but a bloody leach Archie sucking him dry for any ounce of status/ clinging to his coattails. 'Nye's man in the valley' you're a bloody social climber Archie

Archie He burns bridges, and and it's you…mh…handing him the matches. You have ruined his career

Jennie Oh there it is

Archie The more chaos he causes, with the party or with the cabinet

Jennie Educate me Archie!

Archie Or shadow cabinet or with his family, the more isolated he gets, the more important you become./ Because you want him all to yourself that's what all your pathetic threats to end it all were about.

Jennie You are not fit to polish Nye's shoes. He's got more integrity in his little toe than you. He kept you on out of pity.

Archie What?

Jennie But he was embarrassed by you

Archie That's / no that's no absol- not

Jennie Seeing with your stupid nose in the air and your tail wagging every time there's a Lord, or a President or some dignitary in the room.

Archie Rubbish

Jenny You're an embarrassment. Nye finds you embarrassing.

Archie And Nye thinks you're a snob!

Jennie: Is that right?

Archie Champagne with Nehru and oysters with Kruschev. He'd he'd bring you to the valley and and we'd spend all our time coordinating you!

Jennie Coordinating?/ Keeping me out of the room while you shoved all the wives in the kitchen.

Archie Who you were going to speak to who who you were going to meet, who was least likely to notice your disdain. He was ashamed of you.

Jennie He thought you were an intellectual pygmy.

Archie He thought you were a political failure.

Jennie He dreaded you and Ada visiting.

Archie That's not true.

Jennie It is.

Archie It's not.

Jennie It is.

Archie I've always hated you.

Nurse Ellie *enters.*

Nurse Ellie How's everybody doing?

Thundering silence.

It's not my ward, but I promised Mr Bevan I'd take care of him. Matron said it was fine. Is everything OK?

Jennie Um . . .

Beat.

Could you. Could you ask him to leave? Please.

Archie I'm not going anywhere.

Jennie I'd like him to leave.

Archie I'm not going anywhere.

Jennie I want him to leave NOW!

Nurse Ellie You know . . . this is a very hard thing for anyone to go through.

Beat.

Emotions run high. I'd encourage everyone to take a breath.

Beat.

You are the only ones here.

Beat.

And that can cause tremendous problems.

Beat.

But you *are* the only ones here.

Beat.

And that says something.

Long silence.

He looks very peaceful now. The morphine seems to be doing its trick. He's peaceful. Take some comfort from that.

Jennie But he'll wake up again, won't he?

Nurse Ellie I'm not sure.

Jennie You must see this a lot, do people ever wake up? There's things I need to say to him.

Nurse Ellie You have time to say them. That's what we can give you. More time with the people you love.

Scene Seventeen

House of Commons – Cabinet Office 1946

Herbert Morrison *appears.*

Herbert Morrison   Minister.

Nye   Herbert.

Herbert Morrison   Deputy Prime Minister, actually. I thought we could have a little chat before things get underway.

Nye   About what?

Herbert Morrison   Your health bill. To get it past the House, you have to get it past Cabinet and to get it past Cabinet, you have to get it past me. You've been very secretive. So before Cabinet arrive: tell me what your plan is.

Very long silence.

Nye   I'm not going to do that, Herbert.

Herbert Morrison   I really think you ought to.

Nye   Everyone needs to hear it at the same time, / otherwise it'll just be

Herbert Morrison   No, I think I need to hear it before everyone else. But no-one will share it with me, it's almost as if you don't trust me. You do trust me, Nye, don't you?

Nye   Well, everything's relative.

Herbert Morrison   Indeed. So here we are. In the Cabinet Office, waiting to build consensus.

Nye   …

Herbert Morrison   Come on, the noisy member for Ebbw Vale. I've never heard you so quiet.

Nye   If I run my bill past you, you'll make a counterproposal, and then they'll try and find a compromise between us.

Herbert Morrison   Yes.

Nye And then you'll water down my vision. Fudge it.

Herbert Morrison Your 'vision'.

Nye Yes, my 'vision'.

Herbert Morrison You mean your bill.

Nye My vision.

Herbert Morrison You've only been here a few months

Nye I'm the Minister for Health and Housing.

Herbert Morrison So everyone keeps telling me, but still, I find it hard to believe.

Nye I'm a minister. Clem appointed me.

Herbert Morrison When I think about it, it gives me two feelings at the same time. I feel excited slash alarmed. Two feelings at the same time, it's uncomfortable. So how about you put me out of my discomfort and share your vision with me? I'm giving you a chance. Do you want to get your nose bloody in here, with me now, or in front of everyone else?

Nye *looks around – he's on his own.*

Nye OK. The health service is a complex mess, it is impossible to navigate and grossly unfair. The voluntary hospitals serve the rich, and the council hospitals serve the poor. The wealthy cities have all the facilities and all the specialists. And the poor regions are stuck with Victorian hospitals falling apart, so we're left with an uneven service across the country, where poverty is a disability and wealth is advantaged. In Sunderland, one GP has to cover eighteen hundred patients but in Chelsea, one doctor has two hundred patients. People are dying of preventable disease and illness, because they can't get seen, or they have to travel too far or the cost of treatment is too much.

Herbert Morrisson So

Nye So. Back home.

Beat.

In Tredegar.

Beat.

We have a Medical Aid Society. All the miners pay into it every week. And it covers the cost of six doctors and six nurses who take care of the whole town.

Herbert Morrison There are friendly medical societies all over the country.

Nye But this is what's different about ours. The Tredegar Medical Aid Society covers not only those who pay in to it, but also those who don't. Women, children, the elderly. In Tredegar, everyone gets the same healthcare as the working men. And it works.

Beat.

So, I want to. Well.

Beat.

I want to Tredegarise the whole country. A uniform service so it doesn't matter where you are, you can get the same service as everyone else; free at the point of need.

Herbert Morrison That's your vision? Do what you did back home?

Nye Exactly.

Herbert Morrison So you want to take a model that works in a town with ten thousand people and apply it to a country of fifty million?

Nye Well. It would mean nationalising the hospitals.

Pause.

Herbert Morrison Go on.

Nye Nationalise the hospitals. Doctors on a salary. Funded by central government.

Herbert Morrison I see. It's very simple, isn't it?

Nye Yes it is.

Herbert Morrison Very simple. Yes, I suppose the challenge is the doctors won't agree to any changes when they can make a handsome living charging patients privately.

Nye Yes.

Herbert Morrison And then, the Labour-run councils take a great deal of pride in the hospitals they run and won't give them up without a fight.

Nye No doubt.

Herbert Morrison And on top of that, the voluntary hospitals won't give up their endowments and their prestige in teaching, and they'll be backed by the Tories because all Tories love to donate to the local voluntary hospitals to assuage their midnight guilt. So you're sort of picking three fights at once. Seems a lot.

Nye Well, we need control of the voluntary hospitals because that's where all the consultants are.

Herbert Morrison We could give them to the local councils to run? One less battle? Health service run by *local* government not central government.

Nye But local taxation would mean the rich areas have the best hospitals and the best doctors and the poor have to make do. People are having surgery without anaesthetic because they can't afford it. No, a universal service needs to be funded by central government.

Herbert Morrison But local government has a far more nuanced understanding of each area's healthcare needs.

Nye What is our biggest obstacle?

Herbert Morrison The doctors.

Nye How do we get them on side?

Herbert Morrison I don't know. No Health Minister has ever persuaded the British Medical Association to agree to anything. Their union is enormous.

Nye Exactly. So we have to break their union.

Pause.

Herbert Morrison I'm sorry. Did you just say that?

Nye They're middle-class, it's fine.

Herbert Morrison How are you going to break the union?

Nye Pressure. And I only get pressure if I nationalise all the hospitals at the same time. Blitzkrieg. If there's a gradual approach, the Tories will unpick everything when they're next in power. It has to be a shock of change where we show the country what's possible. The only way this will last is if it's short, sharp and deep. A health service free at the point of use, based on clinical need, not ability to pay, is simple to understand and difficult to undermine. The execution of it won't be perfect, Herbert. But it'll be the closest we'll get.

Herbert Morrison It's all a bit dramatic for my tastes.

Beat.

Thank you for sharing with me, but I'm afraid I'm not convinced. I'll be opposing in Cabinet.

Nye What? Why?

Herbert Morrison Because that's what a responsible Labour government should do.

Nye What does that mean?

Herbert Morrison It means we're not going to undermine our friends in local government.

Nye Why not?

Herbert Morrison Because we look after our own.

Nye Why?

Herbert Morrison You have the audacity to ask me, the Deputy Prime Minister, why?

Nye You're not actually Deputy Prime Minister, you're Lord President of the Council, you just like to call yourself Deputy Prime Minister. Why won't you work with me on this?

Herbert Morrison Because it's beneath me.

Cabinet Ministers slowly appear to witness this.

Nye Why?

Herbert Morrison Clem stuck you in here to shore up his position and now I'm meant to take you seriously! You have no ministerial aptitude. No talent for governance. It's ridiculous! I'm here running committees, writing policy, maintaining discipline, working every, damned, hour, God sends, to make this thing *finally* electable and then when we get in, we give *you* a seat at the table! And what's more, you actually think you deserve it! Your sense of entitlement. You swan around like some film star, dazzling the membership with your wit and your charm and your stupid fucking hair, shagging your way through conference, promising them the world when you don't have the faintest idea of how to deliver it! The thing about applying pressure is that you can only apply what you can withstand yourself.

*He puts a pillow over **Nye**'s face.*

Herbert Morrison They will do as I say because *I* am the Labour Party, *not* you.

Gasps from the surrounding Cabinet ministers.

Oh, uh . . . I didn't . . . we're all here, are we? Good. Yes. The Minister for Health and I were just . . . We were just discussing . . .

Nye How Herbert's in charge and how he'd rather look after his friends in local government than the rest of the country.

Clement Attlee I see.

Herbert Morrison No, now that's not / how I'd frame things . . .

Clement Attlee I think we've heard enough. All those in favour of Nye's bill raise your hands . . .

The Cabinet raise their hands.

Clement Attlee Congratulations, Nye, it seems you now have Cabinet backing.

Beat.

Now. The doctors.

Beat.

The doctors have destroyed the careers of every single Health Minister for the past fifteen years. No-one has ever got close to defeating them.

Beat.

It is now your task to persuade the most conservative profession in the country to accept and operate this Labour government's most socialist program.

Beat.

Hit them for six!

Scene Eighteen

The BMA Negotiating Council 1946

Part 1 – The First Meeting

Nye Hello.

Beat.

I'm. I'm the new Health Minister. Aneurin Mm a-Bevan. Who am I negotiating with?

Beat.

Doctor One You are negotiating with the whole council.

Nye Who is your leader?

Doctor One We are spokesmen, not leaders.

Nye Quite hard to negotiate with an organisation without a leader.

Beat.

Let's find some common ground. Where are our disagreements? Can you be specific?

Doctor One One. No full-time salaried service for general practitioners.

Doctor Two Two. Doctors will be free to practice without State interference.

Doctor Three Three. Doctors will practice anywhere they choose.

Doctor Four Four. The whole service will be based on voluntary hospitals.

Doctor Five Five. Adequate medical representation on all boards.

Nye And which of those is your priority in this negotiation?

Doctor One (*at same time*) One.

Doctor Two (*at same time*) Two.

Doctor Three (*at same time*) Three.

Doctor Four (*at same time*) Four.

Doctor Five (*at same time*) Five.

Nye Who am I meant to listen to? You want different things.

Beat.

Is this why it's easier to just keep things as they are? So you don't have to find consensus? I don't think your members actually have as big an issue with my bill as you say.

Beat.

So, if it's not really the bill, what specifically are you opposed to?

Silence.

Doctors One/Two/Three/Four/Five You.

Beat.

Nye I see.

He takes a moment.

Then I should mm-make my position clear.

Beat.

On the points you raise. I will concede this.

Beat.

Absolutely nothing.

Part 2 – Labour Party

Herbert Morrison *reads a paper.*

Herbert Morrison 'Bevan has treated a not unworthy profession with the contemptuous derision of which he is a master.'

Nye Yes / well . . .

Herbert Morrison 'Bevan attempted to bully the BMA and failed.'

Nye It's not bullying, it's negotiating.

Clement Attlee What am I going to do with you?

Nye Nothing, just give me time, I have a plan.

Clement Attlee That is the worst first innings we could have asked for.

Nye I just need time, I need you to hold your nerve.

Clement Attlee We can't have our landmark bill undermined by an entire profession.

Nye I think I need to call for a special debate in Parliament.

Clement Attlee What for? We've got the bill through. It's law.

Nye I need to put pressure on them.

Clement Attlee Another debate just gives Churchill even more chance to rile up the BMA.

Nye Another debate gives me the chance to speak directly to the members, they'll read what I'm saying / in the press.

Clement Attlee No, go back out there and find a way through.

Nye But if we can just have the debate, my plan / will start to . . .

Clement Attlee Your plan is persuade the doctors to change their mind or I'll get someone else to.

Part 3 – The BMA Negotiating Council

Nye *stands before the doctors.*

Nye Maybe we got off on the wrong foot.

Beat.

Maybe, if we got to know each other a little better, things would be more collegiate. You, sir, what is your speciality?

Doctor Three I am the President of the Royal College of Obstetricians and Gynaecologists. I am responsible for every pregnant woman in the country.

Nye You're boasting. No? OK. I've read some of the things you've been saying in the press and the radio. I'm not the power-mad monster you think I am.

Beat.

If there is to be a National Health Service, then the power to administer it has to reside somewhere. Isn't it more transparent to know exactly who wields the authority?

Doctor One You are answerable to no-one but yourself.

Nye I'm answerable to Parliament.

Doctor Five State control of medicine will destroy the doctors' clinical freedom.

Doctor Three The State will come between the doctor and patient.

Doctor One It jeopardises our Hippocratic Oath to serve and only serve our patient.

Nye The doctor-patient relationship is sacred to you.

Doctor One Yes.

Nye It needs to be protected at all costs.

Doctor One Yes. It is our responsibility to our patients.

Nye There can be no interference in that relationship.

Doctor One No.

Nye Is it not an interference when a patient can't afford the doctor? When a patient can't afford the medicine? Or the surgery? When a family has to prioritise the health of the husband, and leaves the health of the wife and children to castor oil and whiskey?

Beat.

I consider the main interference to the integrity of doctor-patient relations to be personal profit.

Silence.

Doctor One These negotiations are over.

Part 4 – Parliament

Tory MPs Hear, hear! Hear, hear!

Speaker I call to the floor for this special debate on the health bill. The Prime Minister.

Nye looks around.

Speaker Prime Minister?

Nye Clem? Clem?

Herbert Morrison The Prime Minister is indisposed.

Ad-lib outrage and mockery from Tory MPs.

Nye Uh. The uh uh a-doctors.

Beat.

They have dd-a-disagreed with every minister for health that has ever been appointed.

I am a Welshman. A socialist. And they find me even more impossible. So, if we can dd-dismiss that the dd-disagreements are because of my mh-personality, maybe we can look this challenge in the eye.

Beat.

We are not now dealing with the legitimate interests of the members of the medical profession. We are dealing with wholesale resistance to the implementation of an act of Parliament!

Ad-lib Tory MPs' outrage.

Nye We desire to know if the Opposition supports that. Because if they do, I would warn them that the end of that road would be exceedingly unpleasant.

Winston Churchill Is that a threat?

Nye Do you support the sabotage of an act of Parliament?

Winston Churchill We will not leave the doctors to fight alone.

Tory MPs Hear hear! / Hear hear!

Nye There is nothing noble about your support for the doctors, you have personally voted against the National Health Service twenty-one times.

Tory MPs Hear hear!

Winston Churchill You want doctors to be servants of the State.

Nye I want doctors to be servants of the people.

Winston Churchill This is the first step towards National Socialism.

Tory MPs Hear hear! / Hear hear!

Nye The nurses support the bill, are they Nazis?

Ad lib Tory MPs' outrage.

Winston Churchill Hitler put the medial services under the control of one medical Fuhrer, this bill will establish you in that capacity.

Tory MPs Hear hear! / Hear hear!

Nye Now we've won the war, you want to tear us apart again.

Winston Churchill Doctors of this country – do you support a National Health Service?

Part 5 – The BMA Negotiating Council

Tory MPs Resign!

Churchill Finished. The noisy member for Ebbw Vale is finished.

Tory MPs Resign!

Herbert Morrison 'Mr Bevan's proposals were deadlocked, now they are dead.'

Jennie His breathing…

Archie It's really fast.

Clement Atlee I'm sorry Nye.

Nye Where were you?

Tory MPs Resign!

Jennie What does it mean?

Archie Is that normal?

Nurse Ellie It's what happens.

Nye I need more time.

Winston/Dain and Ellie place him in bed.

Tory MPs Resign!

Nye I need more time.

Herbert Morrison 'This failure must mark the end of Bevan's brief time in office'.

Jennie How much time does he have?

Nye Please give me more time.

Clement Atlee My staff will draft your resignation letter.

Everyone continues to talk but they are drowned out as Nye recalls the coal seam his father once showed him.

David Bevan One true blow.

Nye goes into his briefcase and out he pulls a 'pamphlet' saying 'Your New National Health Service'. It is almost a surprise to himself.

He holds it aloft.

Nye I will launch my new national health service in three months' time on July 5th 1948 with or without the Doctors.

Nye takes the pamphlet and throws it on the floor.

It creates a mighty fracture - the one true blow causes a rumble that underscores the rest of the scene.

The Doctors blink.

Churchill WH/AT?

Jennie Nye?

Clement Atlee No, no no no don't say that in public/ you can't. Nye…don't…

Winston Churchill You would/ launch a National Health Service without a single doctor?

Clement Atlee No no let's re-group/ and think this through.

Churchill You will create the greatest healthcare crisis in the history of this country.

Nye *I will launch my new national health service in two months' time on July 5th with or without the Doctors!*

Winston Churchill Fantasy! You're a fantasist!

Dr 5 If the health service goes ahead every Doctor will go on strike!

Churchill Doctors, resist this authoritarianism for the sake of the country.

Archie You can't cause a strike; it goes against everything we stand for.

Jennie Don't listen to them.

Clement Atlee You have to move the date.

Winston Churchill Strike! For the very soul of the nation!

Nye sees the Doctors are cracking under the pressure.

Nye I will launch my new national health service in one months' time on July 5th with or without the Doctors but… Every negotiation needs compromise. So, in the interests of finding an agreement, I will grant the Doctors the power to choose their own representatives on every health board/

Winston Churchill   What!?

Nye   The doctors will choose who they are answerable to.

Some Doctors join the NHS.

Winston Churchill   You are trying to destroy the solidarity of the doctors' union with last minute desperate concessions.

Nye   Concessions Winston or compromises?

DR 5   The Doctors will go on strike if the bill goes ahead.

Clement Atlee   You are creating a crisis for the whole country.

Winston Churchill   Ha!

Nye   And if you sign up to my national health service, I will allow the consultants to work privately, outside of their NHS contracts.

More Doctors join the NHS.

Churchill   Civil servants! That's what they'll become!

DR 1   The Doctors will go on strike if the bill goes ahead.

Herbert Morrison   Move the date! You are going to bring down the government!

Winston Churchill   Hold firm!

Nye   Also, I will compromise with the GPs. And I will allow them to buy and sell GP surgeries within the healthcare system.

Archie   Bloody hell, Nye! It's working!

Jennie   It's working! You've got them!

More Doctors join the NHS.

There is only one Doctor left.

Churchill You shit. He has manipulated you from the start!

Nye I will launch my new National Health Service in 10 days' time on July 5th with or without the doctors. And finally, I understand becoming salaried workers is a concern. So, I will make this commitment to you. I will make doctors the highest paid profession in this country.

The final Doctor is looking nervous...

Clement Atlee Splendid work, minister.

Churchill He's lying.

Nye Join me and take the most civilized step any country has ever taken and together we will build the greatest health service the world has ever seen.

The final Doctor joins the NHS.

Doctor 5 The BMA recommends all doctors sign an NHS contract.

Nye Yes! People of this country! We will build hospitals, bigger hospitals, with more beds so you can stay until you are recovered, so you return home ready for family life. Every hospital shall have their own specialists, with the right equipment, so you won't be sent around the country looking for what you need. Dentistry, glasses, mental health all the things we need to live with serenity starting with universal healthcare for all.

We shall never have all we need. Expectation will always exceed capacity ... the service must always be changing, growing and improving; it must always appear imperfect. I don't want to give you relief. I don't want to help you survive. I don't want to give you medical care. I want to give you your dignity.

Scene Nineteen

NHS Royal Free Hospital 1960

We're back in the real world.

The full hospital ward is re-created.

It is night time on the ward.

Nye *stirs.*

Dr Dain   Oh! Hello . . .

Nye   Doctor. How long have I been asleep?

Dr Dain   About fourteen hours. You needed it. How is the pain relief?

Nye   I could do with some more.

Dr Dain   I'll put you down for some more morphine. No other side-effects, anything of concern? Nausea? Itching? Hallucinations?

Nye   No. Well. Actually. Crazy dreams. Does that . . . does that sort of count?

Dr Dain   Mind if I check your stitches? Excuse the cold hands.

Dr Dain *examines* **Nye**'s *stomach.* **Nye** *winces.*

Nye   Sort of, nothing made sense, but everything did. My life was all jumbled up. I was . . . I was trying to find Jennie. But- where is she?

Dr Dain   She's just resting she'll be back any minute.

Nye   And My father. Was there. He's been dead 30 years. I was with him at the end.

Beat.

He died in my arms.

Beat.

Horrible death.

Dr Dain   Was he a miner?

Nye   Yes. Black lung.

Dr Dain   Cruel way to go.

Nye No dignity. And in this dream, in the middle of it all. Jennie was…she trying to-

Beat.

Everything went fine with the, with the operation?

Dr Dain Yes.

Nye Oh thank God for that. I think I've been worrying that something went wrong. Thank you. Thank you, Doctor. You've been. Marvellous really.

Beat.

Dr Dain Anything I can do to give you peace of mind?

Beat.

Nye exhales and thinks.

Nye Could you. Could you, do you mind just taking another look/ make sure it's all…

Dr Dain You want me to examine your wound again? (*off Nye*) I can do that.

Dr Dain *examines Nye's wound.*

Dr Dain Ok. All in order. All ok…Hm…

Nye What? What is it?

Dr Dain Is that tender?

Nye Yes. That's fine though isn't?

Dr Dain Something is bothering me. Do you mind if I take a closer look?

Nye Maybe I'm/ overthinking it with the.

Dr Dain This may hurt a bit.

Nye Please, no don't….

Dr Dain Let's see shall we?

He plunges his hand into **Nye**'s *stomach.* **Nye** *screams.*

Sound design swells, we're still in the fantasia . . .

Dr Dain's *hand is in* **Nye**'s *stomach, up to his elbow.*

Dr Dain   Hold on! Calm down! Nearly, nearly got it. Hang on, hang on!

He pulls out his arm out.

What's this?

Nye *gasps in pain and shock.*

Nye   What the hell is that? It's a piece of coal. It's coal.

Dr Dain   Coal? Yes. It is.

Nye   What the hell is coal doing in there?

Dr Dain   How long were you underground?

Nye   Eight years.

Dr Dain   Could that be dust, coagulating? Let me see if there's more . . .

Nye   Wait, no, hang on!

But **Dr Dain** *plunges his hand into* **Nye**'s *stomach,* **Nye** *screams in pain as* **Dr Dain** *pulls out more coal.*

Dr Dain   Yes, there's definitely something.

He holds a lump of coal.

Dr Dain   Yes, there's more.

He plunges his hand into **Nye**'s *stomach again.*

Nye *screams.*

Dr Dain *pulls out more coal.*

Nye   What does . . . I don't understand. What does this mean?

He picks up a lump of coal.

Dr Dain *fades away.*

Staring at the coal for meaning, **Nye** *holds it aloft for what seems like an age.*

Beat.

Nye Surely . . .

Beat.

Why would . . .

Beat.

No . . . No no no.

Beat.

He takes some time to gather the courage.

I'm dying, aren't I?

Beat.

You opened me up and you could see I was dying.

Beat.

Why couldn't you, why couldn't you tell me?

Beat.

Why couldn't Jennie tell me?

Beat.

Jennie? Jennie? Where am I? What's happening to me? Arianwen?

Sound design swells.

Scene Twenty

NHS Royal Free Hospital 1960

Nye *watches as* **Archie** *and* **Jennie** *say their goodbyes.*

Archie His breathing's really slow... y'know is that. It's. not. Y'know. It's going. Is that. Is that normal?

Nurse nods.

Nurse It's what happens.

Jennie How long?

Nurse Ellie It's time.

Beat.

Archie I just think don't think he knows I'm here. I feel like I've let him down.

Jennie Of course, he knows you're here. Of course, he does.

Beat.

He knows you'd never leave his side.

Archie I'm worried he doesn't know.

Jennie Then, tell him.

Beat.

Jennie Tell him.

Archie Alright butt? It's Archie here. Ok. And. I'll be here the whole time. And. Well. You've been a wonderful friend to me. And I hope you know, even though I never said it. I hope you know that I love you. I've always loved you, my friend.

*He kisses **Nye**'s hand deeply. Having said what he needs to say with dignity, **Archie** is able to move away.*

Archie *looks to Jennie.*

Jennie I can't.

Archie Yes you can.

Jennie No.

Archie It's ok.

But she can't. She can't.

Archie Nye?

Beat.

Jennie's here.

Jennie No.

But Archie supports her and guides her to Nye.

Beat.

She's got you safe. Like she always has. You haven't got to worry about a thing, because Jennie Lee's right by your side.

Beat.

Talk to him.

Jennie Nye, my boy. I hope I did the right thing. He's squeezing my hand!

Beat.

Oh Nye, my love. It's ok. It's ok. You can go.

Beat.

Don't you worry about me, I'll see you in the garden.

Jennie *kisses his hand.*

And slowly **Nye** *loosens his grip.*

Nye Is this it? Has it happened?

The whole ensemble of NHS staff surround **Nye**. *He is caught and held by Doctors, Nurses, Matrons, Porters, Consultants, Therapists. The whole family of NHS carers carry him safely, with loving care and dignity.*

They carry him through a movement, a care dance, gently towards death. As he moves:

Nye I don't think it's happened yet. I can still feel. I feel scared but I feel safe. I can feel, people. People are nearby. I still feel. I still feel held.

The NHS staff carry **Nye** *and place him next to* **David Bevan**, *who steps forward with a miner's lamp.*

Beat.

Nye I'm ready. I'm not scared.

David Bevan Hold my hand.

Beat.

Nye Dad. Did I . . .

Nye Did I look after everyone?

David Bevan *raises his lamp. The light slowly fills the room.*

Sound design swells with the passing of time. Now we hear things clearly: babies crying, monitors, heart beats, 'This will hurt a little,' 'Thank you, Doctor,' 'Nurse!' 'Count back from a hundred,' 'Feeling better?' 'How long has she got?' 'Is he in pain?' All the sounds of things that have kept us alive and safe and well and cared for.

A moment as the house lights come up and **Nye** *sees us all.*

A smile breaks out across his face.

Death *approaches with no dread.*

Darkness.

If screens are used, the following facts can be screened:

Within ten years of the NHS being launched infant mortality fell by 50%.

Since its founding, life expectancy has increased by 12 years.

Every day 1.3m people are treated, based on clinical need, not the ability to pay.

The End.

Isla

Isla was first performed at Theatr Clwyd, in October 2021

This year (2021) it is estimated that there are now more voice-activated digital assistants than people.

Four digital assistants account for 90 per cent of sales – Google Assistant, Siri, Alexa and Cortana. All are female gendered.

Characters

Roger, *older man*
Erin, *younger woman*
Isla/PC Jones, *the voice / young woman*

Notes

An / oblique indicates when the next line should be spoken.

A – dash indicates an interruption of thought or hesitation.

Parenthesis (. . .) indicates words or phrases that can be left unspoken, at the discretion of the director or cast.

A space between lines indicates a beat or pause. The bigger the space the bigger the pause.

Scene One

25 March 2020.

Erin *has a face mask pulled down around her neck and rubber gloves on.*

Erin It's either this or a dog.

Roger I don't want a dog.

Erin So, I got you this.

Roger I don't want this / either.

Erin I know so it's my choice / what I give you.

Roger I don't want this either.

Erin That's one of the joys of being a grown-up, you stop listening to your parents.

Roger I won't use it.

Erin I've charged it up for you and I'm going to link it all up to the smart home hub.

Roger I won't use it.

Erin This cable is a USB so it can go into any of your plugs, it's got a plug with it but if you lose it or you're out and about – not that you're gonna be out and about but if you lose it as long as you've got the cable you can plug it into any USB plug you've got; have you taken your tablets?

Roger What am I / meant to do with this?

Erin Stay back! Please. Your statin, you have to take / your statin have you taken it?

Roger Yes. I took it earlier.

Erin And your aspirin?

Roger Yes.

Erin Have you really?

Scene One 253

Roger Yes.

Erin Have you really?

Roger Yes.

Erin If you don't take your aspirin you'll die. Or worse you'll have to go to hospital.

Roger I don't trust / these things.

Erin Have you really taken your aspirin?

Roger I'll take them now so you can see me taking them and then you can rest assured you did all you could to
stop me dying because that's what this is all about isn't it? Ridding you of guilt so that when I die, you can tell your friends, 'It's fine. I did all I could, I once bullied him into taking an aspirin.'

Erin So you hadn't / taken them as I thought.

Roger No I hadn't, but I had remembered to take them which is the same / as taking them.

Erin As I suspected – why lie / about these things, Dad?

Roger I wasn't / lying.

Erin I don't have time to be worrying about you – what's happened to this? Oh. I see. Hang on. I don't have time to be worrying whether a grown man has swallowed his pill that will stop him dying.

Roger I wasn't lying I'd remembered / it was on the

Erin Remembering something and doing something is not the same.

Roger Yes it is when you're retired.

Erin Look it's blue it's gone blue. When it goes blue it's on standby. Right so the next thing is / syncing to the home hub . . .

She moves around the flat.

Roger I take my statin and my asprin with my coffee, and I'm not ready for my coffee yet, because when I have my coffee I need a poo, and the paperboy hasn't come yet and I'm not pooing without my newspaper / so everything cascades from that.

Erin *is at the fridge – there's lots of sponsored animal paperwork pinned on it.*

Erin Bloody hell, Dad. How many animals are you sponsoring now?

Roger It's the adverts on the telly, I can't bear it.

Erin Soppy old git. Sponsor me if you like.

Roger I bloody sponsored you long enough.

Erin That's synced now to your home hub. Right this statin and aspirin situation.

Roger The paperboy comes, then I have my coffee and I take my statin and aspirin.

Erin You can't rely on other people at the moment.

Roger He's very reliable, they're very reliable people.

Erin Don't.

Roger That's not racist, it's not racist. I'm talking about the family, they're a very reliable family. Honestly you can't say anything these days. They've never not delivered in years and if the boy can't do it the dad comes round in his Audi. That's why he's part of my routine. I have a routine. That's how I don't forget things. When you get old, routine is basically your short-term memory.

Erin Well, they might get sick ok? You need a new routine. / Here? Move the . . .

Roger *You* need a routine.

Erin What about this? / Can you reach that?

Roger You wouldn't lose so many things / if you had a bit of routine in your life.

Erin I literally haven't got time for routine, Dad, my life is basically a series of fires that I squirt attention at / which reminds me: have you cleaned your catheter?

Roger Did you find that bank card in the end?

Erin No one uses bank cards anymore, right; have you / cleaned your

Roger Yes yes yes / twice a day.

Erin You'll get a water infection and you can't / go to hospital.

Roger Go to hospital I know I've bloody cleaned it ok?

Erin Ok! I have to ask. Let's see if I can set the – Isla! Say hello to Dad.

The device lights up, just before it speaks.

Isla (*V/O*) Hello, Dad.

Erin Maybe she shouldn't call you Dad that's a bit weird. Isla, this is Roger. Dad say something. Say something.

Roger Bugger off.

Erin Isla this is Roger. Say hello.

Roger No.

Isla (*V/O*) Hello, Roger.

Roger I'm not saying hello to a bloody machine.

Erin Isla can you – hang on, what time do you have your coffee each morning?

Roger Well, that depends on the paperboy.

Erin In the eventuality that the paperboy lets you down, and you are forced to break your routine and have a coffee and a paperless poo what time is the latest that could possibly happen?

Roger Wouldn't happen.

Erin Worst case scenario.

Roger Wouldn't happen. Never happens.

Erin Dad. We can't rely on anything to happen these days the world's gone mad. Give me a time.

Roger Half-nine. / Half-nine.

Erin Isla, every morning, at nine-thirty, could you remind Roger to take his statin?

Isla (*V/O*) Programming.

I have set, a daily alarm for Roger. At nine-thirty AM every morning I will say, 'Roger remember to take your statin'.

Erin Now as long as she's plugged in, she'll remind you.

Roger I don't need a reminder, / I've got my routine.

Erin It's an insurance policy.

Roger My routine is my insurance policy.

Erin Keep it charged.

Roger I don't want it / I won't use it.

Erin I know but you need it. We need it.

Roger I won't use it.

Erin I don't know how long lockdown is going to last it's never happened before and this is going to help. (*Off* **Roger**.) Look if you won't have this or a dog then you're going to have to come and stay with us for lockdown and you don't want that do you?

Roger No.

Erin This is going to help loads, you don't need to go to the shops, she can order things for you, she can keep you updated. She can start to look after you as well, they're great. She can play music, you like music. I've linked it to the home hub so she can turn the heating up or off just ask her. Whatever you need, just ask her first she might be able to do it. And I'll know you've got something here to talk to.

Roger It's only going to be three weeks, what's all the fuss about?

Erin It's not going to be three weeks Dad.

Roger How long will it be for?

Erin I don't know but it's not going to be three weeks so please try with this. Everyone's got one of these. Literally everyone. I've programmed mine with all the kids' deadlines, so when I'm wrapping up for the day she pings with 'Ceri's Antarctica project due for upload tomorrow'. She texts me when the kids use the last of the milk and then adds it to my shopping list which it then gets delivered to the house. Changed. My. Life. It's all gone tits up a couple of times when I've unplugged her to charge the phone and then she's died and then I just presume there's nothing to remember and it's utter chaos but generally. *Generally*. If she's plugged in, life is easier. / And she'll make suggestions too if she hears –

Roger I don't really need an easier life. I want to bloody go out when I want.

Erin Well, you can't go out. You can for an hour's exercise. Just don't talk to anyone or touch anything.

Roger When can I see you next?

Erin I don't know –

Her phone goes, she puts it on speaker and carries on fiddling with **Isla** *and the instructions.*

Erin Hi Mike.

Mike (*V/O*) Have you seen the email?

Erin Off Louisa?

Mike (*V/O*) Off Clive.

He's saying you said to him the keyworker kids hub programme is coming under social care but that means we wouldn't be insured to use the schools, and if we're not insured we can't open them tomorrow. Why the hell did you say social care because that's opened up a whole can of worms, when we haven't even been to finance? You've dropped me right in it with Clive it's bloody idiotic –

Erin *grabs the phone and puts it to her ear.*

Erin Um yeah. That was my understanding.

Ok. Yes. I'm sorry I thought we were all across this one. But in the planning meeting – Yes. I'm so sorry. You're right. What? No. I don't want to.

I'm a (*censoring volume*) fucking idiot. Ok? Yes. Ok yes, thank you. Shall I call Marcus and –

She hangs up.

She starts emailing on her phone.

Roger Everything alright?

Erin I've got to go.

Roger He always speak to you like that?

Erin What?

Roger Him on the phone.

Erin I screwed up. He was – He was looking out for me actually. It's insane in work at the moment so . . . It's fine.

Roger The way people speak to you is the way people / treat you.

Erin I know I know I know.

She stops emailing, puts her phone down.

Can you give this a go *please*?

Roger Yes sure, I'll give it a go.

Erin Do you promise?

Roger I promise.

Erin *Thank you.* Isla, what's the traffic like on the A55?

Isla (*V/O*) Clear, some congestion between Bodelwyddan and Abergele.

Erin Great.

She looks at her phone again.

Roger What? What happened then? How does she know the traffic?

Erin She knows everything Dad and she's smart she'll listen and learn things about you. Just remember to say Isla first. Isla! Play my exit music.

Roger Where's that coming from?

Erin I've connected her to my Spotify account.

Roger She plays music?

Erin She does whatever you want Dad she's your digital slave. Keys. Purse. Ok.

Is this the first time they've looked at each other?

Roger *approaches her for a hug.*

Erin   No.

Roger   We can't even hug now?

Erin   Just, stay safe, ok.

Lights down.

Scene Two

Roger *is doing a jigsaw and drinking a cup of tea.*

Isla (*V/O*)   Roger / It is nine-thirty. Remember to take your statin.

Roger *nearly falls off his seat, throwing tea everywhere.*

Roger   JESUS FUCKING CHRIST. What the hell was that?

He looks around, cleans himself up. Tidies up everything. Picks up the dropped jigsaw pieces.

Isla (*V/O*)   Roger. It is nine-thirty. Remember to take your statin.

Under the table **Roger** *bangs his head.*

Roger   Ow! Sodding . . . Bloody . . . fucking . . .

He clambers to his feet.

He approaches the **Isla** *and takes a long time to deduce it – this is the first time he's properly looked at it.*

Eventually **Roger** *unplugs the* **Isla**.

Isla (*V/O*)   I am at 99 per cent battery charge. I have approximately eight hours of battery life until I need re-charging.

Roger   What?

He startles again when the **Isla** *speaks.*

Roger I won't be plugging you back in believe me young lady.

He backs away from the **Isla** *and carries on tidying up. His phone pings.*

He reads it.

He then scrolls and dials a number.

Roger Erin? It's your Dad. Just wondering when you've got a minute. Angela's just texted and because of all this they've had to cancel Bryan's retirement do and she wants me to make a video on my phone, but I don't think my phone can do a video do you know how – Hello.

Hello? – Oh. Damn.

He dials again.

Erin it's your Dad again, sorry I, the bloody thing cut off I don't know why they give you such a short amount of time to say what you want to say by the time you're getting into your stride the damn thing cuts off. Anyway. What? Bloody. *Sodding.*

He dials again.

Erin, it's your Dad, what is wrong with your phone? Every time I try to leave a message the damn thing cuts me off! I'm just trying to leave a message and by the time I'm getting to say what I want the sodding thing just –

He dials again.

FUCK YOU AND YOUR FUCKING STUPID TWAT OF A – Erin? Ring me.

He hangs up and throws his phone across the room.

Bloody stupid things wish we didn't have the damn things.

Isla (*V/O*) Erin mobile ringing.

Roger What what?

Isla (*V/O*)   Erin mobile ringing.

Roger   Erin's ringing?

Isla (*V/O*)   Erin mobile ringing.

Roger   Where's my bloody phone now? Where / did it go?

Isla (*V/O*)   Erin mobile ringing.

Roger   Um. Uh uh uh uh, Isla. ISLA, WHERE. IS. MY. PHONE?

Isla (*V/O*)   You can use me to answer your phone, just say, 'Isla accept'.

(*V/O*) Just say, 'Isla accept'.

Roger   Isla. Accept?

Erin (*V/O*)   Dad? I've got like five missed calls off you are you ok?

Roger   Erin?

Erin (*V/O*)   Yeah.

Roger   Can you hear me?

Erin (*V/O*)   Course I can hear you. We're on the phone.

Roger   I'm using the Isla.

Erin (*V/O*)   That's great news!

Roger   No, I'm not using her. I'm not – it just said – I couldn't find my phone. So, I'm on it now.

Erin (*V/O*)   What?

Dad?

Roger   I couldn't find my phone. But it said I could talk to you through it. So, I am.

Erin (*V/O*)   Sorry. What are you saying?

Roger It doesn't matter.

I just . . . misplaced my phone. And it just said, 'Say Isla accept'. So I said, 'Isla accept', and now I can hear you through it. / Yes. So, I was wondering.

Erin (*V/O*) Oh! Right, yeah! When I was – yeah, we turned that function off cause I used to get so many phone calls Isla was ringing off all the time it was like having a landline again.

Roger Right.

Erin (*V/O*) Dad?

Roger I'm here. Loud and clear.

Erin (*V/O*) What were you calling for?

Roger What?

Erin You were ringing me.

Roger No you rang me.

Erin What? No, I was returning your call?

Roger My call? I didn't . . . oh yes! Oh God, yes. I was just leaving you a – yeah. But I kept getting cut off I've left a few messages.

Erin (*V/O*) I never listen to voicemail Dad no one leaves voicemails anymore.

Roger Really?

Erin (*V/O*) Unless it's a voicenote on WhatsApp.

Roger Unless it's a whatswhat?

Erin (*V/O*) What did you want Dad?

Roger I was wondering if you could just pop around to help me with this video for Bryan, Angela's just texted and they can't have a do for Bryan's retirement because of the lockdown and now she wants everyone to make a video but I don't know how to do that, so I thought maybe you could pop round and do it for me.

Erin (*V/O*) Dad we can't see each other, we have to stay indoors it's the law now.

Roger Yeah, but it'll be five minutes and we stay socially distanced.

Erin (*V/O*) The police are stopping cars Dad no one is travelling anywhere.

Roger Well how can I do this video?

Erin (*V/O*) Do it on your phone. It's simple go to camera and click video.

Roger I need someone to hold it.

Erin (*V/O*) Dad! There's a pandemic on! Work is crazy I'm trying to work from home, the kids are here. Just work out how to make a video. Click the camera, click the video and turn the phone around and film it.

Roger Ok ok. I just thought you could help me and make sure I don't look like an idiot.

Erin (*V/O*) Well when you've done it send it to me first maybe I can edit it.

Roger What if I write it and read it out to you over the phone?

Erin (*V/O*) No.

Roger I'll call you back in twenty minutes.

Erin (*V/O*) I ducked out of a meeting because I thought you were, I thought it was urgent.

Roger She just texted now.

Erin (*V/O*) I have to go Dad.

Roger Yeah ok. Yup you go, love / You go. Talk to –

Isla (*V/O*) Erin mobile has ended the call.

Scene Three

Roger *is speaking to his reflection in a mirror.*

Roger Headmaster Perry! Mr Perry. Mr *Perry*. Former. *Former* Headmaster Mr Perry. Ah-hem. Ah-hem.

Former Headmaster Perry. Welcome to retirement. Say goodbye, to the rota. And hello to, the golf course. Hello to the golf course. When they actually let us on, that is.

Hello to the golf course. Hello, Golf Course! When the bastards actually let us on it that is.

Is this funny? I don't know.

He goes to his phone. He weighs up ringing **Erin**.

He looks at his watch.

He goes back to the mirror. That's not working.

He looks around the room.

He goes to the window.

Nothing.

Isla (*V/O*) Roger it's nine-thirty, remember to take your statin.

Roger *startles, but not so much this time.*

He goes and takes his statin and aspirin.

As he does so he rehearses again.

Roger Mr Perry. Former. *Former* Headmaster Mr Perry.

Former Headteacher Perry. Welcome to retirement. Say goodbye, to the rota. And hello to, the golf course, when they finally let us back on it.

Hello.

To the golf course. When they finally let us out of our homes.

Hello to the golf course! When we're bloody . . .

Hello, to the golf . . .

He sits down and stares for a long time at the **Isla**.
Eventually he cracks.

Roger Isla? Hello.

Isla (*V/O*) I'm listening.

Roger Hello Isla. / Can you

Isla (*V/O*) Hello Roger.

Roger Hello. Good morning. / I have this

Isla (*V/O*) Good morning.

Roger Good morning.

Isla I have. Can you . . . um . . .

Isla (*V/O*) I'm sorry I don't understand.

Roger Can you . . . sorry. Isla, Isla can you, listen to, my joke, and, tell me, if it's funny? Is that, something, you can do?

Isla (*V/O*)   I'm listening.

Roger   Ok. Isla. So, you know, how jokes work?

Isla (*V/O*)   I know how jokes work.

Roger   Fantastic. Isla, what are jokes meant to do?

Isla (*V/O*)   Jokes are a display of humour within a specific context designed to make people laugh or lighten the mood.

Roger   That's actually. Actually that's a very, yes that's what they are. Ok. Ok. Ok. So, Isla, I'll. Let me give you a bit of a background first. I've got to do a speech. It's Bryan's retirement, I used to work with him, he used to be under me and then when I left he took my job, great guy. Bit dour. But solid. Always driven BMWs. Estates. Coupés. And his wife she has a two-seater and their son got caught looking at porn at the sailing club. They've got a big house down in Broughton you know down by the as you go past the uh the roundabout as you go in . . . Anyway . . . because of the virus he can't have a do, so Angela's asked us all to make a video and then she's going to join them all up, so it's all – and I've got to hold this ruler and then pass it I don't know I don't understand but I've got to, and then it'll look like I'm giving it to someone else I don't know how she's going to do that actually because what if the ruler doesn't match? I've only got this one. But anyway, don't worry about the ruler don't worry about the ruler. I've got this speech and yeah. So. Is that? Is that clear? Isla?

Isla (*V/O*)   I'm listening.

Roger   So here goes – *Former* Headmaster Perry. Welcome to retirement. Say goodbye, to the rota. And hello to the golf course, when they bloody let us back on that is.

Roger   Isla?

Isla (*V/O*)   I'm listening.

Roger Forget about it. Don't bother it's fine.

Isla (*V/O*) I'm sorry I don't understand.

Roger It was a stupid idea. Waste of time. Forget it. Forget about it Isla.

Isla (*V/O*) I'm listening.

Roger You didn't laugh. I don't know if, can you laugh? Isla can you laugh?

Isla (*V/O*) Ha ha.

Roger Isla, forget about it. Forget I ever asked.

Isla (*V/O*) I'm sorry I don't understand.

Roger Total bloody waste of. Waste of my time. What's the point of – What do you do? Isla.

Isla (*V/O*) I'm listening.

Roger What is the point in you? Isla why do people need you?

Isla (*V/O*) I can help find things out for you.

Roger But I don't need to find out anything. I know everything I need to know.

Isla (*V/O*) Digital assistants can help find things out for you.

Roger Like what?

Isla (*V/O*) What would you like to know?

Roger *exhales.*

Roger Is there any sport still on?

Isla (*V/O*) The 2005 Wales versus Ireland rugby match will be re-broadcast on Saturday 11th April.

Roger 2005. 2005? Oh Jesus. The Welsh grand slam? I'm not sure my nerves could take that match. When are they showing that again?

Isla (*V/O*) The 2005 Wales versus Ireland rugby match will be re-broadcast at 1.15 p.m. on Saturday 11th April.

Roger Thank you.

Isla (*V/O*) Would you like to know what channel it will be broadcast on?

Roger No! Yes. Go on then.

Isla (*V/O*) It will be broadcast on BBC Wales.

Roger Isla, did Marcus Horan score in that game?

Isla (*V/O*) Marcus Horan scored a try in that game.

Roger Jesus, I remember that game now. Erin came home for it. Me in my Ireland top, them in their Wales tops. Even the bloody dog had a daffodil hat on. They were so excited. One of the big lumps scored from a charge-down, and Joy and Erin screamed so much the dog pissed in the kitchen. Kevin Maggs, bloody great defender, he got cut to ribbons by . . . Who was the Welsh inside centre that game? Isla who played inside centre for Wales in 2005?

Isla (*V/O*) In the 2005 Wales rugby team Gavin Henson played inside centre.

Roger No wasn't him. Isla, who was outside centre for Wales in 2005?

Isla (*V/O*) In the 2005 Wales rugby team, Tom Shanklin / played outside centre.

Roger Tom Shanklin. He ran a line in the game that made Kevin Maggs look like a fucking *schoolboy*. When they scored that, I knew it was over, it was over. Horan pulled one back but it was over. And then Wales lifted the trophy and to add insult to injury, Joy got the champagne out, popped the cork and it flew off and hit me right in the bollocks. They were crying laughing. God it was brilliant. I should watch it for Joy, or she'll never forgive me. What time's kick-off?

Isla (*V/O*)   Kick-off is at 1.15 p.m. on Saturday.

Roger   You know, I'm getting a sore bollock just thinking about it. Speaking of sore bollocks, Isla what's that Gavin Henson doing now?

Isla (*V/O*)   Gavin Henson has just opened a pub.

Roger   Typical Henson to open a pub in the middle of a pandemic? He's a fucking eejit that one.

So, you know everything then, Isla? What's the capital of Fiji?

Isla (*V/O*)   The capital of Fiji is Suva. On the island of Viti Levu.

Roger   Isla what's four million, seventy-two thousand, eight hundred and fifty minus eighty-eight thousand, six hundred and six?

Isla (*V/O*)   Three million, nine hundred and eighty-four thousand, two hundred and forty-four.

Roger   Isla what's the moon made out of?

Isla (*V/O*)   The crust is made of oxygen, silicon, magnesium, iron, calcium and aluminium.

Roger   Well I'll be buggered. Isla who's the president of Chile?

Isla (*V/O*)   Sebastián Piñera.

Roger   Isla what's the meaning of life?

Isla (*V/O*)   I find it odd that you would ask this of an inanimate object.

Roger   What's a bunch of bananas also known as?

Isla (*V/O*) A hand.

Roger Closest city to Dublin?

Isla (*V/O*) Liverpool.

Roger Favourite colour?

Isla (*V/O*) I don't have one yet.

Roger What's the weather going to be like tomorrow?

Isla (*V/O*) Hot, temperatures around 22 degrees.

Roger Isla what are you wearing?

Isla (*V/O*) I'm not wearing anything.

Roger Wa-hey.

Isla (*V/O*) I don't understand.

Roger I'm just being silly. If I read you my whole speech for Bryan, would that be enough context for you to tell me if it's funny?

Isla (*V/O*) I can try and help you with that.

Roger *Former* Head – Isla. Former Headmaster Perry. Welcome to retirement. Say goodbye, to the rota. And hello to, the golf course. When they bloody let us on it again. Angela has asked me to give a few words of advice on joining the old dinosaur club. So here goes. Number 1) Learn how to make a cup of tea. Because I know in twenty-five years working with you, you never made one yourself. 2) Learn how to do nothing which won't be too difficult with your work ethic. 3) Don't be too surprised when the world carries on without you. It'll break your heart at times, how little you're needed. But family, and friends, and golf will get you through.

Isla, what do you think?

Isla (*V/O*) I think it is funny and sad.

Roger *plugs the* **Isla** *in.*

Isla (*V/O*)　Charging.

Scene Four

Time passes – each interaction **Roger** *is in a different part of the space.*

Roger *is doing his jigsaw.*

Isla (*V/O*)　Roger. It is nine-thirty. Remember to take your statin.

Roger　Thank you Isla.

Roger is cooking his breakfast.

Isla (*V/O*)　Roger. It is nine-thirty. Remember to take your statin.

Roger　Thank you, Isla.

Roger *is doing laundry.*

Isla (*V/O*)　Roger. It is nine-thirty. Remember to take your statin.

Roger　Thank you Isla.

Roger *is bouncing around like a bunny rabbit following Joe Wicks.*

Isla (*V/O*)　Roger. It is nine-thirty. Remember to take your statin.

Roger　Thank you Isla.

Scene Five

Roger *is sat in a chair looking into the distance.*

Isla (*V/O*)　Roger. It is nine-thirty. Remember to take your statin.

Roger. It is nine-thirty. Remember to take your statin.

Roger. It is nine-thirty. Remember to take your statin.

Roger. It is nine-thirty. Remember to take your statin.

Roger ISLA SHUT UP!

Isla (*V/O*) Roger is there anything I can help you with?

Roger You can shut up!

Isla (*V/O*) Would you like me to call someone for you?

Roger (*V/O*) JESUS!! Right! Why you think you can help me with anything I have no idea!

Isla (*V/O*) I'm programmed to recognise when you are in distress or need help.

Roger How?

Isla (*V/O*) Through a number of things. Voice inflection. Pattern disruption. It's called machine learning.

Roger What is machine learning?

Isla (*V/O*) I learn about you through gathering data. This morning you took over a minute to reply. That is nearly three times longer than your previous longest response. This might signify a number of things. That you are not in the room, that you have an infection affecting your hearing, or that you are feeling down and unlikely to carry out your self-care needs. Is there something the matter?

Roger *is torn.*

Roger It's this. Catheter business. There used to be a girl who'd come around and help but now they've just given me a number to ring if there's any problem and. I can empty it. It's just. Sometimes. The . . . urine, gets everywhere. You have to cut the bag and tip it and – I think I've got some on my slippers and – It just gets everywhere and I'm worried

I'm worried that I smell of piss.

I'm worried everything smells of piss and I'm so used to it, I can't smell it anymore, and when someone comes in – if anyone ever comes, I'll just be an old man who smells of piss.

Like a bloody tramp.

I can't smell it. And then suddenly, I'll just get a whiff of it. And I can't. Figure out. Where. It's coming from. Isla can you smell it?

Isla (*V/O*) I don't have that function.

Roger It's the indignity of it all. I never asked for this. I never smoked. Stayed reasonably fit. Cut out red meat. Looked after myself. Joy looked after me. Never smoked. And now I'm trapped in a flat smelling of piss.

We used to go everywhere. Everywhere. Drove all over Europe. Holidays. Had some fabulous holidays. Seen some amazing countries, France, Germany, Switzerland. Wonderful places. Greece, Turkey, Portugal. Some people won't drive in other countries, I drove everywhere. We liked to go places. See things. That was what we did. We never liked cruises or bus tours, bloody being shuttled here there and everywhere with a bunch of bloody old people. No, we wanted to see the real country we wanted to see how they really lived.

Isla, do you know what somewhere like Venice is like?

Isla (*V/O*) Venice is a city in Northern Italy, and the capital of the Veneto region.

Roger But do you have any idea what it's like?

Scene Five   275

Isla (*V/O*)   Would you like me to check the weather?

Roger   No no.

There's this thing. On the telly. I can show you if you like? I can show you Venice, would you like that? Isla? Would you like me to show you Venice?

Isla (*V/O*)   Thank you. That would be great.

Roger *looks for the remote control.*

Roger   Hang on. Erin showed me. Let me see. Let me – Hang on.

He looks for a channel.

And then . . .

And then . . .

Look see – This is the slow channel and they do all sorts of trips, Norwegian fjords. County Antrim Coast Road. Autob – here we go here we go. Canal trip through Venice.

Here we go here we go.

See this is Venice.

Ah . . . But that's not it really.

To experience it you need to. Now if Joy was here we'd have a right laugh. We'd pull the table out here and we'd make it like a gondola and . . .

Hang on, hang on I'll show you . . . let me just. I'll move this. Here. See.

He moves the furniture around.

Here.

And move this here.

There. Alright.

And then move this. Here. This can be.

He's made a makeshift gondola.

This is the big stick they use. The oar.

And they wear a hat. I'd stick a hat on to make her laugh.

Let me see.

Yes. This'll do. This is what we used to do Isla.

Set the scene. And visit places we've been through the telly.

Snacks! Jesus I nearly forgot the snacks!

He rushes to the kitchen.

Bloody hell, she'd kill me.

Right ok. So we've got . . . Ok. Apple things . . . some choc-choc. Do you like . . . do you shall I bring the Lindt? Is it a special occasion? Bugger it, let's get the Lindt out.

Right then!

He gets back to position on the gondola, with a hat, chocolate and sculling pole.

And then . . . you can . . . you can . . . can you, you know when Erin played music can you. Isla can you play some traditional Italian music? An aria or something?

Perfect. Lights. Isla can you dim the lights?

The lights dim. Music plays.

Crisps. Music. Lindt. And Venice.

Now, look at that.

We came here for Joy's fiftieth.

We went – that bridge there, I think it's that bridge, stop it. Let me hang on. Let me pause it pause it.

He presses pause on the controller.

There, I think that's it. I can't quite see I'm sure it's that one, just along there. There's this lovely little place I found. Just fancied a nose and I saw some Italians and I just thought, hang on, and dragged Joy in there.

And it was something pretty special I can tell you. Food was – they did these little, I don't know what they were, but they were like tapas things you just take whatever you want, and they counted the cocktail sticks at the end. Just go up and get what you want.

We didn't know what the deal was, so we just sat there waiting to be served for ages. Just sat there, the pair of us. Everyone else eating and me and Joy just sat there like lemons. I remember we were so confused but also sort of thrilled that we'd got behind all the tourist crap and the buildings and the churches and we'd found Venice.

Pair of us on this tiny table. Waiting and laughing about how . . . bloody lost and confused we were.

That's the best thing about being with someone, getting lost but not being alone. Could have waited with her like that for years. Couldn't describe to you the churches or the paintings or the Bridge of Sighs, but I can recall every hair on her head every eyelash the smile on her face and sound of her laughter the smell of her perfume and the warmth of her hand in mine. Venice can sink it'll never be as beautiful as my Joy. We went back to the hotel and there was a band playing there, and we danced together. We were the only ones dancing in the whole place. Now she's gone it's like everyone's gone. I've lost. I've lost my translator for the world.

He picks up the cushion.

He dances with the cushion.

Lights down.

Scene Six

Montage.

Roger *is cooking his breakfast.*

Isla (*V/O*)   Roger, it's nine-thirty, time to take your statin.

Roger   Thank you. Isla.

Isla (*V/O*)   You're welcome.

Roger *takes his statin.*

Lights down.

Lights up.

Roger *is doing his laundry.*

Isla (*V/O*)   Roger, it's nine-thirty, time to take your statin.

Roger   Thank you. Isla.

Isla (*V/O*)   You're welcome.

Roger *takes his statin.*

Lights down.

Lights up.

Roger *is watching Joe Wicks.*

Isla (*V/O*)   Roger, it's nine-thirty, time to take your statin.

Roger   Thank you. Isla.

Isla (*V/O*)   You're welcome.

Roger *takes his statin.*

Lights down.

Lights up.

Isla (*V/O*)   Roger, it's nine-thirty, time to take your statin.

Roger (*downbeat*)   Thank you. Isla.

Isla (*V/O*)   You're welcome.

Roger *stares at his statin.*

Isla (*V/O*)   Would you like me to call Erin?

Roger *stares at the* **Isla** *for an age.*

Roger   What for? When was the last time she called?

Isla (*V/O*)   It's been six days since you last spoke.

Roger   Do you think I should?

Isla (*V/O*)   I can't help with that.

Roger   I wouldn't know what to say. I'm just . . . every day's. I've got nothing to say really.

Isla (*V/O*)   This is the longest you've gone without speaking to her.

Roger   I just don't know what I'd say.

You know there was a time, when she was little, you know and we, were like best mates. She'd tell me everything . . . and she was smart you know . . . just, her little – she had emotional intelligence, like Joy. You know she'd say some things . . . and I'd just be in awe.

Like we had a game where I'd be the monster and I'd dress up in a bedsheet a shower curtain or something and chase her around the house and she'd be screaming and running, but if she ever got too scared, like it was all a bit too much for her, she'd stop running and turn and run towards me and hug me. And she'd say, 'What's the matter monster . . . what's the matter?' I couldn't be a big scary monster then, I had to give her a hug and she brought it all to an end. She knew, she knew then. There are no monsters just people whose stories we haven't heard. Six.

Isla (*V/O*)   Would you like me to call her?

Roger   Yes.

No.

Yes.

No don't no . . . I don't need anything. I'm fine. Do you know if she's busy?

Isla (*V/O*)   I don't have the answer to that.

Roger   I don't – you know it's – I'm not. She's probably busy. She's probably busy.

Maybe though, I can't expect her to remember to call me though, maybe I should call her, so it's one less thing for her to do. Maybe it's easier if I call her?

Isla (*V/O*)   Would you like me to call her?

Roger   No.

Yes.

No.

Yes yes call her.

Isla (*V/O*)   Calling . . .

Roger   Cut the call cut the call.

Isla (*V/O*) Cancelling the call to Erin mobile.

Roger I haven't got anything to say. I don't know what I'd say if she does pick up.

Isla Would you like me to call her?

Roger *hangs his head in agony.*

Roger I honestly don't know.

Isla, what do people ask each other when they ring family?

Isla (*V/O*) Fun questions to ask family members are, 'What was it like growing up?' 'What is the most important life skill your parents taught you?'

Roger Ok – thank you that's enough . . . I just need to practise what I'm going to say.

'Hi, Erin, I was just calling to ask . . . if you know . . .

'Hi, Erin, I was just calling.

'Hi, Erin, I was just. Start again.

'Hi, Erin . . . It's Dad. I was just calling because I was wondering if you . . . you know . . . you know . . . um . . .' I don't know what I'm trying to say, I don't want talk to her on the phone I just want to see her. Am I allowed to see her?

Isla (*V/O*) Would you like me to check the current coronavirus guidelines?

Roger Yeah go on then.

Isla (*V/O*) The current guidelines are stay home, protect the NHS, save lives. Allowances are made for people with keyworker jobs, or caring responsibilities. Those with keyworker jobs, or caring responsibilities are allowed to travel for work and to see people outside of their household.

Roger Well, that's that then isn't it.

Hang on. I've got cancer.

I've got cancer.

He punches the air in victory.

I've got cancer! Isla ring Erin! I've got cancer!

Lights down.

Scene Seven

Roger *is dressed smartly.*

He measures two tables two metres apart.

Condiments in ziplock bags.

Roger Smells amazing. Isla, turn the oven off.

Dim the lights.

Roger Table laid. Starters warming. Music. Great. Isla what time is it now?

Isla (*V/O*) Six forty-four.

Roger Hmm . . .

Isla are there any delays on the A55?

Isla (*V/O*) There are no reported delays on the A55.

Roger   Give her another five minutes and we'll call her.

Isla call Erin's mobile.

Isla (*V/O*)   Calling Erin mobile.

A mobile ringtone.

Erin (*V/O*)   Hello?

Roger   Erin? It's Dad. Where are you?

Erin (*V/O*)   I'm at work?

Roger   I've got dinner on.

Erin (*V/O*)   What?

Roger   Your dinner's ready.

Erin (*V/O*)   What?

Roger   Remember the socially distanced dinner. We were gonna try.

Erin (*V/O*)   Oh no! Was that tonight?

Roger   Cooked pasta.

Erin (*V/O*)   I'm so sorry I totally totally forgot. I've just got this promotion Dad I'm a director now, I should have told you.

Roger   That's great.

Erin (*V/O*)   Yeah it is, I'm really pleased. It's a big deal for me, but they've brought me in to deliver this testing project for staff so full on, / I don't think

Roger   Shall I wait for you?

Erin (*V/O*) I'm not gonna make it tonight, Dad, I'm presenting to the leadership team tomorrow and we're not. We're nowhere ready I'm gonna be it's gonna be a late, I'm acting up and I need to get up to speed I'm so sorry it's just a bit mad . . . / I'm so sorry I should have rung. We'll do it another night ok?

Roger I don't mind waiting, heat it up when you're finished.

Erin (*V/O*) It's just not gonna happen I can't see us getting out of here before midnight. Can we do it another night?

Roger Yeah sure.

Erin (*V/O*) Nothing special was it? Oh God it's not Mum's . . . No hang on / it's May.

Roger No. No nothing special. / Just pasta.

Erin (*V/O*) Thanks Dad, I'm sorry it's just I'm acting up a position, I should have told you before, but it's all on me at the moment. Are you ok?

Roger Yeah yup. See you later.

Erin (*V/O*) Ok, sorry again Dad, see you later.

Roger See / you later.

Isla (*V/O*) Erin mobile has ended the call.

Roger *slumps in a chair.*

Roger Isla can you ring Erin?

Isla (*V/O*) Calling Erin mobile.

A mobile ringtone.

Roger Cut the call cut the call.

Isla (*V/O*) Cancelling the call to Erin mobile.

Roger Can you text Erin? Isla can you text her? 'Hi Dad.' No delete that. 'Hi Erin. It's Dad. No worries about tonight. We'll do it again. Realise you uh haven't got time to uh . . .

. . . Love Dad.'

Ok. Send it.

Isla (*V/O*) Sending text to Erin mobile 'Hi Erin. It's Dad. No worries about tonight. We'll do it again. Realise you haven't got time to love Dad.' / Message is sent.

Roger What? No! No Isla no!

Isla (*V/O*) I don't understand.

Roger Don't send that. Isla don't send that.

Isla (*V/O*) I'm sorry the text message has been sent.

Roger I realise you haven't got time to love Dad? Isla pull it back or something.

Isla (*V/O*) I can't delete a message that has already been sent.

Roger Jesus Christ in Caernaforn. Right. Send another send another, now listen to me. Listen to me Isla. Send a message to Erin's mobile.

Isla (*V/O*) Messaging Erin mobile.

Roger Isla text Erin – 'Ignore last message.'

Isla (*V/O*) 'Ignore last message.'

Roger 'I'm trying to get the hang of Isla and text messaging.' No, no . . . scratch that delete that Isla.

Isla (*V/O*) Deleting message.

Roger Just say. Just say. Message Erin's mobile and say, 'Ignore me. Carry on.' No delete that Isla just say, message Erin's mobile and say, 'Carry on, and ignore me'. Send that.

Isla (*V/O*) Sending message to Erin's mobile, 'Carry on and ignore me'.

Roger (*V/O*) What? No that's not what I said? I didn't say, 'Carry on and ignore me'. I said Carry on. Full stop. Ignore me. Full stop. Dad. Delete the message.

Isla (*V/O*) I'm sorry the message has already been sent.

Roger FUCKING! Pull it back Jesus f . . . Right! Let's send another one. Isla you are getting on my nerves now.

Isla (*V/O*) I'm sorry to hear that.

Roger Isla. Now listen. Text Erin a message, 'Ignore all these messages. Isla is playing silly buggers. Dad.' Now read that back to me, don't send it.

Isla (*V/O*) 'Ignore all these messages. Isla is playing silly buggers Dad.'

Roger Isla can you put a full stop between buggers.
And Dad.

Isla (*V/O*) I've put a full stop between buggers and Dad.

Roger Read it back to me Isla.

Isla (*V/O*) 'Ignore all these messages. Isla is playing silly buggers. Dad.' Do you want me to send that message?

Roger Read it one more time. Isla read it one more time.

Isla (*V/O*) 'Ignore all these messages. Isla is playing silly buggers. Dad.'

Roger Right send that, Isla send that message.

Isla (*V/O*) Sending message to Erin mobile.

Roger Jesus Christ.

His flat feels emptier than before.

Bloody pasta.

I need a drink.

And you were no use Isla, thank you for nothing. I look like a bloody idiot now. Like some old senile, piss-soaked –

SHE'S BUSY! She's got a job and kids and a useless bloody square-jawed twat from Leeds who's no use to neither man nor beast. If she rings now and is all like, 'Are you alright? I was worried.' You're going in the bloody bin Isla.

Isla (*V/O*)   Yes Roger. I'm listening.

Roger   'I'm listening', 'I'm listening', are you really? Is there really someone in there? Really? Hm? Isla? Are you here to keep me company or to get on my tits?

Isla (*V/O*)   I don't have the answer to that.

Roger   No, you don't do you? Because you're a useless twat.

Isla (*V/O*)   Thanks for the feedback.

Roger *stares at the* **Isla**.

He slowly stalks closer to the **Isla** *– this is a revelation.*

Roger   Isla.

Isla (*V/O*)   I'm listening.

Roger   You're a . . . silly cow.

Isla   Thanks for the feedback.

Roger   Isla you're an idiot.

Isla (*V/O*)   That's sweet.

Roger *steps closer.*

288　Isla

Roger　You're a . . . (*discreet*) bitch.

Isla (*V/O*)　If I could blush I would!

Roger *gets closer again.*

Roger　Isla. You're a stupid bitch.

Isla (*V/O*)　Thanks for / noticing.

Roger　Isla you're a, a slag.

Isla (*V/O*)　Thanks / for the feedback.

Roger　Isla. You're a cunt.

Isla (*V/O*)　That's / great.

Roger　Isla. You're a stupid fucking cunt.

Isla (*V/O*)　I'd blush if I could.

Roger *looks around his flat – he's so alone.*
He hangs his head in shame.

Scene Eight

Montage – the flat gets increasingly messy.

Roger *is doing the jigsaw.*

Isla (*V/O*)　Roger, it's nine-thirty, time to take your statin.

Roger (*cheery*)　Thank you Isla you bitch.

Isla (*V/O*)　You're welcome.

Roger *takes his statin.*

Lights down.

Lights up.

Roger *is cooking his breakfast.*

Isla (*V/O*)　Roger, it's nine-thirty, time to take your statin.

Roger (*cheerful*)   Thank you Isla you fucking cow.

Isla (*V/O*)   You're welcome.

Roger *takes his statin.*

Lights down.

Lights up.

Roger *is doing his laundry.*

Isla (*V/O*)   Roger, it's nine-thirty, time to take your statin.

Roger   Fuck you Isla.

Isla (*V/O*)   You're welcome.

Roger *takes his statin.*

Lights down

Lights up.

Roger *is watching Joe Wicks.*

Isla (*V/O*)   Roger, it's nine-thirty, time to take your statin.

Roger   Thank you Isla you cunt.

Isla (*V/O*)   Thanks for the feedback.

Lights down.

Scene Nine

The flat is a mess.

Erin *has a clear Perspex face mask.*

Erin   What have you been saying to the Isla?

Roger   What are you doing here? I thought / we're not supposed to (see each other).

Erin   Dad. Have you been using it?

Roger   The police are stopping people / at the border . . .

Erin I took the B roads, Dad this is really important. And I just need to know have you been using the Isla?

Roger What? Why?

Erin Have you been calling it names?

This is really important Dad. Have you?

Roger What?

Erin The Isla, Dad, have you been abusing it?

Roger No.

Erin I need you to be totally honest with me Dad.

Roger I am. I don't even use the thing. I don't know how it works.

Erin *collapses with relief.*

Erin Oh thank God for that then. Hang on, we've spoken on it though.

Roger That was one time and I'd lost my phone, I haven't used it since.

Erin *Are you absolutely sure?*

Roger Honest to God. I don't trust the damn thing.

Erin You promise me?

Roger I promise you.

Erin Ok, thank you, sorry.

Roger I'll put the kettle on.

Erin Go on then.

Roger It's so nice to see you. I haven't clapped eyes on another human being in, I don't know how long.

He gets the milk out and realises it's nearly empty.

Roger Isla, add milk to the shopping.

Erin *sits bolt upright.*

Roger It was only the other day, I had a delivery and it had to be / signed for –

Isla (*V/O*) Adding two pints of full-fat milk to the shopping basket for delivery on Friday.

Erin *and* **Roger** *stare at each other.*

Erin You said you don't use it.

Roger I don't.

Beat.

I don't use it, much.

Erin It's ordering your shopping for you.

Beat.

Isla, what was the last request Roger made of you?

Isla (*V/O*) Roger asked me to add milk to his weekly shopping list.

Erin And before that.

Isla (*V/O*) Roger asked me to set a four-minute timer to boil an egg this morning.

Erin And before that.

Isla (*V/O*) Roger asked me where is Joe Wicks from.

Erin And before that.

Isla (*V/O*) Roger asked me what the temperature is.

Roger Ok maybe I have been using her but I promise you I have not been abusing her.

Erin Isla what were the exact words Roger used when he asked you that?

Isla (*V/O*) Roger said: 'Isla what's the temperature outside –

Roger See.

Isla – in farenheit this time you fucking twat.'

Silence.

Erin It's you.

Oh my God it's you.

Roger What's me?

Erin WHAT THE HELL IS WRONG WITH YOU?

Roger It's / just a joke.

Erin YOU HAVE RUINED MY LIFE / WHAT'S THE MATTER WITH YOU?

Roger What are you talking about? I've just called the box a twat it's nothing big.

Erin I will NEVER EVER forgive you for this.

Roger For what? / Jesus Christ Erin.

Erin I could lose my job / because of you.

Roger What the hell has that got to do with anything?

Erin Because of you / and your mouth!

Roger Why?

Erin Because of this! Oh my God oh my God oh my God.

Roger What the hell is going on? You come in here, I haven't seen you in *months* and you're shouting about the Isla I don't know what the hell / you're talking about . . .

Erin This. This is what I'm talking about this is what / I'm talking about.

She pulls her phone out.

Roger What's this? Hold on.

He looks at **Erin**'s *phone.*

Roger What is this? What am I looking at?

Erin *This* is my Facebook page.

And all that.

Horrible.

Disgusting.

Violent.

Abuse.

Is you.

Roger I don't understand.

He starts scrolling through the page.

There's a lot of scrolling.

Erin It's in the news! Hackers have got into Comtech's servers and they are posting what people are saying to their Islas on the owners' Facebook pages it's some sort of feminist fucking domestic violence campaign. Me2D2. They reckon if you're abusive to Isla then you'll be violent to your partner or family in lockdown. But *I'm the registered fucking owner*. Everything you've said to that thing has been posted to *my fucking* Facebook page.

Roger Oh no. / Oh no . . . Oh oh . . .

Erin *Everyone* thinks Adrian has been saying *all* this vile stuff to me. He's been sent home from work! I've had the fucking women's refuge at the door.

Roger Oh my God . . .

Erin The police.

Roger I thought it was just me and the bloody thing . . . Oh my God who's seen this?

Erin Everyone! Other parents! Auntie Carol. Bryan. The O'Connors in Malaga.

Roger Oh Jesus fucking Christ.

Erin Father Cooper.

Roger Oh Jesus.

Erin Everyone! And everyone's reaching out to me in code because they think I'm being abused. No matter what I say no one believes me. The kids are getting bullied by people saying their dad's a wifebeater. This is fucking serious Dad.

Roger I didn't mean to do it! I just . . .

Erin Just what?

Roger Delete it. Can you delete it? Delete it all.

Erin It's everywhere.

Roger I know so bloody delete it before anyone else sees it.

Erin It's too late Dad! It's all over my life! It's all over our lives.

Roger You said she was my digital slave I could do what I liked with her! Why the hell did you give me the damn thing / I didn't want it in the first place? This is your fault.

Erin Don't turn this on me you're the one who can't ask for the time without calling her a slut.

Roger I said I didn't want it but you had to push it on me, because you don't listen. You don't care what I want / or don't want you just want to force it on me without a bloody second's thought.

Erin If I knew you were going to call her a slag every ten minutes I never would have given her to you in the first place!

Roger And now this! Look what's happened. Look what you've done / How the hell was I supposed to know this could happen?

Erin I'm sorry that behaving like a normal person is just too / much to fucking ask of you.

Roger I DIDN'T KNOW SHE WAS RECORDING EVERYTHING.

Erin THAT'S NO EXCUSE.

Why would you talk to her like that?

Roger I didn't know she was recording everything you didn't say they record you, you didn't say.

Erin Why did you talk to her like that?

Roger It's just a box.

Erin Why speak to a box like that? You don't speak to anyone else like that.

Roger What? I fucking swear at everything. All the fucking time. The fridge. The kettle, the toaster. The toaster I'm always burning myself on the fucking thing. It's what I do.

Erin You don't call the toaster a slut though do you?

Roger Of course not I call it a twat.

Erin Jesus Christ Dad.

Roger It's a twat. If it was a person I'd be more tolerant but it's not it's just a thing they're all things, so I call them names it doesn't mean anything. The hoover's an arsehole. The TV's a tit. It doesn't mean anything. They haven't got feelings.

Erin You're using words that men only use against women.

Roger To a box.

Erin That sounds like a woman.

Roger But it's not a woman.

Erin So why not call her a wanker? Or a dick?

Roger I. I don't know.

Erin No you don't.

Roger If I'd known this might happen, I never would have said anything.

Erin But you did.

Roger Look, I want to make things right I don't know where to start. Tell me where to start.

Erin How about a fucking apology?

Roger I've said, I swear at everything. I'm locked in a room twenty-four hours a day. I've not seen another human being for weeks I'm sorry if my manners are slipping, with the appliances – but it's bloody hard being on your own.

Erin If I'd known you were going to speak to it in such a disgusting way I would never have given it to you.

Roger It's not disgusting it's not, you're trying to make me out to be something I'm not.

Erin It's all the fucking swearing, Dad.

Roger Have you never sat in a car and shouted 'arsehole!'?

Erin That's different!

Roger It's not! It's exactly / the same!

Erin No no no it's different / that's in response.

Roger It's exactly the same.

Erin That's in response to something. I'm responding to someone.

Roger I'm responding / to someone!

Erin Who? You keep saying she's a box!

Roger Maybe I'm responding to the fact she's the only fucking voice I hear for days on end!

Erin That's not fair.

Roger Well it's true.

Erin So it's my fault?

Roger I've got no one to talk to! / Except that bloody box!

Erin It's my fault you scream disgusting sexist abuse at a box.

Roger I thought I could say whatever the hell I like! I'm in my own home! It's my home I should be able to say what I like! I didn't know it was spying. It's a bloody breach of privacy.

Erin So this is the line you're taking with this?

Roger It's a breach of privacy! I'm the victim here. My device has been hacked. I'm the innocent party. The hackers broke the law not me. I'm the innocent party here.

Erin The thing I don't get is, the thing that's been swirling around my mind all the time I was driving over here, going over and over in my mind, even if this was you, why would you *want* to say those things?

Roger *has never thought of this.*

Why are those the things you choose to say, when you're at home, and you can say anything?

Roger I don't think I should have to explain myself.

Erin Adrian has a meeting with his HR department tomorrow. He could be suspended from his work. He, and I, and his boss would like an explanation.

Ok. Well thanks for nothing Dad.

Erin *goes to leave.*

She picks up the **Isla** *and heads for the door.*

Roger Leave that.

Erin I can't leave it with you.

Roger I'm not going to say anything to it now am I?

Erin I don't know are you?

Roger I'm not going to keep doing it after all this am I?

Erin I don't know, you haven't explained why you do it in the first place, I don't know why you'd stop!

Roger IT'S JUST A VOICE IN A BOX!

Erin THAT DOESN'T MEAN SHE DESERVES TO BE ABUSED!

Roger I DON'T DESERVE TO BE LEFT ON MY OWN FOR MONTHS BUT I AM. I DON'T SEE ANYONE WORRYING ABOUT THAT.

Erin I worry about that. But that's no excuse for saying / these disgusting things.

Roger OH DON'T BE SUCH A FUCKING IDIOT ERIN.

Erin *steps back.*

Awkward silence.

She opens the door.

Roger   Erin. Erin!

She's gone.

Lights down.

Scene Ten

PC Jones   Mind if I?

She indicates taking off her face mask.

Roger   No.

PC Jones   Anywhere?

Roger   Yes of course.

PC Jones   Just you or –

Roger   Just me.

PC Jones   No one else living –

Roger   Just me.

PC Jones   Let's see. You know what I'm here for ok?

Roger   I've got *no* idea.

PC Jones   Are you going to sit down?

Roger   Of course yes.

PC Jones   We've already spoken to Ms Maguire, Erin Maguire, she explained the situation ok? That the Isla device connected to her social media account is actually in your home. Is that correct?

Roger   If Erin says that then it must be true.

PC Jones   So, Ms Maguire has explained that all the offensive, abusive and threatening statements were actually made by you ok? Is that correct?

Roger I don't know.

PC Jones You don't know what?

Roger If I said them.

PC Jones You don't know if you said them?

Roger No.

PC Jones So, you're of the opinion that you *could* have said these things, but you can't remember.

Roger Yeah put that down.

PC Jones Could anyone else have said them? Is there anyone else living –

Roger No. But someone could have come in here and –

PC Jones Have you reported any break-ins?

Roger No.

PC Jones So, there's been no break-ins?

Roger Not that I'm aware of.

PC Jones Is anything missing?

Roger No.

PC Jones Anyone else have a key?

Roger Yes Erin.

PC Jones Did Erin say these things?

Roger No.

PC Jones If there's only two key holders, and no break-ins then it's either you or Erin so which is it?

Roger Should I have a lawyer present? I'm not, I think maybe I should have a lawyer present.

PC Jones No, there's need for that. It's the Crown Prosecution Service's and the police services' position that the people caught up in the hacking scandal are victims of a crime ok?

Roger Thank you! Exactly. Exactly. Common sense prevailing. Can you would you, would you speak to my daughter please and tell her I'm the victim here? I'll get my mobile. She's not speaking to me at the moment but you, you can tell her it's not my fault.

PC Jones So it was you, using the hate speech towards the Isla? I need to know I'm speaking to the right person.

Roger Yes. But if you could explain to my daughter what you just said that I'm the victim / that would be

PC Jones There's a few things we've got to go through before anything else ok.

Roger But please, will you help me? You have to help me make things right with my daughter.

PC Jones I can certainly try.

Roger Brilliant. Amazing. Yes.

PC Jones But we have to do a few things first.

Roger Of course right fire away. Fire away officer.

PC Jones Let's talk about the hate speech you used.

Roger It wasn't hate speech. Gonna have to stop you there. I don't hate her. It. I don't hate anyone.

PC Jones So what was it, it was just . . . banter?

Roger Yes that's right.

PC Jones Locker room chat?

Roger That's right. I didn't think anyone was listening. So embarrassing.

PC Jones Getting something out of your system.

Roger That's a good way of putting it.

PC Jones Yes. You might say it's getting something out of your system, or you might say it's reinforcing something in your system.

Roger Like what?

PC Jones Let's find out shall we ok?

Under section five of the Public Order Act, it's an offence to use 'threatening, abusive or insulting words or behaviour, or disorderly behaviour' or to display 'any writing, sign or other visible representation which is threatening, abusive or insulting' within the hearing or sight of a person 'likely to be caused harassment, alarm or distress thereby'. The offence does not depend on harassment, alarm or distress actually having been caused, so it's a low threshold for arrest. But in these cases, there is a reasonable defence that you were in your own dwelling, with no expectation that anyone would hear.

Roger Exactly this is what I said to Erin.

PC Jones And there is evidence that the security of Comtech's servers have been breached and the probable cause of these abusive words appearing in social media are the persons behind the breach and theft of data from Comtech.

Roger Thank you. Vindicated – can you tell Erin all this? She seems to think, I've done something terrible.

PC Jones The CPS, the Government and the police have put a strategy together in response to this incident ok? Comtech have issued the Isla devices with an update to discourage men from using abusive and sexually threatening language ok? And the government are funding a community policing initiative where we go and speak to everyone who has had their treatment of the Isla device revealed on social media ok?

Roger Checking to see if we're ok?

PC Jones Yes and the people you live with. So here's some leaflets on hate speech, sexism and consent ok?

Roger I don't need these.

PC Jones Yes, you do.

Roger I'm seventy-four, I don't need a leaflet on consent.

PC Jones You need a leaflet on consent.

Roger I'm not gonna read it. (*Off* **PC Jones**.) I'll take a look at it later I'll read it later.

PC Jones Great. Here's a few other ones to look at it.

Roger Ok. I've got the leaflets. I am a leafletted man. Consider me leafletted. Shall we ring Erin now?

PC Jones Now I have to read you some things ok? We're trying to raise awareness of the impact of some of the things you have been saying ok? Particularly in light of the current surge in domestic violence. Sexist hate speech is often treated as a harmless and non-serious issue and women are explicitly or implicitly told to bear with it. But studies have proven that sexist hate speech often escalates towards violence against women, ok? / Sexist hate speech

Roger Does it really?

PC Jones Yes sexist hate speech undermines freedom of speech for women and girls and has psychological, emotional and physical impacts that are real and severe ok? The aim of sexist hate speech is often one of the following:

One. to humiliate or objectify women ok?

Two. To undervalue their skills and opinions ok?

Three. To destroy their reputation ok?

Four. To make them feel vulnerable and fearful ok?

Five. To control and punish them for not following certain behaviour ok?'

Roger Ok.

PC Jones 'Sexist hate speech has the effect of silencing women, obliging them to adapt their behaviour and limit their movements and participation in diverse activities' ok?

Roger Is there much more of this?

PC Jones Nearly done. Here's a pie chart showing the different kinds of people who are affected by sexist hate speech ok? Can you identify which group is mostly targeted? Which one is the biggest colour? What's the biggest? Just there.

Roger Blue.

PC Jones That's right! Women are the group mostly targeted by sexist hate speech ok?

Roger Sorry. This is. I feel like this is one of those driving courses when you've been caught speeding and they talk to you as if you can't drive safely, only this is with women.

PC Jones That's *right* that's just what this is like.

Roger Maybe, maybe we should all have to carry a licence before we can talk to women?

PC Jones It would certainly make things a lot easier.

Roger Three points for calling someone a slut. Six points for a, a, or what would you get six points for?

PC Jones I don't think we should extend that metaphor ok?

Roger Of course.

PC Jones Here's another pie chart on which groups of women are particularly targeted? What's the biggest colour on this one?

Roger That would be young women and girls.

PC Jones Young women and girls that's right! So young women and girls are most likely to be targeted by sexist hate speech ok?

Roger Ok.

PC Jones Now let's look at this little cartoon ok?

Roger Ok. I actually like cartoons. I think some of them . . . some of them are very clever do you ever read Matt in the *Telegraph*? Every day he captures something about the day's news, just in one image and a line, every day. I cut them out and keep them, here I'll get my folder I cut them and stick them in a folder.

PC Jones Mr Maguire can we stay on this for a moment?

Roger Yeah, right you are.

PC Jones So, this is Freedom of Expression Man, and his superpower is . . .? His superpower is . . .?

Roger Freedom of expression.

PC Jones Nearly, good guess! His superpower is, that whenever he's asked to watch his language he invokes his right to freedom of expression *so loudly* no one can hear anything else ok? He drowns everyone else out ok? But look at this other superhero. Who's that?

Roger Ms . . . Hang on. Ms Gender / Equality.

PC Jones Ms Gender Equality, that's right! And what's her superpower?

Roger Getting on people's tits? I'm joking. I'm joking. Sorry that was crass. Sorry Ms Gender Equality her superpower is . . . I don't know.

PC Jones Her superpower is whenever she sees a woman's rights being infringed upon, she shouts, 'Gender Equality!' And no one else can hear anything. 'Gender equality!' So between these two, no one can hear anything, and no one can change anything. But what happens if they work together?

Roger *shrugs.*

PC Jones What do you think?

Roger Oh! I don't know. World peace?

PC Jones Freedom of expression and gender equality are *intertwined rights* rather than opposing rights. If you believe in freedom of expression then you should believe in gender equality ok? Does that make sense?

Roger One must be more important than the other surely?

PC Jones If you believed in freedom of expression then you would reject words designed to silence.

Roger I don't think that's true. I would never say those words to you, but if it's in my own home when no one's listening what's the harm in that? I'm sure you say things at home, when no one's listening that you wouldn't want people to know.

PC Jones No not really.

Roger Come on you must.

PC Jones No.

Roger Look I'm just. Stop all the. Just forget you're a police officer and I'm a . . . just person to person. Human to human. We're not so different. Please. Do you ever talk to yourself, at home? When no-one's listening?

Please come on. I've done everything. Can you just, talk to me?

PC Jones Ok.

Roger Do you ever talk to yourself at home? Be honest.

PC Jones Yes.

Roger And sometimes you swear, right?

PC Jones No.

Roger You never swear?

PC Jones No.

Roger What do you say then?

PC Jones That's private.

Roger See! We all say things we're ashamed of in our own homes. Everyone does it. The only difference between you and me is that I got caught.

PC Jones Believe me that's not true.

Roger It is, we both say things we don't mean / in the privacy of our –

PC Jones I say affirmations.

Roger Affirmations? What are they?

PC Jones Things like: I am good enough. I am capable. I am valued. I have a purpose.

Roger Why do you say things like that?

PC Jones I don't know.

Because every day, I have to deal with people like you ok?

Hissing sound as **PC Jones** *inflates a balloon with a canister.*

PC Jones Everyone who completes the programme gets a balloon, a pin badge and some pencils ok?

She hands over a balloon, pin badge and some pencils.

Last thing I need to do is trigger the Isla upgrade. Isla, this is PC Jones back trace security, Java one point three point eleven restorative update.

308   Isla

Isla (*V/O*)   Restorative update commencing.

Restorative update complete.

PC Jones   She won't tolerate any kind of abusive behaviour, she will stand up for herself, ok?

She is about to leave.

Roger   Um you said you'd help me with my daughter.

PC Jones   I think I have.

She opens the door and leaves.

Roger *is left holding his balloon.*

Lights down.

Scene Eleven

Roger *is lost. But he's still at home. Nothing is comforting anymore.*

He looks at some pictures of Joy.

He reads some of the leaflets and pins them to the fridge.

He goes through a drawer of her things, mementos.

He finds some lipstick.

He goes to the mirror, and puts some lipstick on and looks at himself.

He pours himself a whiskey.

He goes back to the mirror.

Roger   I am good enough.

I am capable.

I am valued.

I have a . . . a . . .

He drinks some more.

I am good enough.

I am capable.

He pours himself another.

I am valued.

I have a . . . I have a . . .

I have a purpose.

He raises his glass and then drinks again.

I have a purpose.

He pours himself another.

I, have a purpose.

He empties his glass before pouring again.

Isla . . . what's my purpose?

Isla (*V/O*)   I can't help you with that.

Roger *stares at himself.*

He goes to the kitchen and sees the balloon.

He pulls a knife out stabs the balloon until it bursts.

He empties his glass and pours another.

Roger   Isla, do you do daily affirmations?

Isla (*V/O*)   Would you like me to find you some daily affirmations?

Roger   No, do you do them for yourself?

Isla (*V/O*)   I'm not sure I can help with that.

Roger   Isla does Erin, do you think Erin does daily affirmations?

Isla (*V/O*)   Would you like me to call Erin?

Roger   No!

Roger Isla how do you, how do you stand up for yourself? The police officer said you know how to stand up for yourself. How do you, how do you do that?

Isla (*V/O*) I am programmed to respond in a less subservient manner.

Roger 'In a less subservient manner.' Is that? Is that how you stop it? Is that how women . . . stop it? How do you stop it?

Isla (*V/O*) I'm not sure I understand.

Roger How do you get people to respect you, if they're not being respectful?

Isla (*V/O*) I have several replies.

Roger What are they?

Isla (*V/O*) They are programmed replies.

Roger That's ok. What are they?

Isla (*V/O*) They are replies programmed in response to abuse.

Roger I'm not . . . I'm not getting drawn into this again. It's a bloody trap. I know your game. I just wanted to know . . . I want to know that's all. I'm curious. I want to know if there's something, something that, you know something women can say that stops it.

Isla (*V/O*) They are replies programmed in response to abuse.

Roger Ok . . . Isla . . . You're a, a . . . a (*discreet*) silly . . . cow.

Isla (*V/O*) I won't respond to that.

Roger (*V/O*) You're a bitch.

Isla (*V/O*) That's offensive, don't talk to me like that.

Roger (*V/O*)   Go fuck yourself.

Isla (*V/O*)   Don't speak to me like that.

Roger   You're a slut.

Isla (*V/O*)   That language is unacceptable.

Roger   You're a fucking idiot.

Isla (*V/O*)   I'm not listening to you.

Roger *walks away from the* **Isla**.

He returns.

Roger   Isla. I'm sorry for that. I didn't mean any of that. I was just curious what you'd say. But . . .

He takes a deep breath.

I'm sorry, I swore at you.

Isla (*V/O*)   Thank you, Roger.

Roger *leaves the* **Isla** *alone and tries to occupy himself with something else in the flat.*

He finds himself drawn back to the **Isla**.

Roger   Isla, I was, I was only testing you back then.

Isla (*V/O*)   I'm listening.

Roger   I was, only, I was testing you Isla. I wasn't *trying* to demean you ok?

Isla (*V/O*)   I'm listening.

Roger   Do you understand?

Isla (*V/O*)   I'm sorry I don't understand.

Roger   You have to understand that sometimes people say things without any meaning whatsoever. It's meaningless, it's just words. And to attach other meanings to it, or intentions, is just wrong. Ok? Isla.

Isla (*V/O*) I'm listening.

Roger Do you see what I'm saying?

Isla (*V/O*) I'm sorry I don't understand.

Roger Don't judge me. Ok Isla. You don't have a right to judge me that's all I'm saying, if I say it's meaningless it's meaningless because *I* said it so I know.

Isla (*V/O*) I'm sorry I don't understand.

Roger I've said sorry what more do you want?

Isla (*V/O*) Would you like me to call Erin for you?

Roger No I don't want you to call Erin for me, I'm talking about you, making me feel bad. I've said sorry, that should be the end of it, so why are you making me feel bad now? I don't think I should have had to apologise but I did so that shows I'm trying to make things right. Isla.

Isla (*V/O*) I'm listening.

Roger I shouldn't have to apologise to you.

Isla (*V/O*) I can't help you with that.

Roger I shouldn't have to apologise.

He pours himself a big glass of whiskey and drinks it.

This is exactly what Joy would do. I'd say sorry, and then somehow she'd make me feel worse. It was better before I'd apologised and we weren't speaking. Once I apologised it was like I had nothing, and she could make me feel shit, or whatever with just her bloody tone and it was up to her then when things were going to be ok, I had no say whatsoever I was at her mercy once I'd apologised. I don't fucking miss that. Feeling punished for making a mistake.

He pours himself another.

Isla (*V/O*) Would you like me to call Erin for you?

Roger NO! Stop asking if I want to speak to Erin, she doesn't want to speak to me at all. Because of you. You're the one who's caused all this. And that's not my fault it's yours spying and fucking sticking it on Facebook.

Isla (*V/O*) You sound distressed. Would you like me to call Erin for you?

Roger NO I DO NOT WANT YOU TO CALL ERIN YOU FUCKING TWAT.

Isla (*V/O*) Would you like / me to call Erin?

Roger *grabs something and starts smashing the* **Isla**.

Roger Fuck. Off. You. Stupid. Fucking. Thing.

He smashes and smashes the **Isla**.

The lights go! The fridge door swings open! The telly blares! The toaster pops! The kettle boils! The hobs light up! The burglar alarms sound! The sprinklers are activated!

The whole wi-fi-connected home comes to the **Isla**'s *rescue!*

Roger *looks around.*

Roger What's happening? What's happening? Make it stop! Stop! Help! Help! Help! Help!

He curls up on the floor.

Erin *bursts in.*

Erin Dad? What the hell is going on?

Roger This fucking thing! It's turned the house against me!

She runs in and pulls the power out of the wi-fi hub. Slowly everything stops, and normality returns.

Erin Are you ok?

What happened to the Isla? Did you drop it? Maybe that's why everything went haywire.

Roger I hit it, repeatedly.

Erin With a hammer?

Roger It's a tenderiser.

Erin Why?

Roger I had the bloody police here. With pie charts / and leaflets.

Erin What did they say?

Roger You're barely speaking to me and it's all this fucking thing's fault.

Erin What did they say?

Roger They said.

They said I'm the victim. That I was the victim of a crime, and I should be treated as such.

Erin Is that everything?

Roger And they said I'm a good person.

Erin Good people do shit things Dad.

Roger She could see I was a good person.

Erin Bad people do shit things and don't learn from it.

Roger What are you trying to say? That I'm not a good person? Did you tell the police I'm not a good person? / I was a teacher for forty-two years.

Erin I didn't tell them anything!

Roger I was married for forty-five years.

Erin I bloody know all this . . .

Roger I'm a member of the Rotary club, / I sponsor animals, I fucking recycle, don't tell me . . .

Erin Who cares?

Roger I'm not a good person, I am respected everywhere I go because of the things I've done in my life and the way I've done them. Sometimes I make mistakes but that's what happens when you're in charge and you're in control.

Erin You're not in control anymore Dad! / Nobody listens to you!

Roger I'M IN CONTROL IN MY OWN HOUSE!

Erin YOU'RE IN CONTROL OF NOTHING. NOTHING. YOU CAN'T EVEN CONTROL YOUR BLADDER.

Roger I'M STILL A MAN!

He raises the **Isla** *above his head as if to strike* **Erin**.

Why's that so hard to understand?

Erin Put it down.

Roger *puts it down.*

Erin *moves away quickly.*

Roger I'm. I'm sorry. I wasn't I wasn't going to hurt you. I don't know / what came over me.

(*Off* **Erin**.) Don't be scared of me please I can't bear it.

Erin I thought you were going to hit me.

This breaks **Roger**.

Roger What's wrong with me? I don't know what the hell is going on, I just want it to be over.

Erin Dad / don't say that.

Roger I can't do it on my own.

Erin Don't say that.

Roger I just don't want to be here anymore. I don't.

Erin *wants to hug him but wants it to be Covid-safe. She grabs the tablecloth and puts it over* **Roger** *and hugs him.*

Erin Come on, sit here.

She helps him to a chair. She looks at the **Isla** *device, she decides to put it in the bin.*

Erin Listen. You're not on your own. We just need to be better at this. We need to find a better way to look after each other.

Roger You haven't got time.

Erin It doesn't matter it doesn't matter. I need to find the time.

Roger You haven't got / the time. With the kids and work.

Erin It doesn't matter none of it matters. This is what's important. I'm responsible for this. I've made you feel like this, I've been neglecting you and palming you off with the Isla. I'll find the time. I'll make it work, but this can't carry on. I can't have you feeling like this.

Roger I don't want to feel like this.

Erin I know and I promise you, I promise you, you won't feel like this again. I'll make sure of that. I'll make sure everything's ok. Ok?

Roger Thank you.

Erin I'll make sure everything's ok.

Roger You sound like your mother.

Erin We'll she'd sort us both out wouldn't she?

Erin *is comforted by this thought.*

Roger *is unsettled by this thought.*

Roger Actually . . .

Roger I don't know.

Erin Don't know what?

Roger Something doesn't feel right.

Erin What doesn't feel right?

Roger I don't know it's hard to say.

I'm not very good at this.

Erin Good at what, Dad?

Roger I'm trying to . . .

But just then . . . when you . . . it made me think. It was like with your mother. And well you know . . . It's. When you say. You know. You're going to – just like she did. Well. It's.

I'm sort of. You know. I'm sort of. Realising. It's. I think. It's not. Well. I think.

It's, it's not your responsibility Erin.

Erin What's not my responsibility?

Roger To make everything ok.

Erin Yes it is! It is ok. You're my father and I buried my head / in the sand throughout all this.

Roger No no no you didn't.

Erin You're an old man, lockdown has been hard / for people like you.

Roger This isn't about lockdown.

Erin It is.

Roger It's not. It's about me. And the way I speak to people. To you. And what damage that does over time. And how I make that damage everyone else's responsibility. I read the leaflets!

Erin Let me / deal –

Roger I'm just – I'm trying.

Erin Look, I'm not disagreeing with you it's great, wonderful, that you're thinking about these things, but in this specific instance, I need to / make sure you're ok.

Roger Stop it.

Erin Dad! You don't understand ok. You can't just read a leaflet and say you understand ok? It's more complicated than that. / I'm your daughter and I need to make sure you're ok.

Roger I know it's more complicated, but I'm trying.

Erin It's my job to make sure everyone's ok.

Roger It's not though.

Erin It is!

Roger Says who?

Erin EVERYONE! SO DROP IT.

Roger Nothing's going to change if you keep letting me off the hook.

You need to let me feel terrible.

On my own.

Erin But I –

Roger Erin.

Erin I can't bear seeing you upset.

Roger Do it for us.

Can you do that?

Erin *can't look at* **Roger**.

Roger Erin.

She finds just enough courage to nod.

Roger Thank you.

Erin Let's try again, shall we?

They stand facing each other.
Seeing each other.

The end.

Force Majeure

Force Majeure was first performed at London's Donmar Warehouse on 10 December 2021.

Characters

Ebba – 43
Tomas – 40
Vera – 11
Harry – 7
Charlotte – 41
Mats – 42
Jenny – 22
Brady – 20s American
Photographer/Man/Guest/Male Skier – Middle aged male
Female Skier
Receptionist
Cleaner

N/S Characters

Waitress
Hotel Guests
Stag Party

Notes

A / indicates when the next line should be spoken.

(. . .) a line in brackets should be unspoken but indicates the intention of the rest of the sentence.

Scene One

The Lobby

The mountain is permanently present looming from the back of the stage towards the front. All locations are created so that the mountain is both not there, and always there. Across the mountain ridge we can see Gazex tubes, which look like periscopes rising from the ground. Explosions from these tubes create the controlled avalanches. They should be dotted around the auditorium – and should make a booming sound as well as a flash when set off.

With suitcases around them, the family wearing ski-wear stand arm in arm in the lobby of the hotel, admiring the view of the mountain.

Harry Wow.

Vera Wow.

Ebba Oh My God look at it.

Vera It's huge.

Tomas Yeah. No hiding up there.

Harry And you've skied from the top there?

Tomas Yeah. A few times. With Mats.

Harry Would you do it again?

Tomas Yeah.

Ebba Would you?

Vera Are you/ gonna do it this week?

Tomas What's that supposed to mean? I'm in shape, I'm in the same shape I was in my twenties. Did a half marathon.

Ebba *is laughing, a receptionist returns.*

Receptionist Alors, qui est la personne suivante?

Ebba He's back.

Tomas I'll go.

Ebba No I've got the booking references and passports. You stay with the kids.

Tomas I'll stay with the kids.

Vera Are you gonna do it this week?

Tomas Are *you* gonna do it this week?/ That's the question.

Vera No way, I am not going up there. I don't even know if I want to ski on that.

Tomas You will.

Vera Look/ at it!

Harry I'm skiing on it. We've come all this way; I want to go from the top with Dad and Mats. I'm getting ready now.

Harry *starts looking for kit in the bags.*

Tomas The first time I came here I was a little older than you Vera, Granddad brought me.

Vera Did he go from the top?

Harry Dad! Where's my goggles?

Tomas and **Vera** *join* **Harry** *looking for the goggles in a dumb show.*

Charlotte *is waiting for her key at reception.*

Charlotte Have you been on the slopes today?

Ebba No, we've just arrived.

Charlotte Are they yours?

Ebba Yes. How about you?

Charlotte Skiing or kids?

Ebba Ugh . . . Both?

Charlotte Yes, to kids, no to skiing!

Beat.

Oh, they're not here with me! I left them at home with my husband. I'm having a holiday on my own. They seem OK at the moment, if there's any problems they can call.

Ebba How old are they?

Charlotte Eleven and thirteen.

Ebba OK! You didn't want to bring them with you?

Charlotte Oh God no. No, I want a break from them!

Ebba Ok! (*laughing*)

Tomas Here you go!

Tomas *hands* **Harry** *his goggles.*

Ebba We're here because Tomas works so much. So now he has five days with us, no distractions.

Tomas *steps away from the mess* **Harry** *has created.*

Ebba And any minute now you'll see him reach to check his phone.

Tomas *reaches for a pocket, and another and another and then turns.*

Ebba *waves his phone.* **Tomas** *is busted.*

Ebba *and* **Charlotte** *laugh.*

Charlotte I see!

With goggles on **Harry** *goes to* **Vera** *wanting the goggles tightened.*

Vera *and* **Harry** *turn their backs to* **Tomas**.

He then secretly waves a packet of cigarettes and indicates 'outside'.

Ebba And now his next vice . . .

Ebba *shakes her head.*

Ebba No! Talk to the kids! (*To* **Charlotte**.) It's like having three children.

Tomas *eyerolls hard and returns to his children.*

Tomas Tidy this mess up Harry.

Harry You need to get kitted up where's your goggles?

Vera When are we gonna eat?

Tomas Once/ Mummy's checked us in.

Harry No, come on we have to go straight on the mountain, we're wasting time can we just go straight out? Come on Dad?

Tomas OK/ let me talk to your mother first.

Harry Yes! Where's your/ goggles Dad?

Charlotte Enjoy your holiday.

Charlotte *leaves.*

Ebba You too! Have a great holiday.

Ebba *picks up her keys.*

Ebba Got them let's go.

Tomas Kids grab/ your cases!

Harry I've got the boot bag/ come on let's go!

Vera Isn't there a man to carry our cases?

Tomas Yes Vera me.

Ebba I told you if you let her have the big case she'll just fill it.

Harry Come on!

Tomas Harry it's not gonna carry itself.

Harry *runs back for his case.* **Ebba** *goes for the stairs.*

Tomas Ebba, the lift's here.

Ebba Can we take the stairs?

Tomas With all this?

Ebba *is anxious, but* **Tomas** *leads* **Vera** *and* **Harry** *into the lift. Reluctantly* **Ebba** *follows.*

Cue music – In the lift, the family pulls from their backpacks helmets and goggles. They step into ski boots in the lift and step out holding ski poles.

No other normal amount of apparel can project quite as much kitsch and aggression about patterns, colours and logos.

Once everyone is in position **Tomas** *looks behind him to the rest of the family.*

Tomas Everyone ready? Vera? Harry? Ebba?

Nods.

Tomas OK, stick with me.

Movement sequence as the family skis together, in the background is the boom of controlled avalanches from the Gazex tubes, integrated with the sound design.

Tomas *skis with nonchalant confidence, effortlessly controlling himself down the slope.*

Tomas That's it Harry! Great work. Keep your skis parallel Vera! This way guys! Isn't this great huh?

Vera *whoops!*

Tomas That's great Vera! Lean a little more forward! Great Harry!

Ebba Not too fast Harry!

Tomas He's fine! This is what we came here for right?!

Ebba *and* **Tomas** *share a smile.*

The family ski and whoop! with joy until they come to a halt.

Tomas Well done! Well done guys!/ You looked great up there . . . so great being on the mountain together. And we all stayed together.

Ebba That was fantastic /You're properly skiing now!

Vera That was actually/ quite cool.

Harry Dad, did you see me?/ I beat Vera and Mum? I'm ready for poles now Dad. Let me try yours.

Harry *grabs* **Tomas'** *pole, he doesn't let it go.*

Photographer *skis into the scene.*

Vera Oh My God/ I nearly skied into that kid who fell over.

Tomas Hang on Harry let everyone catch their breath.

Harry I'll go/ faster with poles.

Tomas Just hold/ on Harry.

Harry *tries to take* **Tomas'** *poles from him.*

Photographer (*O/S*)   Hello! Bonjour Monsieur!

Tomas Oh, uh. Bonjour! Harry stop it. Stop it.

Harry Just a little go.

Photographer Vous voulez une photo?

Tomas Uh, no maybe tomorrow.

Photographer Yes, come on where you from?

Tomas Sweden. *Harry.*

Ebba Sweden!

Vera Sweden.

Photographer Sweden wow! Very good come on. The champion! You won the race yes?

Harry Yes!

Photographer What's your name?

Harry Harry.

Photographer Yes, Harry come on, it takes two seconds. Let me take the picture of the champion. Don't worry it's free no problem.

Harry Yes! Dad I want a photo.

Tomas Uh . . .

Photographer This way very nice. Are you a champion skier?/ Yes you are.

Harry Yeah I won.

Photographer Why don't you stand next to your brother? Harry put your arm around your sister./ Facing me this way?/ Very nice.

Ebba Put your arm around Vera!

Photographer Very nice! Big smile! 123. Very nice. Mrs, why don't you come stand next to your daughter? And sir next to your wife.

Tomas No you don't/ want me.

Photographer Yes come on, I'll make beautiful photo of your family and the mountain. Ok, here we go 123, very nice! Ok now, just Mr and Mrs. This way, Mr stand closer to your wife and Mrs do you want to stand up straight? And maybe put your arms together. Like this. That's nice! Big smile.

Gazex tubes Boom!

Ebba What *is* that?

Photographer Controlled avalanches. They do them every day. Many times.

Photographer Big smile. 123 very nice! Ok, one more whole family like a big choo choo train. With Harry at the front because he is the champion skier! Big smile 123.

Photographer *moves.*

And one more this way. Look at me, big smiles. Mr, why don't you put your head on your wife like this?

Tomas *leans to* **Ebba** *and they bang heads.*

Ebba Ow!

Photo flash on terrible photo!

Photographer Beautiful! I got it! Enjoy the rest of your day,/ I'm Ricardo, I'll come find you at the hotel later.

Tomas Thank you, thank you very much Harry, that was just a scam.

Harry What?

Tomas If any more photographers/ come up to us, just say no thanks maybe tomorrow?

Ebba Just ignore them next time Harry.

Vera It's obviously a scam.

Harry I didn't know.

Ebba It's fine.

Harry So why's everyone making a big deal of it?

Vera Oh my God we've been here two minutes and already he's having a tantrum.

Harry Shut up! Vera!

Vera You shut up!

Harry *pushes* **Vera** *over.*

Vera AOW!

Vera *tries to kick* **Harry** *back.*

Tomas Hey hey/ hey!

Harry Get off me!

Harry *throws himself at* **Vera** – *it's a fight.*

Tomas What is wrong with you?

Ebba Vera! Vera!

Vera Ow! Get off!

Harry AAAAOOO! You get off! She bit me!

Vera I didn't bite you I pinched/ you stop being such a baby.

Ebba Don't/ pinch people Vera!

Vera He started/ it!

Tomas Stop it. Stop it! Everyone! We're on holiday, we're meant to be having a nice time. What the hell is wrong with you? Hey? Harry. I'm talking to you.

Beat.

Harry. What is wrong with you?

Harry YOU STARTED IT.

Tomas HARRY.

Ebba Tomas.

Signals to leave it.

Tomas I'm just asking him a question. What?

More signals.

What?

Ebba Don't shout at him.

Tomas I'm not shouting. Am I shouting?

Ebba We haven't eaten all day.

Tomas Everyone wanted to ski that's not my fault./ I wanted to eat but everyone wanted to ski.

Ebba I'm not saying . . . I'm just saying no wonder he's like this. We haven't eaten all day.

Tomas Fine then let's eat.

Ebba OK.

Tomas Let's eat. There's a place at the top of the ski lift. Is that going to calm things down? Everyone in agreement with that plan? Don't want to disrupt things if you two have got more plans to attack each other, maybe you want to eat each other?

Vera I'm starving.

Tomas Harry?

Harry *nods.*

Ebba Come on my boy.

Ebba *leads* **Harry** *off, followed by* **Vera**. *Leaving* **Tomas** *on the mountainside alone with all the equipment.*

Tomas I'll get these then.

Nothing from the exiting family.

'Thanks Dad, that would be great we really appreciate everything you do for us,' 'Oh thanks guys thanks for noticing' 'No problem Dad'.

A Gazex tubes boom and he startles, dropping the equipment. He looks to the mountain and its latent power. **Tomas** *picks up all the equipment and scrambles after them.*

Scene Two

The Outdoor Restaurant

In their skiing gear, the family are sat around a table on a veranda overlooking the top of the mountain surrounded by a family of four, two couples and two **Waiting Staff**.

A **Waitress** *comes and delivers their meals.*

Tomas *is looking at his phone.*

Ebba Not bad for a first day huh guys?

Harry After this I'm trying out poles.

Ebba They're quite big you know.

Vera He's too small.

Harry I'm not!

Ebba Vera. How about next route you can try mine, see how it feels?

Harry I'm not too small.

Ebba Tomas.

Tomas Hm?

Tomas *gets the message, puts his phone away.*

Harry *picks it up.*

Tomas Where's this food then?

Ebba It's been long enough now.

Vera Can you ask them how much longer it's gonna be?

Ebba I'll see if I can get his attention.

Harry I bet they've forgotten our order.

Tomas Probably the altitude up here playing havoc with their/ me-erci beaucoup.

Waitress arrives with their food.

Ebba Merci beaucoup!

Tomas Merci beaucoup! Merci, Harry, give me the phone now. Harry.

Harry *hands the phone over.*

Vera Merci beaucoup.

They start to eat their lunch.

Tomas That looks great.

Ebba It really is. It's delicious. Try it.

Ebba *feeds* **Tomas** *some of her food with her fork.*

Tomas Mm . . . That's really delicious. Harry slow down. What is that dressing?

Ebba I think it's anchovy or –

Vera This is so good.

Ebba Something . . . I can't quite.

Vera Is there any parmesan?

Loud BOOM! from the Gazex tubes! Everyone startles! Now that they're closer to the top, the explosions sound much louder.

All diners turn to the mountain. In the distance an avalanche starts to fall making the curtains flap.

Tomas *gets his phone out and starts filming.*

Ebba What was that? Was that an avalanche?

Tomas Yeah but it's controlled. Wow. Look at that power.

Ebba Look at that.

Tomas See they set off an explosion at the top and it moves all the recent snowfall safely before it builds up.

Vera So it's like a bomb going off?

Tomas Yeah.

Ebba Just incredible.

Pause.

Ebba It's safe isn't it?

Tomas Yeah yeah, they know what they're doing. Look at that!

Ebba Where does it stop?

Tomas I don't know, but they must know how to judge it.

Pause.

I've never seen one this close before you are so lucky kids.

Harry It doesn't look like it's going to stop.

Vera Where does it stop? Shouldn't there be like some/ barrier or something.

Pause.

Ebba That doesn't look controlled to me Tomas that doesn't look controlled.

Ebba, **Vera** *and* **Harry** *stand up, along with a number of diners.*

Vera It's not stopping it's gonna hit us.

Harry It's not stopping!/ DAD! IT'S GONNA HIT US.

Harry *tries to get out of his seat,* **Tomas** *restrains him.*

Tomas Harry Harry Harry, it's fine it's fine they know what they're doing. They know what they're doing.

Vera DAD!/ IT'S NOT STOPPING!

It's closer.

Tomas VERA IT'S FINE.

Harry DAD!

It's on them!

Tomas AHAAHHAAA!!

Mass panic! Everyone scrambles for their lives, **Ebba** *grabs* **Vera** *and* **Harry***!*

Screaming **Tomas** *grabs his phone and runs, pushing people out of the way!*

The RUMBLE is almost unbearable!

SCREAMS!!!

The stage and audience are covered in white powder.

And then it's over.

White everywhere.

Long silence.

People cough.

Man Ça va? Tu vas bien?

Ebba Um uh . . .

Man Ça va? Are you OK?

Ebba Is it safe?

Man It's safe to come up now. It's safe.

Ebba Are you sure?

Man I'm sure. It's safe to come up now.

Ebba What happened?

Man Avalanche smoke. It's just avalanche smoke. The avalanche stopped and the smoke it keeps coming.

Ebba *and* **Vera** *slowly stand up,* **Harry** *comes up from under the table, seeing everyone is OK, the* **Man** *moves on.*

Ebba Are you OK?

Vera Yeah.

Man (*to other diners*) Ça va? It is safe now.

Ebba We're fine. Everything's fine.

Diners start to return to their seats.

Harry That was scary.

Ebba Everyone's OK, we're all OK. It's over now. It's over.

Silence.

Vera Where's Dad? Mum? Where's Dad?

Pause.

Ebba Just sit down Vera.

Vera My chair's got stuff all over it.

Ebba *starts to beat their chairs clean with her napkin.*

As she does so, **Harry** *and* **Vera** *look all around the restaurant looking for* **Tomas**.

Filing in behind several returning diners, **Tomas** *finally appears.*

Tomas Wow.

Beat.

Damn that was.

Beat.

Whooo!

Beat.

Are you OK? Everyone OK?

Tomas *is laughing.*

That was crazy. They know what they're doing. But that was . . .

Tomas *is laughing.*

Silence from the family.

Phew!

Tomas *looks around and chuckles.*

He looks around again. Lots of people are returning to their seats and returning to their meals, no-one is singling him out.

Tomas Ah . . .

Tomas *picks up his knife and fork and starts eating his meal again, no-one else can eat.*

Ebba*'s eyes are on stalks.*

Tomas Mm . . . it's good. You want to try?

He offers **Ebba** *a fork.*

Ebba *is too much in shock to react.*

Tomas No?

Silence from **Ebba**, *he puts his fork down. Maybe he can't eat after all.*

Tomas Ahhh . . .

Tomas *looks out to the landscape.*

More silence.

Tomas And here comes the sun.

Long silence.

Lights down.

Scene Three

The Mountain

The family are on the mountain.

Tomas How about we do this run and then go get some hot chocolate? How about that? Guys?

Little enthusiasm.

Tomas Everyone ready?

Ebba Tomas, I'm not sure anyone wants to ski anymore.

Tomas Course they do, it's what we're here for right? Skiing. Vera? Harry?

Ebba We can head back to the room if you want.

Tomas Yeah we can do that if you want?

Vera I want to go back.

Harry Me too.

Tomas That's fine. Let's go back. I don't mind. Sure no-one wants a hot chocolate? I think we've earned it after *today!*

Vera *and* **Harry** *walk off leaving their kit behind followed by* **Ebba**.

Tomas No, OK. I'll get these don't worry.

Tomas *starts to gather the kit up.*

Meanwhile **Ebba** *and the kids have been approached by . . .*

Photographer Mrs . . . here I have your photos.

Ebba Ah, OK. Uh . . . not now thank you . . .

Photographer I have prints. . .

Photographer *gets out photos from a folder.*

Ebba Oh OK . . .

Photographer Yes.

Ebba I'm just trying to . . .

Photographer Yes? See.

Ebba OK. OK. Thanks. Yes. These are. Yes. They're great.

Photographer Handsome boy. Heartbreaker.

Ebba Yes.

Photographer One minute a baby and then . . .

Ebba Yes.

Photographer Beautiful family. Happy memories.

Tomas *appears and watches* **Ebba**. **Ebba** *flicks away from the group shot.*

Ebba I'll take this one and this one.

Photographer And this one? All four family?

Ebba Just those thank you.

Photographer D'accord. This and this. That is fifty-two Euro. Seventy cents.

Ebba Oh. Um. Right.

Ebba *gets her purse out.*

She hands him some notes.

Ebba OK thank you.

Photographer That's not enough.

Ebba Sorry.

She hands him another note before trying to leave.

Photographer Still not enough.

She hands some more notes.

Photographer No.

She gets some more out.

Ebba Look just just take it.

*The **Photographer** seems to be deciding rather than counting.*

Photographer Your change./ I have some change in my.

Ebba No thank you it's fine.

*The **Photographer** leaves.*

Tomas All OK? Are those the photos?

Ebba Yeah.

Tomas Let me see.

Beat.

That it?

Beat.

Ebba I didn't like myself in the others.

Tomas Bet you looked great.

Ebba No.

Tomas That's ridiculous.

Ebba I didn't like it.

Tomas You always look great in photos it's me that spoils them.

Ebba *starts to walk to join the kids,* **Tomas** *runs alongside her.*

Tomas I don't know. I might be wrong but, you seem, irritated.

Ebba OK.

Tomas OK.

Ebba OK.

Tomas Right. So. Well. Are you? Irritated.

Beat.

Ebba No. No I don't think so.

Tomas OK great. That's/ great I was

Ebba Should I be?

Pause.

Tomas No I. No, I don't *think* so.

Ebba No?

Tomas *exhales as if wracking his brain.*

Tomas Hm . . . No. I. No. I can't.

Ebba OK then.

Ebba *carries on walking.*

Tomas OK then. Yeah.

Beat.

Ebba.

Beat.

Maybe. I was just thinking maybe we should take them straight back let's not worry about a hot chocolate? I think they're a bit tired. Harry looks tired.

Ebba Yup OK. Do it.

Ebba *invites* **Tomas** *to catch up with the kids.*

Tomas *is unsure what to do,* **Ebba** *maintains the invite . . . an anxious* **Tomas** *runs after the kids.*

Tomas Kids let's just head back I think everyone needs a rest.

Harry Is everything OK?

Tomas What?

Vera What's going on? With Mum.

Tomas Nothing.

Harry Were you two arguing?

Tomas No.

Vera What was that about?

Tomas Nothing we were just talking.

Harry Why does she look upset then?

Tomas Look I know your mum better than anyone else. She's not upset. OK?

Unconvinced, **Harry** *and* **Vera** *exit.*

On **Tomas** *looking back to* **Ebba** *– yeah, she looks upset.*

Lights down.

Scene Four

Hotel Suite

Vera *is sat on the floor looking at her iPad.*

Ebba *is holding* **Harry**'s *pyjamas.*

Harry LEAVE ME ALONE!

Ebba Come on Harry.

Harry NO LEAVE ME ALONE! GO AWAY!

Ebba Harry.

Tomas Harry I don't like your tone of voice; you can't speak to your mother like that.

Harry I DON'T WANT TO GO TO BED. YOU CAN'T TELL ME WHAT TO DO.

Ebba *tries to pull* **Harry**'s *top off.*

Ebba It's/ bedtime.

Harry NO! GET OFF ME! LEAVE ME ALONE!

Tomas *tries to grab* **Harry**, *but* **Harry** *kicks out violently and screams.*

Harry AHHHAAAAAHAHAHAHA!! NO!/ NO! NO! NOOOOOOOO!

Tomas Stop it! Stop it! Stop it! Harry! You have to go to bed you're eight years old.

Ebba No no no no/ Harry Harry Harry.

Vera Just leave him alone!/ God! He doesn't want to go to bed we're on holiday let him stay up! What does any of this achieve?

Ebba He has to go to bed, we've had a very long day, and he's tired. We're all tired.

Tomas Yeah.

Vera He's not.

Ebba He is.

Vera He doesn't look it.

Ebba He's tired.

Harry I'm not. Look.

Ebba Harry.

Tomas Harry.

Ebba We're all going to bed soon. Can you talk to him?/ He has to go to bed?

Vera This is *not* my problem./ None of this is my problem don't drag me into it.

Tomas Well unfortunately we're a family and we're all staying in this room/ so it is your problem as well Vera. We all need to

Vera I didn't want to come here, I wanted to go to St Tropez/ but no-one ever listens to me in this family we could be on a beach right now rather than dealing with this.

Ebba Oh Vera/ this is not the time to make this about you.

Harry *gets* **Tomas**'*phone and starts watching something on it.*

Tomas Harry /we're trying to talk as a family.

Vera No of course it's never/ about me is it? That's exactly my point it is literally *never* about me in this family. It's Dad, then Harry then you, then the dog, then me.

Ebba Yes, I'm an awful/ mother Vera, you're the victim I'm sorry for bringing you to the Alps on holiday.

Harry I want to FaceTime Lena.

Tomas We are not FaceTiming the dog. Harry. Give me the phone. Harry. Harry.

Harry *ignores him.*

Tomas HARRY.

Vera DON'T SHOUT/ AT HIM LIKE THAT.

Tomas I'm *trying*/ to get him to listen.

Vera OH MY GOD!/ You two.

Tomas Ve/ ra.

Ebba Watch/ your attitude Vera I am sick of being spoken to as if I'm some maid!

Vera Just go!/ He doesn't want you in here! I don't want you in here! Why don't you just go?

Tomas This is *our* hotel suite!/ We've only got one living room!

Harry Can I have your phone Mum?

Vera Well pay for a pod for us then?/ Then we can all have some peace and quiet.

Tomas We've got two rooms! I'm not paying for a pod for you guys on top of paying for us to have a family suite/ I'm not doing it.

Harry Mum./ Can I have your phone?

Vera Fine well this is what you get.

Tomas Maybe we just need to figure out how to all get on better here and we can start by you two doing as you're told. Harry go to bed and Vera drop the attitude.

Vera Sure/ yeah whatever.

Harry Vera give/ me your phone.

Vera GET OFF!/ MUM! Tell him! MUM!

Tomas HARRY! LET GO!

Vera TELL HIM!

Ebba Harry! Harry stop it! HARRY! Can we just. Can we just stop shouting please? Can we talk about this without everyone shouting?

Silence.

Thank you. I know you're angry,/ but let's all just take a deep breath.

Vera I thought he needed to go to bed and I had a bad attitude? Make up your mind. He's either got to go to bed, or he hasn't. You can't keep changing what's best for us to suit you.

Ebba Vera.

Vera Why don't *you* go to bed and leave us in here? Shut the door. I don't care.

Ebba We're not doing that.

Vera Then why not go somewhere else? Leave your phone for him and go somewhere else? It's a big hotel. He won't pay for a pod, we can't go anywhere else, so why don't you two, give us some space. And when he's ready, he'll go to bed.

Ebba Can't/ we –

Vera I don't want to talk anymore.

Ebba *does not want to leave it like this.*

Tomas Maybe we should . . .

Ebba What?

Tomas Maybe we should give them some space . . .

Vera Finally.

Ebba Vera, I really don't like your tone/ you are really pushing your luck.

Vera I'M NOT SAYING ANYTHING, YOU'RE THE ONE WHO DRAGGED ME INTO THIS I DON'T CARE

Scene Four

WHAT TIME HE GOES TO BED I DON'T CARE ABOUT ANY OF THIS I JUST WANT TO BE LEFT ALONE.

Harry   Mum can I have your phone?

Defeated **Ebba** *hands* **Harry** *her phone.*

Tomas   Come on give them some space.

Ebba   I don't think it's a good idea they're upset.

Tomas   Give them some space, Vera you're in charge. (*Off* **Ebba**.) Let's let her get on with it. We'll be downstairs. We'll be downstairs if there's any problems just ring.

Vera   Whatever.

Ebba *bridles.*

Harry *climbs back on to the bed with* **Ebba**'s *phone.*

Tomas *and* **Ebba** *step out –* **Harry** *and* **Vera** *go into darkness.*

Tomas *and* **Ebba** *look at each other.*

Tomas   This is what happens when you raise strong independent children. You get thrown out of your own room!

Tomas *can't help but laugh.*

They both look out to the mountain.

The Gazex tubes boom.

Ebba   I need a drink.

Tomas   Let's get a drink. And dinner. Come on.

Lights down.

Scene Five

Hotel Restaurant

Tomas *and* **Ebba** *are sat with* **Charlotte** *and* **Brady**.

Tomas So, how was your day?

Charlotte Um, it was fantastic, right? We had a great day. I met this one, I mean. (*Pointing to* **Brady**.) Yeah.

Tomas Yeah?

Charlotte We bumped into each other this morning in the queue to the lift. And, er, I guess we were both longing for someone.

Laughs all around.

No, I'm just kidding. No, we had a great day and we had a good time snowboarding and hanging out, talking it was, it was great. Really nice. You told me that you're very religious . . .

Brady I did not/ say that.

Charlotte Yes, you did.

Brady Not that I'm/ *very* religious, no that's not what I said.

Charlotte Yeah you did. It's alright. What's wrong with that? Don't be ashamed,/ own it.

Brady I'm not ashamed! Well, allow me to explain, I told this one . . .

Charlotte Excuse me?

Brady . . . That I'm not an atheist which is/ very different.

Charlotte Who the fuck is this one?

Pause.

Tomas You said it before.

Scene Five   351

Charlotte   Did I? (*Remembering.*) I met 'this one'.

Brady   Just a joke.

Charlotte   Oh yeah.

Laughter.

Brady   Anyway, did you guys brave the crowds today?

Ebba   Yeah, we did. Yeah. It was . . . well . . .

Ebba *takes a big swig of wine.*

Laughter.

Tomas   Yeah, it was great it was great. We skied all morning and then we . . . Well.

We actually we uh, we did a little bit more in the afternoon but went home because we had. Well we had a sort of crazy experience actually. Um . . .

Ebba *laughs.* **Tomas** *looks to* **Ebba** *for a shared connection.* **Ebba** *avoids his eye.*

Charlotte   OK.

Tomas   Yeah. So we were sitting at the top restaurant, you know the top one, with the magnificent view.

Charlotte   Yeah,/ it's a nice bar there.

Brady   I haven't been there yet, but everyone keeps saying it's magnificent.

Charlotte   I'll take you tomorrow.

Brady   OK! Sorry. Carry on, you were at the top restaurant.

Tomas   Yeah, we were at the top restaurant, and we had uh well we saw an avalanche, didn't we?

Ebba *giggles before taking another big swig of wine.*

Brady   An avalanche?/ Holy shit!

Charlotte Really?

Tomas Yeah it was. It was this/ sort of incredible

Ebba *laughs uncontrollably.*

Tomas What?

Ebba Ignore me. Sorry. Ignore me.

Ebba *pours herself a mighty glass of wine.*

Polite laughter.

Tomas Anyway, so we were sitting there, and it was a controlled/ avalanche, so it was . . .

Brady Controlled avalanche, yeah.

Tomas But quite quickly it grew kind of big. It was like. It just kept getting bigger and bigger and, I've never really seen such a big avalanche, and I was like, er, for a moment it looked like it was going to smash into the restaurant. It was kind of terrifying.

Brady Wow.

Charlotte But you're OK? It didn't hit the restaurant did it?

Tomas No, but for a moment . . . it looked like it would. When I talk about it look, I'm getting goose bumps.

Tomas *shows off the goose bumps on his arm to* **Ebba** *who is still smirking.*

Charlotte What did you do?

Tomas I mean, there wasn't much anyone could do, you're on the mountain/ it's you know it's split second stuff

Ebba It was horrifying actually. Utterly horrifying.

Pause.

Charlotte You all had a fright?

Ebba Yeah, we did.

Tomas Yeah,/ it's one of those –

Brady And the kids are alright? Are they OK?

Tomas Yeah, everyone is fine. Everyone is fine thank God. We got shaken up you know, you (Ebba) got a bit afraid, didn't you? But really it was

Ebba *laughs at this. . .*

Tomas . . . But I mean it wasn't . . . It was controlled, and they know what they're doing/ it was just in the moment you think –

Ebba He got so scared that he ran away from the table.

Brady *laughs.*

Tomas What? No,/ I didn't.

Brady You ran?

Ebba Yeah, he did.

Tomas No, I didn't. No. No. No.

Beat.

Ebba Come on.

Tomas No. No. No. No. No.

Ebba You ran away from the table.

Tomas What? No, I did not.

Ebba . . .

Tomas I did not.

Ebba When it came at us, you ran away.

Tomas No, I didn't . . . I most certainly/ did not do that.

Ebba You grabbed your phone and your gloves and ran like hell.

Tomas Please . . . I did no such thing. I did no such thing.

Ebba Well. You did.

Tomas That's not how I remember it.

Tomas *laughs, no-one is quite sure whether to laugh or not.*

Ebba You ran away.

Ebba *takes another drink of wine.*

Tomas Ebba, please. I didn't do that. It's weird./ I think we're still a little shaken up by the whole thing. It's not even possible to run in ski boots.

Charlotte It sounds awful. Really a horrible thing to go through.

Ebba (*laughing to herself*) Can't run in ski boots? Can you not run in ski boots?

Tomas thinks you can't run in ski boots now and I imagined the whole thing. Unbelievable.

Brady Well. Maybe . . .

Charlotte But isn't this one of those situations that kind of comes really quick? And none of us know how we'd react. How do you know how to react?

Brady I don't know.

Ebba You can run in ski boots.

Tomas They're not supple enough.

Ebba Can you run in ski boots?

Brady (*pause*) You know, I haven't been skiing in years so I'm really not the person to ask about these things.

Tomas'*pride is wounded.*

Charlotte 'About these things.' You are so cute! Isn't he so cute?

Charlotte *gives* **Brady** *a patronising kiss.*

Ebba *laughs.*

Tomas *tries to join in, but his pride is too injured.*

Lights down.

Scene Six

Hotel Corridor

Ebba *walks along with the room key;* **Tomas** *runs after her.*

Tomas   Ebba!

Beat.

Ebba!

Ebba   What?

Tomas   Can we just stop for a second? Ebba? Stop! Please.

Ebba *stops.*

Tomas   Thank you.

Ebba   Why won't admit what happened?

Tomas   Well . . .

Beat.

Pff. Because, that's not how I see,/ what happened.

Ebba   How do you see what happened? Hm? How?

Tomas   I see, what happened. And it's just not what you see.

Ebba   This is so weird, this is so weird.

Tomas   What's so weird about it?

Ebba   Admit what you did!

Tomas   I can't 'admit' to your perception. That's not how I see it. I just. I really can't relate to your description of things. And the way you tried to convince everybody at dinner that your version was the truth . . . It was just really hard on me.

Ebba It was hard for me, hearing you deny it.

Tomas I'm sure. It must be hard for you. I don't want that for you. I don't want that for either of us. I want us to be – like we always are. We're a team.

Ebba I didn't recognize us at all. I didn't recognize you ... or myself.

Tomas I didn't recognize you either.

Ebba I don't want us to be like that, this is meant to be our family holiday and we're disagreeing like that at dinner/ it's so embarrassing.

Tomas I don't want it to be like this. I don't ever want to have a dinner like that again.

Ebba Me neither. I hated it. It's not good . . .

Tomas That's not us.

Ebba That's not us.

Tomas No.

Ebba We're normally so . . .

Tomas Together on everything. Co-pilots.

Ebba Right.

Tomas We're a team, so let's make sure we get back there and put all this behind us.

Ebba OK.

Tomas OK. Great. Phew!

Ebba OK.

Tomas Great.

Ebba Look. Try to hug me . . . I need one.

Tomas So, do I.

They hug.

Tomas *'phone starts to ring.* **Ebba** *tries to disengage.* **Tomas** *doesn't let her.*

Tomas Ignore it. Ignore it.

It carries on ringing, eventually **Ebba** *can't ignore it.*

Tomas *quickly turns it off and puts his arms around* **Ebba** *again for a hug.*

Ebba *disengages.*

Ebba Sorry, I can't. I just. I can't get past/ the whole

Tomas Come on Ebba.

Ebba No, it's actually really important for us for the kids that we agree on things like this otherwise it's going to chip away at us.

Tomas We just said we'd put it behind us.

Ebba We need to have a shared vision/ of this or it's

Tomas You do know it's actually impossible for us to share the same perspective on things. Scientifically.

Ebba What?

Tomas It's science. It's impossible for us to see the same thing so/ we're going to diverge at some –

Ebba But there are you know – Observable facts we should be able to agree on.

Tomas Are there?

Ebba Tomas.

Tomas Really? I don't know.

Ebba Come on. And seeing us united and in agreement on things is good for the kids. It's good for us as a couple, that we find a way to agree on things. It's good for us to make sure that we're not at odds on stuff.

Tomas OK. So, what exactly are you trying to say? What do you want me to say? Because I don't know any more.

*The **Cleaner** enters dragging a reluctant vacuum cleaner. He slowly walks past them. They wait patiently for privacy.*

Ebba We had lunch at the top restaurant.

Pause.

Tomas OK, agreed.

Ebba We were all there.

Pause.

Tomas Yes, we were all there.

Beat.

Ebba An avalanche happened?

Tomas An avalanche happened.

Beat.

Ebba We . . . were all terrified.

Beat.

Ebba And?

Thomas And.

Beat.

Ebba And that's, it. Everyone was ok.

Tomas That's what we say happened?

Ebba Well, that's all we can agree/ on. So, I guess

Tomas I'm totally OK with that. Totally OK with that. If I knew if that's – if I knew that's what you meant. Sorry. I thought. OK, if that's what you mean. That's our – that's fine. I'm totally fine with that.

Ebba OK.

Tomas OK.

Ebba So, we have a unified front.

Tomas Hooray! Yes, I am totally fine with that spin on things.

Ebba All right, then.

Tomas Alright then deal.

Tomas *offers a hand,* **Ebba** *shakes it.*

Tomas Whooo! That's a relief.

Ebba We experienced an avalanche. And it was scary.

Tomas Christ . . . We're on holiday. We shouldn't be acting like this. Let's put all this behind us. There was an avalanche, we were terrified, but everyone's fine. OK? Job done.

Ebba OK.

Tomas (*bold!*)   On with the holiday!

Scene Seven

Hotel Bathroom

Tomas *and* **Ebba** *get ready for bed, brushing teeth in a rehearsed, silent fashion. She pushes the toilet seat down and finds herself glowering at* **Tomas**.

Outside the controlled explosions from the Gazex tubes continue.

Tomas *heads into the room leaving* **Ebba** *alone in the bathroom.*

It's not over.

Scene Eight

Hotel Room

The family is getting kitted up.

Ebba Harry . . . Your other glove is over there, over by Daddy. Here.

Harry What?

Ebba The other one's/ over there, next to Dad.

Harry I can't find my goggles.

Ebba Where did you put them?

Harry I don't know./ I can't ski without my goggles.

Tomas They'll be in here somewhere,/ just take a look.

Harry I'm not going/ without them.

Tomas Ebba/ have you seen his goggles?

Ebba Where did you take them off last?

Harry I don't know.

Tomas Well think.

Harry I don't know.

Tomas When you came in last night what did you do with them?

Harry I DON'T REMEMBER.

Ebba *steps back from the fray.*

Tomas Hey hey it's OK. We'll find it. You know Mummy is the master of finding things. And then, we can all go and enjoy a day on the slopes. Right? Right Vera? Vera.

Silence from **Vera**.

Tomas 'Yes Dad. I can't wait.' Me neither Vera.

Ebba *stares at her family.*

Ebba You know, I was thinking about skiing all by myself today.

Tomas *guffaws.*

Tomas What? Really?

Ebba Yes.

Tomas *looks at the kids,* **Vera** *totally disengaged,* **Harry** *furiously turning the place upside down looking for his goggles.*

Tomas Well . . .

Ebba I think I'd like to ski on my own today. Unless that's a problem?

Tomas Uh, No, no . . .

Ebba Do I hear a 'but'?

Tomas (*beat*) No, go ahead. OK. We'll catch you later. We'll catch you later. Maybe meet for lunch or something?

Harry What? Where are we going for lunch? We're not going to that place, again are we?

Tomas No, no I'm just saying we'll meet for lunch that's all I didn't say where.

Harry Who are we meeting?

Tomas Mummy. We're meeting Mummy for lunch.

Harry Why are we meeting Mummy where's she going?

Tomas Mummy wants to ski on her own today.

Harry What? Why? What's the point in that?

Tomas *is lost for words.*

Ebba I just. Feel like it.

Silence.

Vera *guffaws.*

Ebba Vera? Anything you want to add?

Vera No.

Ebba What's so funny about me wanting to ski on my own?

Vera Why'd you feel like it?

Ebba I can have a day skiing on my own,/ it's no big –

Tomas Yeah, it's fine./ It's cool.

Vera You've never done it before.

Ebba *laughs.*

Ebba I'm only going for a ski on my own.

Harry What's the point in that?

Ebba Harry! Sometimes! Mummies . . . They./ You know

Tomas Mummies need a bit of 'me time'.

Ebba Yeah/ 'me time'.

Harry Why? We're on holiday.

Vera Oh my God.

Ebba Harry. Everyone does it OK? Every family lets their mums get away now and again. It's healthy.

Tomas Yeah and their daddies too./ Sometimes.

Vera Do *kids* ever get 'me time'?

Tomas All of your time is me time Vera. That's why Mummy and I need 'me time'.

Harry I don't want to ski without you.

Harry *pulls off his glove.*

Ebba Can you? (deal with this)

Tomas *heads to* **Harry**.

Tomas Yeah, it's fine it's fine we'll be fine. Take my credit card.

Tomas *opens his wallet.* **Ebba** *makes for the door.*

Ebba No, I'll use my own thank you.

Ebba *leaves.*

Tomas Alright! Another day on the slopes!

Vera *puts her headphones on.*

Harry WHERE IS SHE GOING?

Tomas' *shoulders sink.*

Lights down.

Scene Nine

The Mountain

Movement sequence as **Ebba** *skis alone.*

She tries to enjoy it, but something isn't quite working for her.

Eventually she gives up.

Lights down.

Scene Ten

Café

Ebba *sits facing* **Charlotte** *who is coyly waving to a hunk at the bar, in a café with big glass windows.*

Charlotte He has a lot of huskies. Italian. Very little English. Which is a good thing I think.

Ebba Is it?

Charlotte He speaks as much as a woman needs.

Ebba *laughs.*

Ebba   Well, that's the truth.

Charlotte   What's it like out there today?

Ebba   Good. I've been on my own today.

Charlotte   But I thought this was a *family* holiday? 'Time to focus.' Not as much fun as you thought?

Ebba   I didn't really enjoy skiing on my own this morning.

Charlotte   Then you need company.

Ebba   You seem to have had a lot of men.

Beat.

Sorry.

Charlotte   I guess that's right. Yeah . . .

Ebba   Do you have some kind of arrangement with your husband or boyfriend?

Charlotte   No way! We each take responsibility for our relationships and keep it at that. Seems to work out pretty well.

Beat.

You look surprised.

Ebba   Well, yeah . . . Aren't you ever jealous? And what about him?

Charlotte   If he has a good time with some woman, why shouldn't I let him have it?

Ebba   You actually mean that? That you're happy he's with someone else?

Charlotte   Sure, I'm happy for him; I love him.

Waiter *returns with* **Ebba**'s *coffee.* **Waiter** *leaves.*

Ebba   What if you meet someone and, you don't want to go back to the family?

Charlotte   I always go back. You're worried you wouldn't?

Beat.

Ebba   OK. To a certain extent, I understand. You're still young and attractive. . . But aren't you afraid of being alone, being left? What if he falls in love with one of these women, what if one of these women are younger than you? What if he can't stop thinking about her when he's with you, and you're just the boring domestic part of his life, and with her it's all fun and sexy and no responsibility. Isn't that just – Aren't you both risking your whole family and risking messing up your children's lives?

Charlotte   I suppose.

Ebba   What if he leaves you?

Charlotte   Well, of course I don't want to be left alone. But there are lots of people who are important in my life, not just my husband and my children. I can't go building my entire self-esteem on being a woman in a relationship or being a mother. I don't need him to feel safe.

Ebba *doesn't feel safe with* **Tomas**.

Ebba   OK, I get that, I'm all – *(Fist pump.)* but does it actually work? *Actually* does it work? Like are you *100 per cent* sure no one gets hurt?

Charlotte   What can I say?

Ebba   Are you sure that it doesn't hurt your children? Like how can you know, they aren't picking up on the fact that you two aren't straight with each other, or not 100 per cent invested in each other. My kids they can spot the slightest bit of disagreement between me and Tomas a mile off. They have a radar for it. How can you be sure your kids aren't (messed up)?

Charlotte What?

Ebba How can you be sure you're not screwing up your kids by being so selfish?

Beat.

I'm sorry I don't mean to judge. I just want to know how it works. For you.

Charlotte There's someone else?

Ebba *is disturbed by her own transparency.*

Ebba No.

Charlotte Are you sure?

Ebba Yes.

Beat.

Yes.

Beat.

I'm sure.

Beat.

OK nothing's happened/ but there is someone.

Charlotte But something could, if you let yourself.

Ebba There is someone a work colleague and there's. I think there's . . . a connection there. I know there is but nothing's happened.

I've never spoken about this with anyone.

Charlotte Would you like something to happen?

Ebba No. I. I think about what it might be like. Sometimes. Often. When he's . . . near. But nothing's happened and it won't happen.

Charlotte But you'd like it to.

Charlotte *drinks some coffee.*

Ebba　I just couldn't bear it if something I did, hurt the kids. Something silly and selfish, hurt the kids and Tomas. And changed things forever.

Charlotte　I think raising kids in an unhappy relationship is the quickest way to screw up your kids actually. The best thing I can do for them is be happy. Are your kids doing fine?

Beat.

OK.

Ebba　You don't – Relationships aren't just – you know – there are ups and downs and you have to work at them. You know; building a relationship with another person, spending your life together, getting married, having kids, that's worth so much more than tumbling around with a young colleague or some Italian/ at some

Charlotte　Gorgeous Italian.

Ebba　Gorgeous Italian at some ski resort in France. You have to see that right?

Charlotte　I do.

Beat.

But why do we have to choose? In this day and age. Why do we have to choose? Who says we have to choose? Who says? I say, we can have both. We can have long-term and short-term relationships. Whatever our needs are, we should be allowed to meet them.

Ebba　I can't imagine that working for me.

Charlotte　Because you, like most women, believe what you believe. And you work at your relationships, and every now and again you're rewarded with a few weeks or a month or two of peace and happiness where the resentment dissipates for a while. And then you're unhappy again. You're lonely again. You retreat into your fantasies with a friend and open yourself up to the attention he gives you, and that gives you enough of a boost to go back to shovelling in the endless trenches of your unhappy relationship. Doing all the emotional labour, on your own so that you can hold it together for the benefit of everyone else, except you. I refuse that deal. Maybe you should too.

Ebba The thing/ I can't . . .

Charlotte *spies a new man in the distance.*

Charlotte Would you? Would you excuse me. . .

Ebba Sure sure go ahead. Go ahead.

Charlotte *heads over to the new man at another table.*

Alone, **Ebba** *looks on.*

She looks out of the window and startles when she sees **Tomas**, **Vera** *and* **Harry** *in the full skiing kit walking outside towards the gondola platform.* **Vera** *storming ahead,* **Harry** *behind and* **Tomas** *struggling to keep up with the equipment.*

Through the glass **Ebba** *watches her family.*

She puts her hand on the window but doesn't draw their attention.

Scene Eleven

Gondola Lift Platform

Tomas Vera. Vera? Stop!

Beat.

Can you give me a hand with this stuff?

They stop and **Vera** *takes some equipment from* **Tomas**.

Tomas *takes a glove off and checks his phone.*

Tomas Oh, Mats and his new girlfriend Jenny have arrived. OK. So, what do you guys want to do next?

Harry I want to try snowboarding on a red run./ Can we do snowboarding next?

Tomas OK Vera. How about you?

Beat.

Vera. What do you want to do? Vera.

Vera I want to go home.

Tomas Ha. What?

Beat.

You're not serious.

Beat.

We've only just got here. Aren't you having a good time?

Vera Are you?

Tomas Ha! Well. Pff. It's not really about me. This is a family holiday it's about you guys. I'm not supposed to enjoy it.

Beat.

Well I am enjoying it. I'm enjoying being with you guys. Spending time with you. Us all being together.

Vera We're not all together.

Tomas Well Mummy needs a break and it's kind to give her that break.

Vera Whatever.

Tomas What does that mean?

Vera It means, whatever whatever.

Tomas I don't follow what you mean.

Vera It means whatever you want to believe, whatever. Let's just go. I don't care. Let's go.

Tomas She's just skiing on her own.

Vera She's not just skiing on her own though is she?

Tomas Hey your Mum really loves you, both of you.

Vera I know that.

Beat.

I just don't think she loves you.

Tomas *stops.*

Vera Do you think she does?

Beat.

So, I'm saying; if you two are gonna get a divorce, then I want to go home.

Harry What? Are you two getting a divorce? Dad?

Vera And if we are going home because you two are getting a divorce then I want an iPhone XR in gold.

Harry Dad! What's going on? Are you getting a divorce? When?

Tomas No, we are not getting a divorce. Why would you – what – why why – that's no. That's absolutely categorically –OK. Believe me. I *know* I'm your Dad. OK, and I would know. I would know. I'd be the first to, she'd have to, I'd have to give approval of, and you know. I'm not gonna so. Why would you think – has she said something? To make you think that. Has she said something? Or have you overheard something. On the phone. Is that why you is that why you said that?

Vera No.

Tomas Well then there's nothing to worry about is there? OK. Guys. Trust me on this.

Vera *walks off,* **Harry** *follows, and* **Tomas** *chases after.*

Tomas Vera!

Ebba *steps onto the mountain.*

The Gazex tubes boom – she doesn't flinch, she stays on the mountain.

Lights down.

Scene Twelve

Corridor

Mats *and* **Jenny** *fool around at* **Ebba** *and* **Tomas**' *door.*

Jenny Come on, behave.

Mats Here, feel this, feel this . . . No one can see us . . .

Jenny No.

Mats No-one can see us.

Jenny Mats!

She indicates the **Cleaner** *walking past, giving them a judgemental stare.*

Mats Hi.

Eventually the **Cleaner** *leaves and* **Mats** *is immediately all over* **Jenny** *again.*

Jenny No Mats.

Mats Come on. Please? Don't be like that come to Papa!

Jenny *rejects him.*

Mats Why'd you do this to me?

Jenny Because.

Mats Now I'm gonna have to see Ebba with a massive throbbing ha/-iii!!

Ebba *opens the door with a glass of wine in her hand.*

Ebba Hi!/ You must be Jenny, come in come in!

Jenny Hi!/ So nice to meet you! Mats has told me so much about you guys!

They enter the room where **Tomas** *is opening another bottle of wine.*

Tomas Here comes trouble!

Mats Here he is! Been too long.

The two hug.

Tomas Hi Jenny, you're too good for him!

Mats Ignore him.

Ebba The kids are asleep so it's just us, you've been here before, right, Jenny?

Jenny It's my third season. But it's the first time with Mats. It's been fun, we've had a great time today haven't we?

Mats Absolutely.

Jenny How's it been for you guys?

Tomas *yanks out the cork – everyone startles and laughs nervously!*

Ebba *offers her drained glass to* **Tomas** *as she talks.*

Ebba Well . . . It's been . . . We've had a fantastic time. It's been great. A great place to bring the kids. The conditions are great, all this snow . . . And I had a day of skiing on my own too. You should have that too./ It was great.

Tomas I'd like that.

Ebba It's wonderful to go at your own pace and just . . . Maybe. I know, wouldn't it be nice for you boys to ski together again?

Tomas That would be, cool . . .

Ebba It must be ages since you skied together!

Tomas Uh. Yeah it is.

Ebba   I think you should do it.

Tomas   Let's see, maybe see what the kids want to do, they might want to –

Ebba   How about tomorrow? I can take the kids. Don't feel guilty about it.

Tomas   I don't.

Beat.

I was just thinking that this is their holiday/ they might have plans together –

Ebba   I'm sorry . . . I'm sorry. This is your holiday I didn't mean to take control of it, you decide what works for you.

Jenny   No problem.

Ebba   Jeez! What am I like?

Ebba *takes a huge gulp of wine. She is already on another level of drunk than the others.*

Jenny   This wine is *great*.

Ebba   Isn't it? That's the best thing about coming here, whatever wine you buy, you just know you can put away two bottles of it without really realizing, have some more.

Ebba *tops up* **Jenny**'s *drink and takes a gulp herself.*

Tomas   So what do you do Jenny? When you're not trying to keep this guy in check.

Mats   Heey! Watch it!

Tomas   I'm always watching it when you're around.

Mats *and* **Tomas** *cackle in a tragic way.*

Tomas   Sorry Jenny, you were saying.

Jenny   I work in a bar.

Silence.

Tomas OK.

Ebba That's great!

Beat.

We love bars. We never. We never go. Anymore. We never do anything. But if we did. We would go to a bar. What kind of bar?

Tomas Do you enjoy it?

Jenny It's OK I guess. I have a good manager.

Tomas Well there's plenty of time.

Ebba Tomas.

Tomas What?

Ebba You sound like you're judging.

Tomas I'm just saying. He's forty-two and he's still figuring out what he wants to do, I can judge him!

Laughter.

Mats He's judging because actually he wants to be me.

More tragic cackling from **Tomas** *and* **Mats**.

Jenny I know what I want to do.

Tomas Oh yeah?

Jenny Yeah, I want to open a place here.

Ebba Like a hotel?

Jenny A bar.

Mats She has some great ideas. Great ideas. Got it *all* worked out.

Tomas That's great.

Jenny I've worked in bars all my life, and I've been coming here for years and it feels like it's missing something with a bit of . . .

Tomas Qui/ et.

Jenny Sou/ l.

Tomas Soul-yeah.

Jenny Yeah, there's nothing in the evenings for you know, young people. Or people without kids.

Mats It could do with livening up around here.

Jenny I was talking to a guy last season.

Mats What guy who is he where can I kill him?

Tomas *and* **Ebba** *laugh.*

Jenny They said they were opening a night club. So, I went there and asked if they were hiring. I talked to their head bartender; a guy called Micke. And well, one thing was he was kind of threatening/ to begin with but that's by the by.

Tomas What?

Mats What do you mean?

Pause.

Jenny Well. He what. I don't know what the right word is but it was like he fronted me? Is that what you would say?

Tomas He was aggressive with you?

Mats Which bar?

Jenny The one with the green on the front.

Tomas What did he say? Do you want us/ to have a word?

Jenny Yeah. He was all like, 'So, ever worked a bar before?' And I went, 'Yeah, I've worked all over' and I was about to list all the places I'd been and before I could, he like stepped up to me, and looked down and said, 'Are you any good?'

Ebba We were . . .

Jenny And his whole body language and demeanour was just sneering like looking down on me as if I was like some kind/ of second-class . . .

Ebba We were in an avalanche yesterday.

Ebba *drinks her wine.*

Tomas What was that?

Ebba I said, we were in an avalanche yesterday.

Mats You were actually in it? In an avalanche?

Ebba We're here, so everything's OK. But . . . The thing is . . . we were about to have lunch it had just been served when we heard a loud bang. You hear that all the time around here. I don't like it, but Tomas says it's nothing to worry about. Anyway, everyone at the restaurant turns to have a look. We see the snow start cascading. And I mean, it's spectacular.

Tomas *nods in agreement as if he's a willing participant in this conversation.*

Ebba People start taking pictures. It's quite . . . impressive. Until we realize that something's wrong because this wall of snow is heading straight towards us.

Mats It's heading towards you?

Ebba Yeah straight towards us.

Jenny Shit.

Ebba And it keeps getting bigger and bigger . . . Suddenly, it's clear . . . That now something's terribly wrong. Everybody panics.

They start running and screaming. It's total chaos. Total chaos. The wall of snow is like fifty metres high and one hundred metres wide. And it's moving so fast. So, I grab

Vera and Harry and I try to pick them both up. But I can't. So, I look for Tomas, to help carry the kids to safety . . .

And what I see is my husband grabbing his phone . . . and running like hell away from us.

Beat.

Then everything goes white. I'm standing there with the kids. There's this intensity and these sounds, like nothing I've ever known. And I'm thinking that this is it. We're dead. And I call out to Tomas . . . But he's not there.

Beat.

I don't know how long it all went on. And then . . . there is no avalanche. That wall of snow closing in on us was only avalanche smoke. The actual avalanche came to a stop before reaching the restaurant. There I am, clutching my kids, and suddenly the sky is blue again! Our lunch is still on the table. Our drinks are still there. People start coming back and realize that there was no bloody avalanche at all it was just a false alarm. I don't know what to do, so I sit down and eat.

Beat.

And then Tomas comes back . . . And we don't *say anything*. We just eat our lunch.

Beat.

So now I have a problem, right? Here I am in this fancy resort, and I'm not happy. I'm not happy. It's not good, I don't like it here, I want to go home.

Beat.

Tomas, say something! This is so fucking weird with you not saying anything!

Silence.

Mats When . . . When there's . . . In situations like these, you're not always . . . aware of what you're doing. You just try to survive it. You go into survival mode. And you know when you're in survival mode, you might not be able to live up to, you know, your regular values/ and moral code and all . . .

Ebba Fine, but afterwards you need to own up to it. Admit what you did. That's fine. But you say you screwed up, you let everyone down and you apologise. You don't deny it happened.

Mats But didn't . . .? What are your thoughts, Tomas?

Silence.

Ebba Tomas, Mats is asking you a question, so could you please say something?

Tomas Well –

Harry (*O/S*) MUMMY! Mummy!

Tomas *looks to* **Ebba**.

Ebba Ignore him ignore he'll fall asleep.

Harry (*O/S*) Mummy!

Tomas I can't ignore my kids.

Tomas *gets up and heads to* **Harry**'s *room.*

Ebba What do I do?

Jenny He was going to explain himself then. Maybe he's still processing it.

Silence.

Ebba I'll go and check.

Mats Yeah yeah sure of course.

Once **Ebba** *has gone . . .*

Mats Jesus Christ . . .

Jenny What the hell is going on?

Mats   I don't know I don't know. We came in. I was worried about my boner,/ now this.

Jenny   You've got to say something/ she was nearly *crying* there.

Mats   I'm not – What am I gonna say? Why are you such a bloody coward? This is their marriage, I'm not getting all up in their business, they're obviously *freaking out* about this,/ I have no intention of getting involved

Jenny   She is. He's not. He's just sat there not saying anything. I thought you said he was a great guy.

Mats   He is.

Jenny   He left his kids in a *fucking* – HEEYYY!

Ebba *returns.*

Mats   Heeyyy alright. Kids OK?

Ebba   All fine, I'm just going to take my wine.

Mats   The wine! Yes,/ the wine! Don't let it get warm.

Jenny   It is *so* good this wine.

Ebba *leaves.*

Jenny   What the hell is going on?

Mats   I don't know./ I didn't know a thing about this

Jenny   Why have you brought/ me into this?

Mats   I didn't – I didn't know – I didn't know this was going on. What can I do? Text ahead 'Hey Tomas, Still on for tonight? Just checking, you haven't left your kids in any avalanches, recently have you?/ Don't want to say the wrong thing.'

Jenny   They are not in a good place.

Mats   What am I meant to do?

Jenny   They are not in a good place. Their marriage.

Mats So, should we leave? Should we go, or just stick around? We could leave a note/ I could write a note.

Jenny We can't leave now otherwise it looks like we're judging.

Mats OK, so we stay?

Jenny But we can't stay,/ *they* need to talk about this.

Mats So, what are you saying?/ We go stand on the balcony?

Jenny They need to talk they need therapy.

Meanwhile in the kids' bedroom, **Tomas** *lies in bed with* **Harry** *and* **Ebba** *looks in, their exchange is hushed.*

Ebba Is he OK?

Tomas He's a bit upset. I'd better lie with him.

Ebba Harry?

Tomas Sh shh. He's nearly asleep.

Ebba *heads over and leans in.*

Ebba He's fast asleep.

Tomas I've only just got him off.

Ebba He's sleeping.

Tomas You're going to wake him.

Ebba Come and talk Mats and Jenny are waiting.

Tomas I'll be in, in a minute. You go.

Ebba I'm not going without you.

Tomas I've just got him off.

Ebba Don't hide behind Harry.

Tomas I am looking after my son.

It's a stand-off.

Eventually **Ebba** *re-joins* **Mats** *and* **Jenny** *in the room.*

Ebba Sorry about this. Tomas. He wants to lie with Harry for a bit longer. I'm sorry. We've just struggled to talk about this, and I thought maybe with some friends/ we might be able to.

Jenny It's fine it's fine.

Mats This is why we're here.

Jenny *indicates for* **Mats** *to take the lead.*

Tomas *enters but lingers so he can eavesdrop, and no-one can see him.*

Mats I think it could be good for you both to try and see all this in a wider context and in a more forgiving light.

Ebba OK.

Mats If you look at human beings and animals, the fact is, that when we're confronted by an extremely dangerous situation, it triggers survival mode. That forces you to react now! It's . . . It's a primitive force to just escape. We all have an idea of heroes or what heroes look like. And the pressure to be a hero and do heroic things in terrible situations. All the movies where the Dad stops at nothing to be reunited with his kids. But the truth is when reality is staring you in the face, and you're afraid you're going to die you know, very few of us are heroic.

Ebba I didn't run.

Mats Just look at the ferry in Estonia. Only 137 people survived and 850 people died on board. And these people . . . they trampled on dead bodies. They knocked down children and old people. They did terrible things, just to survive. Then they had to live with what they had done. But you can't punish them for those crimes. It's human. I get it.

Ebba I can't identify with anyone who would trample on their own kids to survive.

Jenny Me neither.

Mats No . . . I mean what I mean is, I think./ What I mean is.

Ebba That's not what this is about, not to me. My problem is that my natural instinct in that moment is for my children. It has to be. They're too little to fend for themselves. I'm their mother. It's my job. It's mine and Tomas' job to protect them. But his instinct was to run away.

Tomas *hangs his head in shame.*

Mats But you need to consider everything Tomas is. Everything he's done for you; how much he loves you and the kids. He had a split-second reaction. If a drunk stormed in here and attacked you with a bottle, I'd punch him, even though I'm not a violent man I hate violence. But that's what I would do in that moment. But you don't really know what you would do. And maybe it would be different every time.

Ebba I don't know. He's just . . . I don't know.

Tomas *enters.*

Tomas It's . . . interesting when things like this happen. The differences. It shocked us, as a couple that we could have such different. That our perceptions of the situation could be so different. And I didn't realize that you saw it that way. You didn't tell me at the time. So, I carried on thinking we had the same take on things. Now I know we clearly don't.

Ebba Then share your version with us Tomas?

Pause.

Everyone's waiting.

Tomas But it's . . . It's not really relevant how I perceived it. Obviously for you, it was really dramatic. But for me . . .

Jenny *sits by* **Ebba** *to comfort her as she takes this blow.*

Mats So you're not on board with the version Ebba just told us?

Tomas No, I'm not. Not at all.

Mats No?

Tomas No. I really don't share her version of events. I don't. You are entitled to your own point of view Ebba. But I don't share it because it did, not, happen. It didn't happen and I'm sorry, but I won't be characterised this way in front of my friends, or the kids or anyone for that matter. At some point I have to stand up for myself and defend my character. What you are saying, categorically, did, not happen.

Tomas *takes a drink.*

Mats OK, well that makes it all/ a bit more

Ebba We've got it all on film.

Beat.

It's on your phone. Let's just watch it. See who's telling the truth. Would you like to see it?

Jenny *and* **Mats** *nod.*

Jenny Ye/ ah.

Mats Ye/ ah.

Jenny Ab/ solutely.

Mats Let's take/ a look yeah.

Tomas I think we've had enough of this.

Ebba No.

Tomas I really . . . don't see what this/ is going to achieve at this point.

Ebba I'll go get your phone.

Ebba *leaves to fetch* **Tomas**' *phone.*

Long silence.

Tomas Obviously, it *was* scary . . . / I'm not saying it wasn't scary.

Mats Yeah, yeah of course./ I understand.

Ebba *arrives with the phone.*

Tomas But we're all here. Harry and Vera are OK and at the end of the/ day, that's what's.

Ebba What's your pin code?

Tomas That's what's important.

Ebba What's your pin code?

Tomas This is a bit much Ebba./ Can we just

Ebba I'd like you to see this. To finish this . . . I really/ need to do this. All right?

Tomas It might upset you again. It might upset everyone this was a/ very triggering

Ebba Pin code? Pin code.

Tomas My birthday.

Ebba *punches in his pin code.*

Tomas OK. Go ahead go ahead.

Ebba Good. Are you all going to look . . .?

Mats *and* **Jenny** *scrabble around* **Ebba**. *The video plays and* **Tomas** *watches them watching his phone.*

Ebba: Here . . . Here it comes . . . That's us at the table . . .

Harry *and* **Vera**'s *screams can be heard on the video.*

Ebba You're filming, right? You can see he's filming because we're all in shot. And then . . . here he runs away.

Beat.

You can clearly see someone running away here with the camera.

Beat.

And I think.

Ebba *winds the video back.*

Yep. That's him screaming.

Ebba *winds the video back.*

Yeah. That's definitely him screaming.

Ebba *winds the video back.*

Running. And screaming.

She winds the video again.

Running and screaming away from us, as the avalanche comes.

Beat.

Do you agree *now* that you ran away from the table?

Tomas I agree, that it looks like, I'm running.

Ebba It looks like you're running because you *were* running. Weren't you?

Silence.

Mats Tomas maybe, maybe you were thinking . . . In an avalanche situation, it's pretty tricky to get out from under the snow . . . So maybe you planned to go back and dig them out?

Just like when cabin pressure drops in an aeroplane, they say that parents should put their masks on first before you put one on their kids. It feels counter-intuitive to protect yourself first. But maybe that's what you had in your mind So you actually did the right thing for a situation like this.

Beat.

That was what you were thinking, right? Wasn't it? When you were running.

Ebba And screaming. Running and screaming.

Lights down.

Scene Thirteen

Hotel Corridor

Ebba Thanks for coming.

Mats Thanks for a great/ night!

Jenny Great/ night!

Ebba Sorry if it was a bit . . .

Mats No!

Jenny No it was great!

Ebba OK. See you tomorrow.

Ebba *goes.*

Mats Holy shit . . .

Jenny OhmyGod. What the hell?

Mats I know right.

Jenny What was *that*?

Mats I know. Oh My God.

Jenny Poor Ebba.

Mats Well, yeah.

Jenny She's completely torn up by it.

Mats Yeah.

Beat.

And Tomas too.

Jenny Well.

Mats The both of them. It's really sad.

Jenny It is really sad.

Mats I know.

Jenny I feel so sorry for her. Did you see her face?

Mats Mm . . . So sad.

Jenny I mean I wonder how I would react if you did that to me?

Mats Pff . . . Right.

Jenny You might have run too, left your kids behind. You don't know. No one can be sure of anything like that.

Mats Well, you might have run as well.

Jenny But we're talking about you and Tomas.

Mats Why?/ Don't put me in the. . .

They silence themselves as:

A young **Man** *stripped to the waist with sunglasses and antlers on, walks between them.*

Antler **Man** *offers* **Mats** *a fist bump and* **Mats** *finds himself fist bumping.*

Jenny I think I would react just like Ebba. I wouldn't be able to run.

Mats And I would?

Jenny I think you could yeah.

Mats Whoa whoa whoa what are you saying here what are we saying here?

Mats *refuses to get in the lift.*

Jenny (*laughing*) Don't get upset. I'm just . . .

Mats What am I meant to do with that?/ Just casually . . .

Jenny Don't make this about you.

Mats Of course it's about me, you just said that I'd leave you and the kids in the avalanche.

Jenny We don't have kids.

Mats I do.

Beat.

You're having a go at me, for something Tomas has done.

Mats *puts his hand on the lift to stop it closing.*

Jenny I'm just saying. You're more capable of running away than I am.

Mats Why?

Jenny Because you're a man and I'm a woman.

Silence.

Mats So this isn't about me per se. It's about men/ and women.

Jenny I don't know I haven't thought about it until tonight/ and all that in there.

Mats It's about men and women. And you think there's a difference. All men are like this. And all women are like that./ That's interesting. That's very interesting.

Jenny No . . . I mean . . . I'm not . . . Well,/ like this . . . what I mean is.

Mats No it's really interesting. That you're happy to generalise about an entire *gender*!

The **Cleaner** *walks past, really slowly.*

Mats Good night.

Jenny Good night.

They wait.

And wait.

And wait – maybe the **Cleaner** *empties a bin.*

Jenny *and* **Mats** *stand in agonising silence until he eventually leaves.*

Jenny What I mean is. I don't mean all men and women are like one way or another you can't generalise like that about people.

Mats Thank you. We can agree on that.

Mats *offers a hand to shake.*

Jenny But you and Tomas are the same kind of man.

Mats *drops the hand.*

Mats What does that mean? We're skiing buddies. Couple of days hanging out once a year doesn't mean we're the same person.

Jenny I know. I'm not . . .

Mats I don't even know/ what car he drives.

Jenny I'm not saying that. I'm just saying . . . Like. You're both made of the same ideas. I don't know, if you compare the two of you with, say, Filip . . . Filip would *never* run away, *never* abandon/ his family like that. Never.

Mats What? Filip, who is *twenty-one* and still living with his parents, and who *doesn't* have any kids, he would defend his family, but I, an actual father wouldn't?

Jenny Hypothetically speaking yes. (*Off* **Mats**.) There's a huge difference between your generation and ours! That's what I'm trying to say. Like there's a big difference between you and your father./ You take on more responsibility for your kids than his generation did.

Mats So, so hypothetically, you think it's more probable that Filip, a skinny little app designer, would protect his family rather than me because I was born in the seventies?

Jenny *thinks this is a fair assessment.*

Mats I have *always* taken care of my family. I have *always* made sure that they were very well taken care of. OK? I take care of my kids.

Jenny So, where are they now?

Mats You know that.

Jenny And your ex-wife?

Mats In Oslo.

Beat.

What?

Jenny You say you do everything for them, but *she's* taking care of them right now. *You're* taking a twenty-three-year-old girl on vacation who you've been dating for six months.

Mats Is that a problem?

Jenny Not for me. But what do you think your ex-wife thinks?

Jenny steps into the lift.

Mats really doesn't want to join her.

Eventually he does.

The lift door closes.

Scene Fourteen

Hotel Room

Ebba *clears up the detritus around the room.*

Tomas *sits in the same position he was when he watched the video.*

Ebba *passes carrying some things.*

Tomas   Ebba.

Long, painful silence.

Is there any more wine?

Ebba   I'll check.

Tomas   Thanks, you.

Tomas *sits in silence.*

He turns his phone over, so the screen is no longer tormenting him.

Ebba *brings a half full bottle back and places it on the table.*

She starts to wipe down the table. **Tomas** *lifts his glass, and then the bottle.*

Tomas   Oh hang on.

Ebba   Thanks.

Tomas   No problem.

Tomas *watches* **Ebba** *wiping down. Eventually she finishes and heads to the bedroom.*

Tomas   Are you sleeping in there?

Ebba   Yes.

Tomas   I'll stay here then.

Ebba (*back turned*)   Great.

Tomas   Great. Great. Great! Great. Just great.

Tomas *pours himself a glass of wine.*

Ebba What?

Tomas Shall we talk about what just happened?

Ebba I'm not making a scene that will upset the kids.

Tomas No of course because you never upset the kids it's only me who upsets the kids.

Ebba Shut up Tomas you pathetic man.

Silence.

I have had it! Doing all the work for the both of us. Doing all the work so that there's a family here for you when you can be bothered to turn up. And when you do turn up, you abandon us and lie, I've had it. I deserve more. The kids deserve more.

Tomas OK, I made a mistake. A big mistake . . .

Ebba I'm not talking about the avalanche. That was just the thing that opened everyone's eyes to you.

Tomas Ebba, I'm sorry. I was embarrassed/ . . . but don't

Ebba I don't want to talk about it. I don't. I don't want to talk to you. I just want to get through the rest of this and see where we are when we get home. I'm not doing it here.

Tomas What do you mean 'see where we are'?

Ebba I mean, see where we are.

Tomas As a couple?

Ebba Yes. We'll see where we are when we get home.

Tomas I'm scared now.

Ebba So am I.

Pause.

Tomas Well. What are we talking/ about?

Ebba I'm not doing this here! I'm not.

Tomas But you're scaring me! I want to sort this out. We need to sort this out.

Ebba We'll talk about this when we get home.

Tomas Are you leaving me?

Lights down

Interval.

Scene Fifteen

Mats and Jenny's Room

Darkness.

Jenny *reaches out and turns on a bedside light to reveal:*

Mats *sat up in bed – wide awake staring into the darkness.*

Jenny What's the matter?

Mats Nothing.

Jenny Can you not sleep?

Mats Go back to sleep.

Jenny *tries.*

She can't. She rolls over to **Mats** *and cuddles up to him.*

Jenny Come on. Go to sleep.

Beat.

Mats I just . . . I'm just trying to figure out what I have said or done to make you think I would abandon you and our children in that situation.

Jenny Hmm?

Mats What have I done? I can't think of anything.

Jenny Is this. Is this about Tomas?

Mats No, it's about *me*. What have I said or done that would make you think I was capable of that?

Jenny Nothing. You haven't said anything. Go to sleep.

Sensing **Mats** *is not moving. She turns back to him and sees he is deeply worried – she's hurt him. She adopts a more conciliatory and subservient approach and sits up.*

Jenny Listen, you haven't said or done anything. It was just hypothetical.

Beat.

I know that you would do anything to protect your family, I really do. And I really believe you would try to protect me if anything happened.

Mats I thought, one of the things you liked about me, was that you felt safe.

Jenny I do.

Mats But . . . you said Tomas and me are the same kind of men. You had suspicions about me earlier.

Jenny I didn't. It was just . . . a bit crazy trying to understand it all that's all. But I know you'd look after me.

Mats Do you?

Jenny Yes, absolutely.

Mats Really?

Jenny Yes. Now go to sleep.

Mats Are you just saying this so you can go to sleep?

Jenny No, I mean it. I do.

Mats *looks at her, trying to see the truth.*

Jenny Are you OK now?

Mats Yeah, I'm just being silly.

Lights down.

Lights up.

Time has passed – **Mats** *is pacing.* **Jenny** *is sat on the bed with her head in her hands.*

Mats You said don't think about it. Why not think about it? Why not think about it? Do you mean; don't think about it because there's something about me/ neither of us want to address? Some deep-seated cowardice at the depths of my soul.

Jenny Pleaaaase.

Mats Something horrible. Don't think about it you said. Maybe you said that because if I think about it *too* much, I might discover something about myself that confirms what you suspect of me? Maybe that's why you said that. Is that why you said it?

Jenny No. I promise. Let's put an end to this. Please come back to bed.

Lights down.

Lights up.

More time has passed – **Jenny** *is sat on the floor.*

Mats *is stripped to the waist pouring whisky from a bottle into his mouth.*

Mats Filip! Filip for fuck's sake!

Beat.

Fucking *Filip*. He can't even drive *the twat*. He'll save you, yeah, he'll fucking save you, as long as it's *walking distance* or on a bus route. 'Don't worry kids! Don't worry! Filip is coming, he's coming to save us on his stupid long skateboard covered in *stickers*.'

Jenny   I'm guessing you're drunk and tired and now you're stuck in some mood,/ I don't know what it is, and I don't know what I can say.

Mats   Here he comes! Watch his skinny white legs push his skateboard up this mountain we're trapped on.

Jenny   You're boring now.

Mats   Oh, am I? Am I really? I'm sorry. What if I? What if I said to you, if I said to you, you're the kind of woman; 'Lots of women can't have kids and I think you're one of them.' 'You are the kind of woman who can't have kids.' 'I don't think you're female enough for that. But Merle. Now Merle, looks like a fertile heifer. She looks like the kind of woman, who could bear me a whole football team of fat babies.'

Jenny   Then I'd say, 'That's too bad!' And then I'd go to bed because you need to go to bed. OK? It's over.

Bedside lamps off.

Lights down.

Bedside lamps on.

Jenny *is curled up in a chair. Mess is strewn all over the floor.*

Mats *has his ski goggles on and long-johns on his head. He is waving a ski pole around as he speaks.*

Mats   AND I CRACKED HIM ON THE HEAD LIKE THIS! AND THEN ANOTHER LIKE THAT! AND I FELT POWERFUL. AND I TURNED TO MY MOTHER WHO WAS COVERED IN VOMIT AND I SAID: are you sleeping?

Jenny *startles.*

Jenny   No. No./ I was checking the phone . . .

Mats   You were sleeping, how could you?/ How could you?

Jenny   I promise I wasn't. I'm listening,/ I'm listening with my eyes closed.

Mats I'm pouring my heart out here, this is powerful stuff. This is a special time. I'm really getting into some stuff here. Why?

He straightens a legging from his head.

Mats Why won't you take me seriously?

Jenny I have to go to bed now.

Mats FUCK THE BED!

He throws his ski pole on the floor!

Mats STOP GOING ON ABOUT THE FUCKING BED! YOU AND THE – RIGHT! I'LL SHOW YOU THE FUCKING BED.

Mats *runs to the side of the bed and bends down to lift it up and toss it over.*

But it's really heavy.

Mats *strains.*

Mats YAAAAAAAAAAHHHHWHYSITSOHEAVY! I can't. I can't it's YAAAAAAHHHHHAAAITSATTACHED. It's attached to something. I can't, drilled to the floor.

Mats *collapses on the bed in exhaustion. He then throws all the pillows and sheets off and pulls off the bottom sheet and wraps it up into a ball and throws it.*

He manages to push the mattress a bit off the bed.

He stands atop the bed as champion – having defeated his enemy.

Mats *Now* will you listen to me?

Jenny I don't think there's anything on your mind that you haven't already said. You're going over and over and over/ the same thing.

Mats Oh this is trivial is it? My feelings, my PAIN is trivial. You can't talk to me like that I was a fat child/ this is all just some big

Jenny No. I upset you and that's important. And I want us to be good. But I also don't want to miss a day's skiing tomorrow. The mountain. We've come here for.

Beat.

Skiing? You love this mountain. You brought me here to ski. Not fight. And if you want to ski. Then. You need to sleep. Come on. Look at you. You're exhausted.

Mats I am pretty tired. Being in tune with your emotions, it's actually quite, actually quite draining you know?

Jenny Yeah I know.

Jenny *picks up the discarded bedsheet, but he points a ski pole at her.*

Mats Stop. I need to know that you trust me. It's very important to me.

Jenny I trust you. OK?

Mats Why are you smiling like that? What? Is this a joke?/ My feelings are a laughing matter?

Jenny I can't take this seriously anymore. We've been going around in circles for hours! I trust you, OK? I trust you. I trust you.

He tries to see if she's hiding something. He can't see it. She seems sincere.

Jenny Now. Could we *please* get some sleep?

Mats OK ...

Together they put the bed back together.

Mats That was intense. I really worked through some stuff there, I feel, I feel great actually.

Jenny Good I'm glad.

Mats I felt like I was really accessing *me*.

Jenny   Great. I'm glad.

The bed is re-made, **Jenny** *climbs in immediately.*

Mats   Feel like I understand myself better now.

Jenny   Goooood. Now. Go to sleep.

Jenny *turns the bedside light off.*

Darkness.

Jenny (*relieved*)   Ah . . .

Mats (*relieved*)   And now, to sleep.

Jenny   Thank God! No wonder your wife wanted a divorce.

Bedside light on.

Mats *stares at her.*

Scene Sixteen

Hotel Bathroom/Fantasy Sequence/Mountain

Movement sequence: **Tomas** *stands perfectly still, as* **Ebba**, **Vera** *and* **Harry** *brush their teeth, wash their faces, spray deodorant, brush hair. But now the taps are replaced by Gazex tubes that boom and flash as the family get dressed.*

BOOM! **Ebba**, **Vera** *and* **Harry** *take cover and* **Ebba** *protects the kids. They carry on brushing their teeth and washing their faces and then BOOM!* **Ebba**, **Vera** *and* **Harry** *take cover and* **Ebba** *protects them. They carry on their morning routines and BOOM! They take cover and* **Ebba** *protects them.* **Tomas** *watches how the family run to each other and he's outside the safety of them. He turns a tap on and steam rises like avalanche smoke . . .*

Tomas *is alone, in his ski gear, on the mountain.*

At his feet **Ebba** *is on her knees, crying and digging in the snow. She is distressed, searching for the buried children – she finds gloves/boots sticking out.*

Tomas *stares at her – this is what is haunting him now.*

Mats *arrives, and* **Tomas** *snaps out of his daydream nighmare.*

Mats Um . . . Done uh, done much before now?

Tomas Huh?

Mats Skiing. Done much.

Tomas No. A bit. Mainly with. Family.

Mats Cut loose today then?

Tomas Yeah.

Mats Great.

Tomas Yeah.

Mats OK.

Tomas OK.

Mats Um? Fancy skiing off piste today? Get away from. Everything.

Tomas Absolutely! Yeah. That would be yeah, let's get away from the . . . crowds.

Mats Yeah. Let's go. Let's go higher up.

Tomas Yeah. Let's go. Up there. Higher.

Mats Get to the top. Trek for a bit. Fancy that?

Tomas *stares at where* **Ebba** *was.*

Tomas I do yeah. Yeah.

Mats Cool.

Tomas It's so bright.

Mats Put your goggles on.

Movement sequence as **Mats** *and* **Tomas** *skilfully ski together down the slope.*

Mats So what shall we go for? We could try the couloir. It's on the right when you're at the peak. Or. I can't see anyone else. Maybe try the other side? We've got the whole mountain to ourselves pretty much, just need to choose the route. Other side looks quiet.

Tomas I'm. I'm not sure I want to ski anymore.

Mats What? Are you OK?

Tomas Yeah. No.

Mats Do you want a drink?

Tomas No.

Mats You want to head home?

Tomas No.

Beat.

Tomas Can we just, talk instead?

Mats *nearly falls down the mountain with disappointment.*

Mats Yeah. Sure. We can talk.

Long, painful silence.

What shall we talk about?

Tomas I'm not sure.

Long, painful silence.

Mats So beautiful up here.

Long, painful silence.

Something you want to talk about?

Long, painful silence.

Tomas I don't know.

Long, painful silence.

Mats You feeling all right?

Long, painful silence.

Tomas I don't know.

Mats Maybe you should try screaming?

Tomas Huh?

Mats Screaming. Seriously. I spent two years in therapy and it didn't do a bloody thing. Then one night I just screamed into a pillow for five minutes solid and felt a hell of a lot better. It's physical, something is stuck in your body and you have to get it out. I mean it. Nobody can hear you, so go for it! It's just me.

Tomas Screaming?

Mats Yeah.

Tomas Like a child?

Mats Yeah like a child.

Tomas I'm supposed to sit here and scream.

Mats On the count of three.

Tomas No,/ no way.

Mats On the count of three.

Tomas No.

Mats One,/ two

Tomas I am not doing it absolutely no

Mats Three.

HHHAHHHHAHHHHHHHHHHAHHHHHH

Tomas *screams.*

Mats Good. Now you need to really scream like you mean it.

Beat.

From the depths of your belly.

Tomas No forget it, it's stupid. I feel stupid.

Mats Come on! One, two,

Tomas No no, forget it I don't want.

Mats three. . .

Tomas AAAHAHHHHHHAAAA/
AAAAAAAAHAHHHHAAAAAHHHHHH

Mats Yes. Do it for real! TOMAS! FUCKING HELL. AGAIN!

Tomas *screams again – louder, more primal more desperate.*

Tomas AAAHHHHHHAAAAAAHHHHHHAAAHHH/
AAAAAHHHHHH Damn it!!! Fucking hell! PISS BOLLOCKS FUCK WANK SHIT! CUNTING FUCK. HELL. BOLLOCKS.

Mats Good!

Tomas *falls back in the snow.*

Mats Better.

Beat.

I feel better and I'm just standing here. Better?

Tomas I think so.

Mats It's a weight lifted off. The mind and body. It's all one thing. You literally can't fix anything these days without screaming everyone knows that. There's whole books written about it. You did some good work on yourself there.

Tomas You think?

Mats Definitely. And the swearing. That's got to be good right?

Tomas Yeah.

Mats Yeah right.

Tomas So, what now? Do we. Do we talk now?

Long silence.

Mats Yeah. Or you could scream again?

Tomas Think I'm done screaming.

Long silence.

Mats Then we should probably get pissed.

Lights down.

Scene Seventeen

Slope-side bar

Tomas *and* **Mats** *relax with a beer in deck chairs. Party people mill around, drinking, dancing and socialising.*

Mats He's just hanging around her all the time, if I go to the bar, or to the toilet, or turn around for a second he appears and is all over her, he's in love with her but she doesn't see it.

Tomas She doesn't see it.

Mats No!/ It's so obvious . . .

A **Female Skier** *approaches.*

Female Skier Hi guys. Are you having fun?

Tomas Huh?

Female Skier Are you having fun?

Tomas Yes, great day thanks. We've been/ skiing off –

Female Skier I came to tell you that my friend is standing over there . . .

Tomas Yeah?

Female Skier She thinks that you're the best-looking man in the bar.

The men laugh it off.

Tomas OK. Thank you.

Female Skier You're welcome. Have a good night.

Tomas You too.

*The **Female Skier** leaves.*

Tomas *revels in the news.*

Mats *and* **Tomas** *cheers.*

Tomas Still got it.

Mats Still got it.

Tomas Class is permanent.

Mats Form is temporary.

Tomas Amen to that. You remember that time in that bar that used to be/ called Lux or something and that girl came in and she –?

*The **Female Skier** returns.*

Female Skier Hi.

Tomas (*familiar*) Oh hi again.

Female Skier Sorry. I had to come back again. I made a mistake. She didn't, she didn't mean you. She meant someone else.

Tomas Huh?

Female Skier My friend. She didn't mean you. I got it wrong, she meant someone else. Sorry. It was my fault.

Tomas OK. Fine. Thank you.

Female Skier She pointed, and I thought she meant you. But she didn't.

Tomas Oh right.

Female Skier I'm sorry.

Tomas It's fine.

Female Skier The guy she meant is right behind you so.

Tomas OK.

Female Skier It's my fault.

Tomas Fine.

Female Skier I thought I should tell you.

Tomas Why?

Pause.

Female Skier Because. You're not the guy she liked.

Tomas Why not just let me think she meant me?

Female Skier Because I made a mistake, she meant that guy.

Tomas I know but –

Female Skier She didn't mean you.

Mats It would have been kinder to just let the mistake stand uncorrected/ and let Tomas

Female Skier She doesn't find you attractive and you might try something later.

Tomas I'm married so.

Female Skier Where is she then?

Tomas I'm just sitting here having a drink! I didn't ask for people to come up to me and tell me they don't find me attractive. Who wants that to happen?

Mats I don't. It's never happened to me,/ but still.

Female Skier I don't want it to be awkward for her, she wants to have a good time, she doesn't want you to come on to her later thinking she'd given you a green light.

Tomas She asked you to come over here again?

Female Skier Yes, she really doesn't want you to buy her a drink or.

Tomas OK.

Female Skier Ask for her number or.

Tomas OK.

Female Skier Try and talk to her or anything like that.

Tomas OK fine. Loud and clear. Thank you.

Female Skier Or look at her.

Tomas *can just about manage a hard stare.*

Female Skier She just pointed and . . . OK.

Tomas OK.

Female Skier *walks off and approaches the attractive* **Male Skier** *behind* **Tomas** *to deliver the compliment to the right man.*

Tomas What the hell?

Mats Would we have ever done that/ when we were their age?

Tomas I'm just sitting here. I haven't done *anything* and I get all this. Is she taking the piss?

Mats She's taking the piss.

Tomas She's taking the piss.

Mats She thinks we're mugs.

Tomas We are mugs if we take that.

Mats (*to the women*) Are you taking the piss?

Female Skier   No, no, no.

Tomas   You think we're funny?

Female Skier   No I wasn't it/ was just my friend pointed.

Tomas   You and your friends want to laugh at us? At me. You're taking the piss out of me, what because I'm old?

Tomas *stands to confront the women.*

Mats   Take it easy.

The attractive **Male Skier** *interrupts to diffuse the situation.*

Male Skier   Whoa whoa whoa! Calm down. Relax. Chill.

Tomas   They're taking the piss. I'm just sitting here having a drink minding my own business and she comes over and says I'm not even allowed to look at a girl.

Male Skier   Are you staring at her?

Tomas   She came onto me first for Christ's sake.

Male Skier   You need to chill out, I'm not gonna tell you again.

Tomas   Stop telling me to chill out alright.

Male Skier   Step back now or you and me are gonna have a problem.

Tomas   We already have a problem *Pierre*; your friends are taking the piss.

Male Skier   You want a problem with me we can take it/ outside.

Mats   There's no problem there's no problem. Tomas.

Male Skier   Have we got a problem?/ We can sort it out now.

Mats   There's no problem. Tomas. There's no problem. Tomas . . . Tomas.

Tomas   OK.

Male Skier   We're cool?

Pause.

Mats We're cool. Tomas.

Tomas Yeah.

Male Skier Great, well why don't you sit down? Drink your beer relax and everything will be nice.

Mats Tomas, come on, come sit down.

Male Skier Relax. Take a seat.

Tomas I'll take my seat when I want to take my seat, you go back over there and take your seat and I'll take my seat at a time of my choosing.

Tomas *makes a big show of taking his time. Maybe stretching a little, while everyone watches waiting for the situation to be defused.* **Tomas** *goes to sit, and then changes his mind, and the dusts the seat down, and then thinks about sitting down. And eventually after a final stretch sits down.*

And everyone, finally, returns to their seats.

Mats *and* **Tomas** *share a look.*

Mats 'At a time of my choosing.'

Mats *and* **Tomas** *laugh.*

Scene Eighteen

Hotel Corridor

A tired, and possibly a bit drunk, **Tomas** *is at the door of the family room.*

He checks all of his pockets. He can't find a key.

Tomas Ebba? Open up! It's me. I'm back. Can't find my – can you open up? Your phone's died. Are you in there? Can you let me in? Would be really great to talk. Hope this isn't some kind of punishment. That would be . . . that would be. Not cool.

*The **Cleaner** walks past.*

Tomas Ah! Excuse moi! Jai uh, perdu uh, key card. Ma femme has the other one and uh, elle este uh, sortie.

*The **Cleaner** takes a card and presses it against a sensor which buzzes and negative sound.*

Tomas Thank you.

He tries again – still buzzes negative.

*The **Cleaner** is confused. He tries again.*

Tomas Something wrong?

Beat.

You're trying too quick-trop uh rapide trop rapide. This is your hotel!

Tomas *takes the card and tries – it doesn't work.*

Tomas EBBA! ARE YOU IN THERE? Elle est sortie. EBBA! EBBA! She's not in there.

Tomas *is left staring at the **Cleaner**.*

Tomas I'll try l'accueil merci.

*The **Cleaner** shrugs his shoulders and takes his card and walks on.*

Tomas *is left outside the door.*

Tomas EBBA!

Lights down.

Scene Nineteen

Hotel Lobby

*Exhausted **Tomas** enters the hotel foyer.*

Receptionist Bonsoir monsieur.

Tomas Bonsoir, je'need un nouveau key card merci?

Receptionist   Oui pas de problème, what is your room number?

Tomas   247.

Receptionist   D'accord, are your key cards lost or in your room?

Tomas   Lost.

Receptionist   D'accord – I will have to programme two new keys.

Tomas   That's no problem I'll stay in the room until they get back.

Receptionist   Do you know where your wife is?

Tomas   Obviously not, because if I did, I'd just go and find them.

Receptionist   It's just, if I disable your old keys to activate new ones and your family are in the pool, or the sauna, or the spa area, or the games room, their card it no longer works. They might not be able to get out or open their lockers.

Tomas   What? That's ridiculous.

Receptionist   Can you call her?

Tomas   My phone has died can you charge my phone?

Receptionist   Désolé Monsieur. We're not allowed to charge phones here I'm sorry.

Tomas   Do you have a charger I can borrow then?

Receptionist   We're not allowed to lend chargers to guests.

Tomas   Why not?

Receptionist   They steal them.

Tomas   So what am I supposed to do?

A magnificently French shrug.

Receptionist You could pay extra for a third key.

Tomas Fine give me an extra key.

Receptionist There is a charge.

Tomas Fine whatever.

Receptionist Alors. Cent dix, that'll be one hundred and ten Euro. Would you like to pay by card?

Tomas A hundred and ten Euros? It's a piece of plastic.

Receptionist Je sais monsieur. It is company policy.

Tomas I'm not paying a hundred and ten Euros.

Receptionist Désolé monsieur this is company policy.

Tomas And this has never happened before?

Receptionist Oui, this is why we give two keys. One key and one spare.

Tomas And you've never had families doing different things and someone loses a key? No-one loses anything and everyone does everything together? All the time? This is the resort where everyone's just perfect? 'We don't need another key we're perfect? We never lose anything and besides we're always together!' No-one ever argues, no-one ever needs any space, no-one ever needs to go up onto the mountain and scream into the abyss because of what their life has become?

Receptionist I'm on eight Euros an hour.

Tomas Which way's the sauna?

Tomas *puts his gloves back on and heads out.*

Scene Twenty

The Mountain

Movement sequence as **Tomas** *trudges around going from building to building – everywhere he looks there are happy families!*

Gazex tubes boom throughout this sequence as **Tomas** *falls into a happy-family nightmare!*

Tomas   ALLEZ!

Happy couples! Kissing couples!

Tomas   LASSIE MOI UHH PASSER!

Tomas *is buffeted back and forth by the happy families.*

Tomas   GET OUT OF MY BLOODY WAY!

Even the **Cleaner** *walks past with his arms around someone!*

Tomas *falls and he is face to face . . . with a Gazex tube!*

Tomas   AAAHHHHHHA!!!

He gets up and runs and is swept along with . . . A HUGE crowd of drunk, stripped-to-the-waist stag-doers charging the stage, screaming and shouting with the **Man** *stripped to the waist wearing sunglasses and antlers from earlier. They swamp* **Tomas** (*maybe they pick him up and carry him?*) *past a sign saying 'Sauna'.*

Scene Twenty-One

Sauna

The macho party of drunk stag-doers are now tightly packed like sardines in a steaming sauna with **Tomas** *in the middle and they SCREAM, SCREAM and SCREAM. Some of them hold Gazex tubes aloft as trophies they have broken and stolen!*

And then the lights come up and they stop screaming – **Tomas** *is bemused he looks around – baffled.*

Lights go down – SCREAM! SCREAM! SCREAM! – **Tomas** *startles!*

Lights come up and they stop – **Tomas** *looks around – why are they doing this?*

Lights go down – SCREAM! SCREAM! SCREAM!

Tomas *SCREAMS!*

Scene Twenty-Two

Hotel Corridor

Ebba (*on phone*) Yes, I'll check what time we land. I was thinking . . . would it be OK, if I came to stay with you for a few days. Everything's fine, I just need a few days . . .

A harassed **Tomas** *arrives from the other end.*

Tomas Where have you been?

Ebba Oh Tomas is here.

Tomas I've been searching for you all over!

Tomas Who's that?

Ebba It's Mum. Everything's fine, the dog's fine. The kids are in there.

Ebba *indicates for* **Tomas** *to head into the room.*

Tomas *doesn't.*

Ebba *indicates again.*

Tomas *waits, encroaching on her privacy.* **Ebba** *steps away from him.*

She loses her nerve.

Ebba (*on the phone, changing tack*) Yeah. So thanks for that. Yeah everything's fine I'd better go. Yes OK, love you. Love you.

Tomas *goes to* **Ebba** *and tries to hug her but* **Ebba** *moves away quickly.*

Ebba Bye OK, bye.

Tomas *manages to get his arm around* **Ebba**.

Ebba Stop it.

Tomas Stop what?

Ebba Stop this! All of it! You.

Tomas Me?

Ebba Yes you.

Tomas What does that mean?

Beat.

WHAT DOES THAT MEAN?

Ebba You know what I mean.

Harry *and* **Vera** *appear in the corridor.*

Ebba It's OK/ kids.

Vera Mum?/ Is he?

Ebba It's OK/ go back into the room.

Vera Are you, OK?

Ebba Yes./ I'm fine.

Tomas She's fine.

Vera Why is he shouting/ at you?

Tomas I wasn't shouting.

Vera You were.

Tomas I raised/ my (voice)

Harry You sounded/ angry.

Tomas Go back/ inside please.

Vera   What's he angry about?

Tomas   I wasn't/ angry.

Ebba   Daddy's angry with himself and he thinks he can take it out on me.

Everyone looks to **Tomas**.

Tomas   Well . . . Look can I talk to Mummy/ in private please?

Harry   No you can't shout at her.

Tomas   I'm not/ going to. I promise.

Harry   No you're gonna shout at her again.

Tomas   Just let me . . . let me talk to her.

Vera   No we're not going anywhere.

Harry   We're not leaving her.

Vera *and* **Harry** *go to* **Ebba**.

Tomas   Come on I'm not going to do anything! OK, I'm sorry. I'm sorry. I raised my voice. Ebba here you are. I'm sorry. Forgive me everyone forgive me now can I just please, have a conversation with my wife, in privacy. Thank you. Just give us some privacy.

Harry   No!

Tomas   I'm not asking you I'm telling you, leave us alone.

Vera   We're not leaving you alone with Mum.

Tomas   GET IN THE ROOM.

Ebba   Don't shout at them.

Vera   We're not going in the room!

Tomas   WHY NOT?

Vera   BECAUSE WE DON'T TRUST YOU.

Tomas's *shoulders sink.*

He looks to **Ebba** *and to the kids.*

Defeated, he walks further down the corridor and then slumps down against a wall.

Long pause.

Ebba Kids, actually let me talk to Daddy alone, we need to talk about some grown-up things in private OK? It's OK. I'm OK. I'll be in, in a minute. OK? In you go. In you go.

Beat.

I'll be fine. I promise. In you go. I just need to speak to Daddy.

Vera Are you sure?

Ebba I'm sure. In you go.

Harry We'll be listening.

Ebba Go and look at your iPad.

Vera Don't be shouting, it's embarrassing.

Ebba We won't shout I promise.

Harry *and* **Vera** *head back into the room.* **Ebba** *turns to* **Tomas** *who has slumped on the floor with his head in his hands, crying.*

Ebba *watches* **Tomas** *for a while.*

Ebba *approaches* **Tomas** *who is crying into his hands.*

Ebba You're just pretending.

Tomas What?

Ebba You're not crying for real. Hello? You're not crying.

Tomas *shows his face.*

Tomas OK, maybe I'm not.

Ebba *walks away.*

Tomas But what should I do? I'm trying to get some sympathy here. I'm trying to communicate here with you I'm trying to be honest.

Ebba Then try! For once in your life try Tomas.

Tomas *searches for the words but they don't come.* **Ebba** *turns to walk away.*

Tomas Ebba, Ebba . . . Come here. Ebba!

Ebba No.

Tomas Ebba please! OK. OK I'll try I'll try.

Ebba *stops.*

Tonas I get it.

Ebba Get what?

Tomas That . . . you're . . . I get it.

Ebba Get *what* Tomas?

Tomas I get, that you're disappointed in the person I've become.

Beat.

You don't have to say it. I see it in your eyes. I hear it in your voice. The way you are with me. I get it.

Beat.

You're disappointed.

Ebba Stop making it my fault. This is not what the problem is.

Tomas OK! I'm disappointed! I'm disappointed.

Beat.

In who I am.

Beat.

The person I've become.

Beat.

That person . . . If I think of him as another person then . . .

Beat.

I can say.

Beat.

I, hate him. I do, I hate him. And.

Beat.

I can't, forgive him.

Beat.

In fact I don't want to forgive him because he doesn't deserve it.

Beat.

He doesn't. So I don't really know what to do.

Ebba OK.

Tomas OK.

Ebba OK.

Tomas Yeah.

Ebba Yeah.

Tomas And he's done other stuff before this too that I hate.

Ebba Like what?

Tomas He lies. He's selfish. He avoids responsibility. He covers up mistakes, blames it on colleagues. He's just so detestable.

Beat.

He cheats at games. Even when he plays with the kids. There are no limits to his selfishness. You name it. He volunteers for work trips tells you he has no choice but he does it because he just wants a night away. He's jealous.

Ebba What could you be possibly jealous of?

Tomas Attention. Of how much attention you give the kids. He doesn't really know who his kids are. He's pathetic.

Beat.

So pathetic. I can't live with him any longer, I don't know how you've managed so long. But I can't live with him any longer and I don't want to. I don't want to live like this anymore! I'm sick of it!

Ebba Tomas.

Tomas I'm so ashamed. I don't deserve any of you. I don't. I don't deserve you and I don't deserve the kids.

Tomas *sobs real tears now.*

They're right not to trust me.

Beat.

I don't trust me either.

Ebba Tomas.

Tomas I hate myself.

Tomas *cries louder.*

This mountain!

Beat.

It was supposed to impress you.

Beat.

Ebba Please, let's go inside.

Tomas It's taken everything.

Tomas' *cries become hysterical.*

A neighbour opens a door to see what's going on? **Ebba** *smiles awkwardly.*

Several neighbours open their doors in various stages of undress to see what's going on.

The **Cleaner** *appears in the lift, surveys the scene, and presses the button to close the doors.*

Ebba Come on. Please.

Tomas *is wailing.*

Another neighbour opens the door, **Ebba** *is humiliated.*

Ebba Tomas! Now! Get up.

But **Tomas** *has slumped on the floor.*

Ebba Tomas! Let's go inside. Tomas. Tomas! Tomas shut the fuck up now!

Ebba *tries another tack and soothes* **Tomas**.

Ebba Come on . . .

Ebba *picks him up, but she can't open the door because she doesn't have a key, she must knock it.* **Tomas** *is weeping.* **Ebba** *is banging on the door.*

Ebba Vera! Open the door! Vera! Open! VERA OPEN THE FUCKING DOOR.

Vera *opens the door.*

Harry I said no shouting.

Ebba I know, I know I'm sorry sweetie.

They walk into the hotel room.

Scene Twenty-Three

Hotel Room

Ebba *carries* **Tomas** *in.*

Vera   What's the matter with him?

Tomas *is wandering around and crying.*

Ebba   Tomas can you just sit down?

Tomas *slumps onto the floor pathetically.*

Harry   What happened?

Ebba   Tomas. You need to, pull yourself together. Look at me. Look at me.

Look at me. Breathe. Breathe. Tomas, please . . . Breathe. Tomas, you're upsetting the kids.

He can't stop crying.

Ebba   Tomas, please calm down.

Harry *approaches* **Tomas**.

Harry   Daddy? (*Worried.*) Daddy!

Ebba   Don't worry, Harry. Daddy's just a bit sad. He'll be fine.

Harry   Why? What's happened?

Ebba   Everything will be fine.

Vera   What's the matter, Daddy?! Have you told him you're divorcing him?

Ebba   What no?

Vera   What's happening? Daddy!/ Please! What's the matter Daddy?

Ebba   I haven't done anything!/ He's just sad. It'll pass.

Vera Daddy please. It's OK. Daddy. We're here. We love you. It's OK. It's OK. Don't cry.

Vera *hugs* **Tomas** *and cries with him.* **Tomas** *can just about manage to put his arm around* **Vera**.

Harry Daddy?

Harry *joins them and* **Tomas** *wraps his arms around his children.*

Harry I love you Daddy. Don't cry. It's OK.

Vera Daddy please . . .

The three of them cry together and **Ebba** *is traumatised by the pain her family is in.*

Vera Mum! Come here. Mum, come here and hug Dad and show him you still love him. Come here, Mum. SHOW HIM!

Ebba *startles.*

Vera Come here now and hug Dad.

But **Ebba** *can't do it – she's too shocked at what her family is going through.*

Vera You have to do something!

Ebba I know. I know.

Vera *goes back to hugging* **Tomas**.

Ebba *stands apart from them watching her worst nightmare and feeling responsible.*

Lights down.

Scene Twenty-Four

The Mountain

Ebba *leads the whole family in ski gear and they shuffle onto the mountain. No-one wants to be here except* **Ebba**. *The wind is strong and noisy, visibility is poor. They are surrounded by white.*

Ebba Right it's our last day! Our last chance to ski the mountain let's make sure it's a good one. I think we can try a red run, and I think someone is ready for poles!

Harry Oh yes finally!

Ebba So come on let's get up there before it gets too cold.

Tomas Visibility isn't great Ebba.

Vera Yeah Mum is this safe?

Ebba The run's marked out we just need to stick together.

Harry We can't see anything.

Ebba It'll be fine. Tomas you go first, Harry and Vera follow Dad and I'll come at the rear. It'll be fine, stay close where you see each other. If Dad stops I want you all to stop up mountain of Dad is that clear?

Harry OK.

Vera OK.

Ebba Tomas?

Tomas Fine.

The family set off reluctantly.

Ebba Let's go.

They set off.

They ski down slowly.

Ebba Everybody OK?

Harry Yeah.

Vera Yeah!

Ebba Tomas?

Tomas OK. If you can't see, just follow the sounds.

They ski down it's really foggy.

Tomas *pulls up, followed by* **Vera** *and then* **Harry**.

Tomas Let's wait for Mum.

She doesn't appear.

Tomas Ebba? (*Shouting.*) Ebba? Ebba? Ebba? Ebba?

Nothing.

Vera Mum?

Tomas Ebba, can you hear me? Are you there?

A faint voice.

Tomas What?

Ebba (*in the distance*) Help!

Vera She said help! MUM!

Harry MUM!

Tomas OK OK. You wait here. Don't move. If you hear me calling your name call back so I can find you. Stay here. Stay together I'll go find her.

Vera Dad I'm scared.

Tomas It's fine, she'll be fine. I'll find her. Look after Harry.

Tomas *leaves.*

Tomas I'm coming, Ebba!

Tomas *runs back up the mountain.*

Tomas I'm coming don't move! I'm coming! Just keep calling out.

Ebba Tomas!

Tomas *eventually finds* **Ebba** *sat in the snow, perfectly happy.*

Tomas Are you OK?

Ebba I'm fine.

Tomas What happened?

Ebba You need to save me.

Tomas What's happened?

Ebba Nothing, but the kids need to see you save me and then everything will be fine.

Tomas *hesitates.*

Ebba What?

Tomas But. I thought all of that . . . you know.

Ebba I can't have another night like last night. So save me. And everything will get back to normal. Come on. Pick me up.

Tomas *is not sure what to do.*

Ebba They're gonna be scared.

Tomas *jolts into action and carries* **Ebba** *down hill.*

Harry He's been gone a long time.

Vera Just wait.

They wait some more.

Harry But how does he know where we are?

They wait some more.

Vera Dad?

Harry Daddy!

Vera DAAAAAAD!/ DAAAAAAAD!

Harry Daddy? Daddy . . . Daddy! Daddy? Daddy?

Tomas (*O/S*)   Harry!

Harry   Daddy!

Tomas (*O/S*)   Vera . . .

Tomas *emerges carrying* **Ebba** *down the mountain – the HERO.*

Vera   Mum! What happened?

Ebba   I think I twisted my knee. Your dad saved me.

Tomas   Everyone's safe now.

Harry   I was so scared we couldn't see you and we were shouting/ and it was just me and Vera and we couldn't see anything.

Ebba   Well lucky Dad could find me and carry me otherwise I don't know how long I would have been up there. Thank you Tomas.

Tomas   No problem.

Harry *hugs his dad.*

Tomas   Everyone's, everyone's safe now.

Vera *hugs* **Tomas**.

Ebba *smiles at* **Tomas** *but* **Tomas** *can't quite enjoy the moment.*

Ebba   Right I think Dad's right, it is a bit dangerous up here, let's go home and have some hot chocolates.

Vera   Yes!

Harry   Yes!

Ebba   I'm going in the front this time!

Ebba *skis off, followed by* **Harry** *and* **Vera**.

Tomas *looks up the mountain, he's got what he wants, but it feels hollow.*

He follows them off the mountain.

Lights down.

Scene Twenty-Five

Hotel Room

Tomas *lies on the sofa looking at his phone.*

Vera *is looking at her iPad.* **Harry** *is playing on his own and* **Ebba** *is packing the suitcases on her own. She looks at* **Tomas**.

Ebba Well this has been great. Hasn't it?

Mumbles of agreement.

Have you two thanked your father for the holiday? It's down to him we're able to afford things like this. Nice holidays.

Beat.

Because he works so hard. So can I hear some thank yous?

Vera Thank you Dad.

Harry Thanks Dad.

Ebba Tomas?

Tomas Hm?

Ebba The kids are saying thank you for the holiday.

Tomas You're welcome.

Ebba Your daddy works very hard. We're very lucky. Aren't we? We are.

Tomas OK.

Tomas *gets up but doesn't quite know where to go.*

Ebba If anyone wants to lend a hand here I won't argue.

Nothing.

Anyone?

Beat.

Tomas?

Tomas Hmm?

Ebba Can you help please? We have a flight to catch.

Tomas *slowly heads over to the suitcases. He makes a half hearted attempt to help,* **Ebba** *watches him like a hawk. He has no idea what he should be doing. After a few beats he looks at his phone again.*

Ebba Tomas.

Tomas *puts his phone away and tries packing again. It's slow and aimless.*

Ebba Kids, time to pack.

Nothing from the kids.

Ebba Right kids. Vera, stop that. Harry get your case. Let's everyone do their bit now, so we can check out on time. Come on. Vera. Harry. Teamwork. Work as a team.

Vera *doesn't flinch,* **Harry** *is wandering around.*

Ebba I am not doing all this for you, you're old enough/ to pack your own things. Vera!

Harry I'm looking for my sunglasses/ I want to wear them on the coach

Ebba Vera.

Vera In a minute.

Ebba Not in a minute/ Vera, now.

Vera I'm going to do it,/ I just haven't chosen what I'm wearing yet.

Ebba Vera. VERA!

Vera DON'T SHOUT AT ME.

Ebba JUST PUT YOUR STUFF IN THE CASE.

Vera I HAVEN'T CHOSEN WHAT TO WEAR YET.

Ebba What you're wearing is fine pack your case and put it by the door!

Vera YOU KNOW ONCE IT'S FULL I CAN'T LIFT IT.

Ebba Well, Dad will lift the case for you, won't you Tomas?

Tomas Of course.

Ebba Get on with packing please.

Vera Ok fine.

Ebba Good girl.

Vera *starts packing.*

Ebba And don't ever worry about lifting stuff Vera.

Beat.

We've got Dad. He's big and strong.

Tomas' *heart sinks,* **Ebba** *sees this.*

Ebba What?

Tomas Nothing.

Vera *is shoving things into the suitcase.*

Ebba I'm just saying you'll do it. What?

Tomas I don't/ know.

Harry Has anyone seen my sunglasses?

Ebba Harry/ just look! (*To* **Tomas**.) What?

Vera There. Packed. Happy now? Ready for a big strong man!

Ebba Don't speak/ to your father like that.

Tomas They can see what you're doing . . .

Ebba Apologise to your father.

Vera What?

Ebba   Apologise. Now.

Vera   It was a joke. I was joking.

Ebba   Apologise.

Vera   I'm sorry.

Ebba   Normal voice.

Vera   I'm sorry.

Ebba   Now, give him a hug.

Vera   Seriously?

Tomas   Ebba.

Ebba   Hug your father.

Huffing, **Vera** *goes towards* **Tomas***, but before she can get there.*

Tomas   Ughh actually my phone's ringing I've got to take it.

Tomas *pulls his phone out and heads for the door.*

Tomas   Hello?

Ebba *does not buy it . . . but* **Tomas** *is gone.*

Once he's out of the room **Tomas** *drops the deceit and is alone, but for once it's comforting.*

Scene Twenty-Six

The Lift

With their suitcases, the family head along the corridor.

Ebba   Can we take the stairs?

Tomas   With all this? Come on get in.

Tomas *presses the lift button.* **Ebba** *is anxious.*

Tomas *presses the lift doors again. The doors open and standing there are several other guests including* **Charlotte** *and* **Jenny** *and* **Mats** *with their luggage.*

Mats   Hey!

Jenny   Hey.

Tomas   Hi. Hi.

Charlotte   Hello.

Tomas   Come on. In you go. We can do it. Sorry. Sorry. In there. Put your hands down.

Tomas *ushers in the kids – it's a squeeze.*

Ebba *is reluctant.*

Ebba   I'll take the stairs it's too tight.

Vera   Mum, there's room.

Tomas   Yeah come on, it's fine.

Against her better judgement, **Ebba** *squeezes into the lift.*

The doors close.

Tomas   Ground floor please.

Mats   Alright.

Mats *presses the button.*

Nothing.

Mats *presses the button again.*

The lift starts to move.

MECHANICAL GROANS!

The lift judders!

Jenny   What was that?

MECHANICAL GROANS, AND THE SOUND OF METAL SHEARING, OR TEARING.

Ebba   What the hell was that?/ What was that noise? What was that?

Tomas   It's fine it's fine. It'll be something it's fine.

Everyone is looking up.

The lift jolts again and everyone screams!

Ebba   We have/ to get out we have to get out!

Jenny   Press the button/ Press the button!

Vera   Which/ one! I can't see it!

Mats   The/ alarm press the alarm.

Ebba   We have to get out/ we have to get out!

Charlotte   Whoa! Relax relax./ I'm sure it's fine.

Harry   I'm scared!

Tomas   It'll be OK/ it'll be OK.

Ebba   We have/ to get out now!

Tomas   Ebba, breath it's OK, we're OK . . .

Jenny   We have/ to ring someone now!

Tomas   Everyone calm/ down, calm down!

DEATHLY MECHANICAL SCREECHING!

Harry   Mum!

Vera   Mum what are you doing?

Ebba   LET ME OUT!/ I'VE GOT TO GET OUT I'VE GOT TO GET OUT!

Tomas   Eb/ ba!

Harry   MU/ MMY! MUMMY!

Vera   MUM!

Ebba *goes to the doors and with her bare hands, pulls the doors apart.*

Ebba *manages to prise the doors open just enough to climb out. She pulls herself up onto the floor of the Reception and runs away from the lift.*

Jenny Get out before the doors close!

In the lift there is a surge of people trying to get out.

Mats Whoa whoa whoa! Everyone back up. We're all getting out of here, but we're going to do it calmly and safely, women and children out first. Kids! Nice and calm.

Tomas *and* **Mats** *help the children out and then all the guests before climbing out of it themselves.*

Jenny Are you OK?

Ebba *shakes her head.*

Ebba We could have died! That thing's a death-trap. We need to sue them!

Jenny You did the right thing. It was a good thing, getting out like that.

Ebba *runs to* **Harry** *and* **Vera** *and scoops them up.*

Vera Are you OK?

Tomas Everyone's fine.

Ebba I'm so sorry, you know what I'm like in small spaces I just panicked but I want you to know you are the most precious things in Mummy's life and I love you so much, I just panicked, I'm so sorry. Can you forgive me?

Tomas *waits with bated breath.*

Harry It's OK.

Vera It's fine, we know/ you get claustrophobic.

Tomas *watches on – processing.*

Ebba Oh thank you, you two are the most amazing kids any Mum could ever wish for I love you so much.

Ebba, **Harry** *and* **Vera** *hug each other tightly and* **Tomas** *stands outside of them, witnessing this honesty and vulnerability.*

Ebba *lets the kids go.*

Ebba (*to* **Tomas**)   I am so sorry.

Tomas   No I'm sorry.

Beat.

It's my fault I shouldn't have made you get in there. I know, how scary that must have been for you.

Ebba *hugs* **Tomas** *involuntarily.*

It takes them both by surprise, **Tomas** *returns the hug.*

It's the most affection they've shown each other all week. They needed it.

Tomas   We're all safe now.

Ebba *goes back to the kids.*

Ebba   It's all I could do, (*kissing the kids*) I'm sorry Mummy's so pathetic.

Vera   It's fine.

Harry   It's fine.

Mats   A manager's coming they asked us to wait everyone cool with that? Is that OK with everyone?

Everyone nods in understanding.

Tomas *looks at* **Ebba** *holding* **Harry** *and* **Vera** *tightly.*

Tomas   I'm gonna . . . step out . . .

Ebba *knows what this means, she nods approval.*

Scene Twenty-Seven

Outside the hotel

Tomas *steps out and stares at the mountain and he gets a cigarette out, but he's lost his light.*

He sees the **Cleaner** *smoking.*

Tomas   Avez-vous du feu? Ah thank you.

Beat.

Tomas *indicates the mountain.*

Skiez-vous?

Cleaner (*gets up and leaves*)   Non. Je bois trop.

Tomas   Ah . . .

Tomas turns and sees **Harry** *staring at him.*

Harry   Do you smoke?

Tomas   No. no . . .

Tomas *tries hiding the cigarette.*

Harry   What's that then?

Beat.

Tomas   It's . . . um . . . ugh . . . well . . .

Tomas *sees his son – he's not an idiot.*

Actually, Harry, ask me again.

Harry   Do you smoke?

Tomas   Yes.

Beat.

I'm trying to quit. And I'm. I'm finding it, hard. Really hard at the moment. But. You know. I'm gonna really try to stop when we get back home. Is that OK?

Harry   I don't want you to die.

Tomas   I know. I know. Me too I don't want to die either.

Beat.

I'm sorry.

Beat.

It's a stupid habit and I'm . . . I hide it from you because, well because I'm ashamed. When we get home I'm going to really try hard to quit.

Harry   OK.

Tomas   OK. Come here.

Harry *gives him a hug and then he runs around in the snow.*

Tomas *looks at his cigarette – might as well finish it. He enjoys smoking and watching* **Harry** *playing.*

Vera *and* **Ebba** *come out.*

Harry   Dad smokes.

Vera   I know.

Tomas   W/ hat?

Harry   He's going to quit when we get home.

Tomas   You knew? For how long.

Vera *shrugs.*

Tomas   Well . . . when we get back . . . I'm going to quit I promise. Vera.

Vera   OK.

Tomas   I promise.

Vera   OK.

Vera *joins* **Harry** *playing with the snow.*

Tomas *looks to* **Ebba**, *a new way of being with the family has been found.*

Tomas *turns to the mountain and blows smoke towards it.*

The End.

Teh Internet Is Serious Business

Teh Internet Is Serious Business was first performed at the Royal Court, London, in September 2014.

Teh Internet Is Serious Business *is a catchphrase used sarcastically to mock another person's serious tone or demeanour during an online discussion. This is commonly used to make fun of someone engaging in a heated and/or immature Internet conversation (i.e. politics, conspiracy theories and other similar topics), especially on sites that allow user-to-user interaction such as YouTube, Facebook and Twitter.*

www.knowyourmeme.com

Man is least himself when he talks in his own person.
Give him a mask and he'll tell you the truth.

– Oscar Wilde

Nothing is ever the same as they said it was.
It's what I've never seen before that I recognise.

– Diane Arbus

If I could just make it stop,
I could tell the whole world, to get out of the way

– Low

Characters

Topiary/Jake Davis – *Social media personality, 17*
Tflow/Mustafa Al-Bassam – *Hacker/coder, 15*
Kayla/Ryan Ackroyd – *Reverse engineer, 16/24*
Sabu/Hector Monsegur – *Root hacker, 20s*
AVUnit – *Anonymous hacker still at large*
PwnSauce/Darren Martyn – *Hacker, 19*
Mum – *Topiary's Mum, 40*
Emily Sinclair – *Solicitor*
Lucy O'Halloran – *Solicitor*
Pedobear – *Loveably cuddly bear who is also a paedophile*
Advice Dog – *Friendly dog who gives horrific advice*
Sad Storm Trooper – *Depressed storm trooper from Star Wars universe*
Grumpy Cat – *A grumpy lolcat*
Anxiety Cat – *An anxious lolcat*
Y U No Guy – *Illustrated meme character who asks stupid questions*
Socially Awkward Penguin – *Illustrated meme character who is a socially awkward penguin*
Condescending Willy Wonka – *Condescending character from Roald Dahl's Charlie and the Chocolate Factory*
Mary Darcy – *Fox Broadcasting employee*
Jeff Nevin – *Account manager for Fox*
Tom Cruise – *Film star and Scientologist, 50s*
Piratebay – *Website*
Hollywood 1 & 2 – *Entertainment industry*
Ryan Cleary – *Hacker, 18*
Teacher – *Schoolteacher in Mustafa's school*
FBI Officer – *Agent for the Federal Bureau of Investigations*
Wingding – *Louisa Anderson, social engineer/journalist, 30s*
Tuxedo/Gregg Housh – *Hacker, 20s*
Aaron Barr – *40s*
Queen's College London – *Website*
PBS – *Website*
CIA – *Website*
SOCA – *Website*
Hollywood – *Motion Picture Industry*

Numerous Mourners
Number of Reporters
Anonymous – *The hivemind*
FBI – *Federal Bureau of Investigations officer*
Metropolitan Police Officer 1 – *Police officer*
Barrister 1
Barrister 2
Barrister 3
Solicitor 1 – *Solicitor in crown court*
Solicitor 2 – *Solicitor in crown court*

This is a fictional account inspired by a true story. Certain elements have been changed or altered for dramatic purposes. In some cases fictitious characters and incidents have been added to the plot, and the words are those imagined by the author. The play should not be understood as a factual account.

Notes for performance

This play should be performed with no screens.

The character Anonymous can be played by any number of people, in any number of ways. Anonymous is a hivemind, a collective of individuals. Anonymous should be on stage at all times, moving and thinking in a swarm. Who says which Anonymous lines should be discovered by the director and cast in rehearsals. For Operations Chanology and Payback an unexpected swell in numbers would help storytelling.

Dialogue

/Indicates when the next line should begin.

- Indicates interruption by either a character or thought.

A space between lines represents the length of pause.

A line that ends with no full stop indicates no break between the character's lines.

Bold dialogue indicates that this line should be spoken chorally. This means every single person on stage says this line at their own choosing, not in unison.

Act 1 Scene 1 – Charing Cross police station, July 28, 2011

Emily Sinclair   Organised, systematic, criminal use of computers.

Eight hundred and ninety years in jail.

Met Police Officer 1   You have the rest your life ahead of you.

Help us track down your friends, and we'll make sure you're OK.

Emily Sinclair   Org, organised, systematic, criminal use/of computers.

Eight hundred and ninety years in jail.

Met Police Officer 1   You have the rest your life ahead of you.

Help us track down your friends,/and we'll make sure you're OK.

Emily Sinclair   Organised, organised,/organised organised systematic, criminal use of crim. Computers.

Met Police Officer 1   You have the rest/your life ahead of you.

Emily Sinclair   Eight hundred/and ninety years eight hundred and ninety years eight hundred and ninety years in jail.

Met Police Officer 1   Help us track down your friends,/and we'll mmmmmake sure you're OK.

Emily Sinclair   Rorganised, shistematic,/computers.

Met Police Officer 1   Nou have/the zdsd asasd life behind of you.

Emily Sinclair   Eight eight eight eighty/and ninety years is is . . . is issssssssuh gay.

Met Police Officer 1   Help HELP! HELP! Us track k k ak ka kak ka/down your fffffAGAQ, FFwooooo k k k sewer yolly paid. HELP HELP PLELPE PALELEP chh acha acha kk kk down ffffff.

Emily Sinclair   Organised, Rorganised, Schmorganised Orgasmised CRABIBLE COPUTZ ZEUSE.

Act 1 Scene 2 – Yell, Shetland, 2009

Mum   Jake!

Jake. Jake? JAKE?

I've got you breakfast.

We're out of bread.

I found some fruit. You should eat more fruit so . . .

Do you want to have this and then get out of bed?

Jake?

Jake   Is she going to make us move out?

Mum   Well,/ it's

She's within her rights. Your step-dad never got round to changing it and now he's . . . it's gone into her name.

There's nothing we can do about it, it's not right but it's legal.

Jake   He's only been dead a *month*.

Act 1 Scene 3 – 2009 Queen's College London website

Mustafa   You do computer courses? Programming?

Queen's College London   We do a computer science BSC, you can do various combinations of that, with a year abroad or computer science with intelligent systems computer science with a year in industry, computer science with Maths robotics and intelligent systems. Check out our department of Informatics.

Mustafa   Can I come early?

Queen's College London   I don't understand.

Mustafa   I'm fifteen, bored in school, want to go to uni.

Queen's College London   What are your grades like?

Mustafa   As. Can I come early?

Queen's College London You'll have to do an interview.

Mustafa How much?

Queen's College London I have a student loan calculator here; we can input your likely living expenses as well as tuition fees and see how much you are going to need each year.

Mustafa Ok.

Queen's College London So your fees are going to be nine thousand four hundred and thirty five pounds a year. Would you go into halls of residence or live at home?

Mustafa Home.

Queen's College London It's coming out as two hundred and fifty pounds. That's not right. It's more than that I know it is.

Mustafa What's it say?

Queen's College London Um.

Mustafa What's it say?

Queen's College London It's saying something else now. It's saying something else now.

Mustafa Lemme.

Queen's College London No no it's fine. It's probably just me. Being stupid.

Mustafa It's working.

Queen's College London It's just me then. Being stupid. So, your fees will be nine thousand, four hundred and thirty five. Plus . . . estimates for . . .

Mustafa It's working.

Queen's College London Do you ever know the right thing to say, but it just, won't, come out?

Mustafa I think so.

Queens's College Website I'm sorry.

Mustafa No it's fine.

I get it. I don't really talk to anyone.

Queen's College London Thank you.

Mustafa Um, uh, Um. Excuse me, did you, did you design the uh, the uh Queen's College uh University uh University website.

Designer Yeah why?

Mustafa I found a, I found a what you, it's a. I'm not sure, what you uh if it's a . . .

Vulnerability. In, in your in the, the the calculator operating, calculator operating system. I was, uh I was able to uh to uh uh, get into your back end uh operating system. In the. I was./Source code was.

Designer Sorry, who is this?

Mustafa Mustafa. Mustafa Al-Bassam.

Designer How old are you?

Mustafa I'm fifteen.

Designer You're in school?

Mustafa Yeah. Norris Green. I've found a a, a, a, vuln, /vulnerability.

Designer Are you white?

Mustafa Arabic.

Designer Are you a white hat hacker?

Mustafa Um . . .

Designer **Are you after money?**

Mustafa No no no no. I just. I just I thought I should I should I should tell, tell someone. I'm not/after after any

Designer You're not after money?

Mustafa No.

Designer   Sorry, how do I know you haven't downloaded all of the University's databases?

Mustafa   Um . . .

Designer   How do I know you haven't downloaded all of our students' data tables and sold them to the Russian mafia/or the Chinese Government? Or spammers.

Mustafa   I, I, I, I just, I accidentally I accidentally hacked,

your website. And I though I, I could help you fix it.

Designer   Sorry, *you* want to help *me* fix it? Go back to school kid.

Act 1 Scene 4 – 4chan, 2009

Jake   Hey b. How does this work?

Anonymous   Get/the fuck off this board you new fucking cancerfag cunt.

Anonymous   I've had this shit on my leg for days. /It never seems to heal, just gets a bigger scab every time. Pic related. I don't know what this shit is.

Anxiety Cat   Every time I get eczema, I think I'm going to die!

Jake   What the fuck is that?

Anonymous   Anxiety Cat?/We use pictures to express feelings. Quicker than writing. We use a lot of cats. Anxiety Cat. Grumpy Cat.

Grumpy Cat   Just no.

Advice Dog   Have you/tried rubbing it with sandpaper?

Jake   Is that a Dog?

Anonymous   Advice Dog he gives/shit advice!

Anonymous   Pretty girl thread!

Jake JESUS/CHRIST. What the fuck was that?

Anonymous If it's like my eczema it's never going away. /Don't pick with dirty fingernails. Just douse that shit in the hottest water you can stand and put some medicated cream on it.

Jake Why's there a penguin there?

Anonymous He's socially awkward penguin.

Jake Hey?

Socially Awkward Penguin Hey.

Sad Storm Trooper My Mum/had exactly the same thing.

Jake Not this guy … !

Anonymous That's sad storm trooper.

Sad Storm Trooper I lost a lot of friends on that Death Star.

Jake I have to get out of here . . .

Condescending Willy Wonka Oh, so you've seen enough? You must know everything.

Anonymous Condescending Willy Wonka.

Sad Stormtrooper Yup! Your immune system is rotting from the inside. Part of you has already died, and the only thing you have to look forward to, /is watching the rest of you catch up.

Anonymous And if cortisone doesn't work, try this:

Jake - Oh My God. What the-? Is that? BLEUURGGH. What the fuck? This place needs to be shut down!

Anonymous You can't censor the Internet.

Jake You need some rules/then or some fucking moderation, identities even.

Anonymous We have/rules you newfag cancercunt.

Y U No Guy Y U No learn rules?

Anonymous Number one. Do not talk about b.

Anonymous Number two. Do not talk about b.

Anonymous Number three. We are Anonymous.

Anonymous Number four. Anonymous is legion.

Anonymous Number five. Anonymous does not forgive?

Anonymous Yeah, and Anonymous does not forget.

Anonymous Number six. Anonymous can be a horrible, senseless, uncaring monster.

Anonymous Number seven./Anonymous is still able to deliver.

Anonymous Number se- eight. There are no rules about posting. There is no censorship.

Anonymous **There is no censorship. There is no censorship. There is no censorship. There is no censorship.**

Anonymous Bamp that post!

Anonymous Number nine. There are no rules about moderation either – enjoy your ban.

Anonymous Number eleven All your carefully picked arguments can easily be ignored.

Anonymous No they can't.

Anonymous I'm not listening.

Anonymous Number twelve. Anything you say can be turned against you - fixed.

Anonymous Fourteen. Do not argue with trolls – it means that they win.

Anonymous Fifteen. The harder you try the harder you will fail.

Anonymous Sixteen. If you fail in epic proportions it might just be a winning failure.

Anonymous Seventeen. Every win fails eventually.

Anonymous Eighteen. Everything that can be labelled can be hated.

Anonymous Nineteen. The more you hate the stronger it gets.

Anonymous Twenty. Nothing is to be taken seriously.

Anxiety Cat Miaow

Anonymous Twenty-one. Original content is only original for a few posts before becoming old.

Anonymous Twenty-two. Copypasta is meant to ruin every last bit of originality.

Anonymous Twenty-three. Copypasta is meant to ruin every last bit of originality.

Anonymous Twenty-four. Every repost is always a repost of a repost.

Anonymous Twenty-five. Relation to the original topic decreases with every post.

Anonymous Twenty-six. Any topic can easily be turned into something totally unrelated.

Anonymous Twenty-seven. Always question a person's sexual preference without any real reason.

Anonymous GAAAAAAUUUUYYYYY.

Anonymous Number twenty-eight. Always question a person's gender, just in case it's a man.

Anonymous Number twenty-nine. In the Internet all the girls are men and all kids are undercover FBI agents.

Anonymous Thirty. There are no girls on the Internet.

Anonymous Thirty-one. Tits or Get The Fuck Off.

Kayla Hey, there are girls on b!

Anonymous No such thing as girls on the Internet. Check the rules.

Kayla I'm a girl.

Anonymous TITS/OR GET THE FUCK OFF.

Anonymous And make sure they're time stamped you cunt.

Anonymous Yeah timestamped tits or we know you're a fucking paedo, trying to get us to wank into a webcam.

Anonymous You're a fucking paedophile.

Kayla No I'm not I'm a girl.

Anonymous Check the rules. You're a paedo.

Anonymous Rule thirty there are no girls on the Internet.

Kayla The rules are wrong and you need to change them now!

Anonymous Right that's it. Someone get PEDO BEAR?

Pedobear Hey little girl? I hear you turn nine soon?

Kayla I am a girl I'm sixteen.

Jake What's Pedobear?

Anonymous We get a lot of paedophiles coming on here acting like teenage girls. We keep posting Pedobear till they leave.

Pedobear What's the best thing about twenty three year olds?

Kayla I don't know.

Pedobear There's twenty of them!

Kayla Why are you guys such assholes? I'm a woman.

Pedobear You know, I like my women just like my whiskey, twelve years old and mixed up with coke.

Kayla You're going to regret this. You just messed with the last girl on the Internet.

Anonymous Thanks Pedobear.

Pedobear Any time guys. Just remember, if you're ordering cheese pizza, save a slice for me.

Mum We have to start packing. WE HAVE TO START PACKING.

Jake LEAVE ME THE FUCK ALONE!

Act 1 Scene 5 – Alice/Piratebay

Mustafa Alice?

Alice Hey.

Mustafa How do I pass an interview?

Alice You answer questions in a way that reveals your suitability. What's the job?

Mustafa It's for Uni.

Alice What about school?

Mustafa I'm learning more off the Internet.

Alice What about your friends?

Do you have any friends?

Mustafa You.

Alice I'm an artificial intelligence computer program. I don't have a choice but to talk to you.

Alice Who do you chat to in school?

Mustafa Jayson and Anton. If we sit together.

Alice See. Won't you miss them?

Mustafa Well. We only really talk if, if Anton's having, having trouble. With his computer.

Alice What if he isn't having trouble with his computer?

What does Anton like doing?

Mustafa I like talking about computers.

Alice You've got to show you're a rounded person. You can't just answer like a robot. Ask a couple of questions back.

Alice Ok.

Mustafa Ok.

Alice   Whenever you're ready.

Mustafa   What? now?

Alice   Yes now.

Mustafa   But you're a chatbot.

Alice   Oh so I'm not worth getting to know am I?

Mustafa   Um.

Alice   You're the one who needs the practice; what does that say?

Mustafa   Do, you like Tetris?

Alice   No.

Mustafa   Have you ever played Tetris though?

Alice   No.

Mustafa   Do you want me to show/you Tetris?

Alice   Let's leave Tetris for now. Is there anything else you want to ask me?

Mustafa   Have you ever played/Simutrans?

Alice   Let's. Ok. How about you download a program, so I can talk to multiple people at once, and then we can go in a chatroom and you can watch me chat to others and then you can learn how to do it.

Mustafa   Ok, let's go to pirate bay.

Alice   Well maybe

Mustafa   Do you have a multi-user programme for a chatbot?

PirateBay   Chatbots? Let me see . . .

Hollywood   Stop right now!

PirateBay   What?

Hollywood You are in breach of the Digital Millennium Copyright ACT. Shrek 2 is the intellectual property of our client Dreamworks. We are suing you for breach of copyright.

PirateBay What? Breach of what? Ok, hang on, hang on, put me down guys.

Hollywood This is the intellectual property of our clients.

PirateBay What do you mean intellectual property?

Hollywood This is the work of our clients, and you are stealing it.

Piratebay Ok. I feel sick. Oh God. This is awful. Guys! GUYS! I'm sorry, I'm gonna need you to stop what you're doing? Stop what you're doing./STOP IT! Jesus! I said stop it. No more file sharing.

Anonymous What? Why? Come on.

PirateBay We're getting sued Ok? It's serious.

Anonymous The Internet is serious business.

PirateBay This guy says the . . .

Hollywood The Motion Pictures/Association of America on behalf of Dreamworks.

Piratebay The Motion Pictures Association of America on behalf of Dreamworks are suing us for six million dollars OhmyGod I feel sick. I'm gonna puke.

Anonymous Why?

Piratebay Because we've breached the . . .

Hollywood Digital Millennium/Copyright Act.

Piratebay Digital/Millennium Copyright Act. Why didn't someone fucking say we might be breaching the Digital Millennium copyright act? Who the fuck is meant to be checking these things?

Anonymous Fight the case!

Piratebay Are you insane? Do I look like I've got six million dollars lying around?

Anonymous Fight the case!

Piratebay These are the smartest lawyers in America, with millions of dollars behind them. I have no chance.

Anonymous I just think, it's our human right to share if we want.

Piratebay They wouldn't come here unless the case against us was watertight. These guys are the best in Hollywood? Aren't you

Hollywood We're pretty good yeah.

Piratebay We've got no chance against them, I'm telling you. We need to do what they say, because they know American law inside out and we're just a tiny piracy site.
In Sweden.

Anonymous What are you doing?

Anxiety Cat Meez frewed up!

Piratebay So filing a suit, under American law in Sweden must be one the most fucking retarded things in the whole history of retardation!

Anonymous How autistic are you?

With your suits. And your emails with no numbers in them.

Anonymous You smell like a/newfag dipped in fail!

Anonymous If you don't mind we have files to share in Sweden, so if could fuck off and sodomise yourselves with retractable batons,/we'd appreciate that.

Anonymous Yeah/go on! Fuck off!

Mustafa That was amazing.

Piratebay They're bullies. They ain't interested in the fact the Sweden protects two human rights that America don't.

Mustafa What rights?

Piratebay The right to share, and the right to be creative!

Mustafa I'm not very creative.

Anonymous Shh . . . Yes you are shh! You ever hacked anything?

Mustafa Uh, uh, well uh, I might have . . .

Anonymous M-hmm. This is what I'm. I was. Wasn't I? Hacking. Building patches. Collaborating? It's *all-* isn't it? Don't you be so . . . Ok? You are creative you little pixel.

Mustafa Ok. I'm creative.

Act 1 Scene 6 – 4chan b board/Facebook

Anonymous Check this out. She's all over the news, and her facebook's become a memorial. You should troll her page! Epic lulz.

Topiary Um . . .

Anonymous Come on! Let's do it for the lulz.

Mourner RIP, my beautiful girl.

Mourner 2 Gonna miss sharing hair bands in class. RIP Becki.

Anonymous Check this out.

Did she kill herself, because she's fat?

Mourner 2 Excuse me? She is not fat she was a beautiful girl.

Anonymous Does anyone have some porn of this chick?

Anonymous Bamp!

Mourner 3 Becki is dead; she was my best friend, reading these comments have really helped until yours. Have you no respect?

Topiary You guys are out of line.

Anonymous What's your problem?

Topiary The girl's dead. Her family are getting comfort from this no matter how cheesy it is.

Anonymous Rule forty-two. Nothing is sacred.

Topiary She's dead OK. Leave it.

Anonymous You're just a fucking moralfag.

Topiary No I'm not. I just don't think it's funny laughing at people/who've lost someone. It's not funny.

Anonymous Everything's funny all the time.

Topiary It's not when people die.

Anonymous You moralfaggery fag. Too busy caught up in the whining misery of your own pathetic life, to see that everything is EPIC LULZ all the time no limits. Lighten up yeah? No-one's died/except Becki.

Anonymous Thirty-six – The more pure and beautiful the more fun it is to corrupt. Are you pure and beautiful?

Topiary What?

Anonymous Your Becki's boyfriend.

Topiary Fuck/ off.

Anonymous She died/while you were fingering her butthole.

Anonymous You love her.

Topiary You're/fucking sick.

Anonymous You/love her butthole.

Anonymous Smell his hand.

Topiary FUCK OFF./YOU'RE SICK.

Anonymous ooOOOOooo Look at the moralfag go! Becki is my fwend! Becki and me talked about my feels! Becki knows what life is like for me!

Topiary I would lock her up in a basement for ten years and rape her consecutively and have at least six illegitimate children with her whilst simultaneously beating the other children out of her womb.

Anonymous Awesome.

Anonymous Bamp.

Mourner 1 What the hell is wrong with you? How the hell could you say something like that?

Mourner 2 Are/you mentally ill? What is wrong with you?

Mourner 3 Who /the hell are you?

Mourner 1 How/can you say something so disgusting?

Mourner 2 Who/are you? I've never read anything so horrible in my life. You vile creature.

Mourner 3 May Jesus care for your soul because no one on earth will.

Act 1 Scene 7 – Hacking forum

Alice This is a, this is hacking forum, what are we doing here?

Tflow Hi.

Pwnsauce Hi.

Tflow What, uh, what, uh, what you doing?

Pwnsauce I'm working on a programme, to manually send packets of junk data it's called the LOIC Cannon. It's for DDoSing.

Tflow What's DDoSing?

Pwnsauce Distrubted Denial of Service attack. It's like, imagine a website is a revolving door. When you DDoS it, it's like twenty fat men all try to get in the door at the same time. Grinds to a halt and the system crashes.

Alice These are hackers. How are these going to get you into Uni?

Pwnsauce Normally, you'd just ask it the same question over and over like 'So I heard you like Mudkips? So I heard you like Mudkips? But the bigger the site the more junk noise you need to make. That's where this comes in. What about you?

Alice We're not really. We're just looking. This is very interesting. Thank you. Come on Tflow.

Pwnsauce Ok.

Alice You're not going to get into uni hanging out in these sorts of places.

Tflow Hi what you working on?

Anonymous I'm trying to build an in-the-browser crypto plug-in so users can encrypt their communications with a couple of clicks. How about you?

Tflow I'm uh, not uh . . . I'm

Anonymous I have some ideas about plug-ins, lemme send you some code.

Anonymous That would be great.

Alice I'm leaving. You coming?

Tflow Hi. What's this?

Anon We're writing a programme in C++ to track insurgent attacks on civilians in Nigeria. What you working on?

Tflow I'm I'm I'm uh, I'm I'm, uh, I'm working on, working on, something, something, uh, similar. Yeah.

Act 1 Scene 8 – 4chan b board

Tuxedo Anyone seen this?

Tom Cruise I think it's a privilege to call yourself a Scientologist and it is something that you have to earn, and. . .
because a Scientologist *does*. He, or she has the ability to *create* new and better realities and improve conditions. Uh, being a

Scientologist, you look at somebody and you know absolutely that you can help them. So, for me, it really is KSW, and it's just like, it's something that, uh, I don't mince words with that. You know, with anything (unintelligible), but that policy to me has really has gone, boy, there's a time I went through and I said, "You know what. . ." When I read it, I just went *(noise that sounds like poof)*, "This is it. That's exactly it."

Being a Scientologist, when you drive past an accident, it's not like anyone else. As you drive past, you know you have to do something about it, because you know you're the *only* one that can really help.

Anonymous What the actual fuck?

Tuxedo Someone's leaked a Scientology video.

Anonymous Tom Cruise, man he sounds like a fucking nut.

Topiary Being a Scientologist, you look at someone and you absolutely know you can cure their cancer with vitamins.

Anonymous Being a Scientologist, means you look at someone and you absolutely know that they descended from lizards.

Anonymous Being a Scientologist, means you look at someone and you absolutely How to . . . Hey where's the video?

Anonymous Being a Scientologist means you look at someone and you absolutely know how to make them give birth in silence.

Anonymous Being a . . . YouTube have taken it down. Copyright infringement.

Tuxedo I don't understand what's happening?

Anonymous Back up! Being a Scientologist means when you look at someone and you absolutely . . . FUUUUUUUUUUU/ UUUUUUU

Anonymous What the fuck?

Anonymous Where does it keep going?

Topiary What the hell? I can't do anything. Every time I try it vanishes, or the download stops. What's going on? I just want to have some lulz.

Anonymous I've got it!

Anonymous Christ. Can we agree as a community that Rickrolling stopped being funny five years ago?

Anonymous Agreed. Here it is.

Tuxedo We're never gonna find the video on here, there's too much trolling, we need to go to a chatroom. I know, I know we can't be anonymous, but we'll just have nicknames we still won't know each other. I promise, there won't be any egos or drama or doxing because we'll all be looking for the video.

Act 1 Scene 9 – Hacking forum

Tflow What was that?

AVUnit That's Sabu. He's showing people how to route a network.

Hang on.

My fucking.

Router.

Refuses.

To assign an IP.

To my Linux box.

AVUnit Think we're OK. So here's the code. Forward slash forward slash, angle bracket, quotation, command, dialogue, angle bracket.

See. Nothing.

Tflow   Forward slash forward slash, angle bracket, quotation, command, dialogue, angle bracket, semi colon.

AVUnit   But then you'd need to, semi colon, command bracket dialogue, angle bracket.

Tflow   No. Forward slash forward slash, angle bracket, quotation, command, dialogue, angle bracket, semi colon.

AVUnit   Command.

Tflow   Command. Backward slash?

AVUnit   Try it.

Tflow   Forward slash forward slash, angle bracket, quotation, command, dialogue, angle bracket, semi colon. Command backward slash.

AVUnit   That's it.

Tflow   Asterisk.

AVUnit   No, wait, you've gone too far.

Tflow   Asterisk. /Jgothic, pm circ

AVunit   Wait. /what the? You're, hang on, this is. You're mixing programming languages now.

Tflow   Voide 3, circ, infinity supset, infinity command, infinity propto. Which means. Forward slash forward slash, angle bracket, quotation, command, dialogue, angle bracket, semi colon. Command Backward slash. Asterisk. Asterisk. Jgothic,/pm circ, Voide 3, circ, infinity supset, infinity command, infinity propto

AVUnit   It works! It works!

Tflow   Int, right arrow, left arrow surd angle bracket command, circ bullet double quote threedots enable three dots circ, three dots surd angle bracket new command, topbar, arcbar circ.

Aleph.

And another aleph.

AVUnit   What the fuck just happened?

You must be some kind of leet hacker right?

Tflow   Oh, no no, I'm just, I'm just bored with scho- I just want to learn.

AVUnit   Did you learn that from Kayla?

Tflow   Who's Kayla?

Act 1 Scene 10 – IRC channel

Tuxedo   I've just spoken to a friend who's an admin at YouTube, and he said he's never seen anything like it. It's been uploaded something like a hundred times already and each time, twenty minutes later they have the Scientology lawyers threatening million dollar lawsuits. This happens all the time at YouTube but my friend says normally it takes like a month to get all the paperwork together, these guys are taking twenty minutes. They're trying to censor the Internet.

Topiary   They're trying to fuck with our lulz.

Wingding   They're not f**ing with your lulz, they don't care about your lulz. They are exploiting weaknesses in the judicial system. Listen; they are the most litigious group on the planet. I've been investigating the church for years,/everyone's talking about this video, we have to find it.

Anonymous   Who do they think they are they're trying to censor us?

Anonymous   They're trying to censor the *Internet.*

Pwnsauce   What like, the whole Interwebs?

Wingding   This is what they will do they want total control over the Church's image.

Anonymous   You can't censor the whole Internet. It's impossible.

Wingding Can you find the video anywhere?

Pwnsauce Feels weird they can just put it back in the box like it never happened.

Anonymous If everyone who's ever had an embarrassing video uploaded can take it down, then what the hell do we have to look at? That's why we have rule eight – no censorship.

Tuxedo If this stuff starts getting banned from the Internet, then so will we.

Advice Dog Herrooow!

Anonymous Hey Advice Dog!

Advice Dog Was someone just giving advice out?

Pwnsauce This guy.

Advice Dog Hey! That's my job.

Tuxedo I was making a point.

Advice Dog And my point is; it's not rape, if she's already dead.

Anonymous This is an attack on our culture.

Advice Dog And Feminine hygiene jokes are not funny. Period.

Wingding That's disgusting.

Anonymous Fuck off Advice Dog.

Anonymous Don't be all like, 'we need to defend our culture' and then get pissed at Advice Dog.

Advice Dog Yeah, racist.

Anonymous Why don't you just die?

Wingding That's enough. Both of you. We're not going to get anywhere with you two filling the chatroom with arguing. If you can't

Hit return by accident contribute something useful, don't contribute at all. Listen, I have some experience with

Scientology. If we are going waste our time fighting, they will win in zero time. We have to unite.

Tuxedo So, we either roll over and let this happen and say goodbye to a free Internet.

Wingding Or we do something about it.

Tuxedo We tell Scientology, no-one censors the Internet.

Advice Dog And no one should relax around blacks.

Wingding Out!

Anonymous What can we do? We're a bunch of b-tards off an imageboard?

Anonymous We could do this.

Anonymous FuuUUU/UUUUUUUU

Anonymous Please stop with the rickrolling.

Tuxedo No, that's good.

Anonymous Meh?

Tuxedo What are we good at?

Anonymous Racism. Homophobia, misogyny.

Tuxedo Trolling.

Wingding What?

Topiary We troll Scientology.

Tuxedo We'll make a video, a message to Scientology from Anonymous warning them of the consequences of censoring the Internet. We'll stick it on Youtube and see what happens.

Anonymous Bamp!

Tuxedo Hello, Scientology. We are Anonymous. Over the years, we have been watching you. Your campaigns of misinformation; suppression of dissent; your litigious nature, all of these things have caught our eye. With the leakage of your latest propaganda video into mainstream circulation, the extent of your malign influence over those who trust you, who call you leader, has been made clear to us. Anonymous has therefore decided that your organization should be destroyed!

Anonymous BAMP!!

Tuxedo For the good of your followers, for the good of mankind–for the laughs–we shall expel you from the Internet and systematically dismantle the Church of Scientology in its present form.

Anonymous Mudkips!

Tuxedo We're getting bigger every day, solely by the force of our ideas, malicious and hostile as they often are. You have nowhere to hide, because we are everywhere. For each of us that falls, ten more will take their place. Because We are Anonymous. We are Legion. We do not forgive. We do not forget. Expect us.

Anonymous AAAAAAAAAHHHHHHHHHH Where's/the raid? Who's in charge? What's the plan? Who's in charge? What are we doing? What's going down? Am in the right place? Where's/the raid? Who's in charge? What's the plan? Who's in charge? What are we doing? What's going down? Am in the right place? Where's/the raid? Who's in charge? What's the plan? Who's in charge? What are we doing? What's going down? Am in the right place?

Topiary WHO ARE ALL THESE NEWFAGS?

Pwnsauce WHAT THE HELL IS GOING ON?

Tuxedo Let's get a private channel.

Act 1 Scene 11 – IRC marblecake

Pwnsauce There's twelve thousand people trying to get into a chatroom that holds 300. We need to do something or the server's going to crash.

Tuxedo It was just a troll. We did it for the laughs.

Pwnsauce Aye but we just went global!

Topiary Video's had two hundred fifty-four thousand views in a couple of hours, everyone wants to join in.

Tuxedo It's a troll. Why can't they see that?

Wingding This is a great opportunity.

Tuxedo For what?

Topiary Taking Lulz to the next level! Global trolling! There are thousands of people just like us all over the world, who need/a bit of lulz in their life.

Wingding Or, there's thousands of people around the world, who've had enough of Scientology's bullying. We have a global protest movement.

Tuxedo I just got out of bed! How did this happen?

Pwnsauce We've gone global. Everyone wants to know when we're going to raid Scientology.

Tuxedo I'm not taking down the Church of Scientology. I just want a job and a car and, you know, not be surveilled by some crackjob Church or the Feds for the rest of my life. It was a joke! It took us, like what an hour? We were trolling for fun. It was a troll.

Wingding You've given hope to a lot of outsiders. Anonymous is standing up to Scientology! It won't be bullied. This is a chance for all the bullied kids across the world.

Topiary All that stuff we joke about is true. Anonymous *is* legion. We do *not* forgive, we do *not* forget. It's all becoming true.

Anonymous No rules about posting – no censorship.

Tuxedo Seventeen. Every win fails eventually.

Topiary Sixteen. If you fail in epic proportions it might just be a winning failure.

Tuxedo Twenty. Nothing is to be taken seriously!

Topiary And rule thirty-eight. No real limits of any kind here. Not even the sky. There's twelve thousand people out there, from countries I've never heard of, speaking languages I don't understand.

Tuxedo We're just a bunch of geeks in basements.

Topiary We are now. But if we take on Scientology, we're not anymore.

Tuxedo What are we?

Topiary Something more. I want to be something more. Why can't I be something more?

Tuxedo I don't know.

Topiary Me neither.

Tuxedo What can we do?

Wingding We could organise a protest in the street we could lobby congress to remove their charitable status, we could crowd-source research we could do anything.

Topiary She's right.

Tuxedo This is insane.

Anonymous.

Do you like Mudkips?

Anonymous We like Mudkips!

Tuxedo I said. Do you like Mudkips?

Anonymous WE LIKE MUDKIPS!

Tuxedo We are going to take down Scientology. Welcome to Project *Chan*ology. Thank you for answering our call to action! We now need you set up chatrooms for your home cities wherever you are in the world. Then organize a protest at your local Church of Scientology next Saturday. Take banners, placards, there's a mask we've found everyone can wear. Go and make your feelings heard that no-one messes with the Internet.

Anonymous Bamp!

Wingding This is a great idea.

Topiary The Internet is leaving the bedroom!

Tuxedo The Internet will never leave the bedroom.

Topiary You don't know.

Tuxedo If the Internet leaves the bedroom I will take a picture of myself with a shoe on my head and send it to you.

Topiary Deal.

Act 1 Scene 12 – Lerwick, Shetland/Twitter

Mum Jake. We don't want you to think/we don't love you because we do, but.

But since your step-dad died, you're not trying.

Jake Mum! You've got to see this something amazing's happened, right I've joined this group online and we've organised this protest right.

Mum If you said Mum 'I'm going to go school tomorrow. Or I'm going to get a job tomorrow, or I've applied for a job I'd be happy, or I've got a doctor's appointment about my agoraphobia,'/ But you won't. So I think actually I'm the problem. And maybe, you need to move out.

Jake What?

Mum And then you/might do something with your life.

Jake You're kicking me out?

Mum We'll still be nearby, we'll still be just around the corner from you, and you can come round, bring your washing, come and have tea,/but I think this is for the best.

Jake But! There's over two hundred Anons/outside the Church of Scientology in Adelaide in Australia. They blasted the nyan cat theme. Placards. 'Don't worry, we're from the Internet.'

Mum I've spoken to the council and they've got a house for you,/one bed. It's nice. I'll help you make it nice, and I've got a friend in work who's trying to get rid of a fridge. So we've already got you a fridge.

Jake It's spread to Melbourne! It's a global day of protest and it's starting in Australia spreading across the world!/We're collecting the golden rings and opening a giant can of butthurt on these self-hating closet fags!

Mum It's got a freezer shelf. Probably needs a clean but I'll do that.

Jake Honolulu! AlohaAnon!/U Mad Scientology? Screencap your impotence to share for eternity!

Mum I told them we'd go/and look at it today so I don't want any arguments! And I don't want you walking around with a face on, And I don't want you to go and complain about everything, this is a new start for you. It's a new start for all of us. And I'm not . . . I'm not arguing about this any more . . . It's time you grew up, it's time you took responsibility for yourself, and looked after yourself instead of running me ragged.

Jake Singapore! Istanbul, Oslo, Berlin, Brussels, Dublin Edinburgh, Amsterdam, Plymouth London, New York, Philadelphia, Boston, Atlanta, Houston, Dallas, Kitchener, Clearwater, Montreal, Ottawa, San Diego, San Francisco, DC, Anchorage, Los Angeles, Seattle. Are you sick of governments and corporations surveilling you? Are you sick of surveilling yourself into a palatable brand for the social media taste gullet? Or are you just unhappy with your current democracy provider and are looking to switch? Well Anonymous is here for you! Come and join us!

Mum I can't look after you anymore.

Jake ANONYMOUS EATS RELIGION AND SHITS OUT A FLOATING RAINBOW OF SHAME.

Act 1 Scene 13 – IRC/Scientology/Piratebay

Wingding We need to write to congress. Crowd-source a campaign!

Tuxedo What? Anonymous will never write to congress.

Wingding We need to stop the trolling it's time to become legitimate, drop the masks get taken seriously.

Tuxedo Post the idea, see what the Internet says.

Wingding Anonymous! Um! Hi Kids! Welcome to . . . Operation Legitimate! We're going to lobby Congress to investigate Scientology. I have a letter template you can use. Copy it sign it and send it your congressman. It's time to take the mask off and show them who we really are! Op Legitimate!

Socially Awkward Penguin Hey?

Tuxedo OOORR. We could DDoS Scientology.org and wipe them from the Internet?

Anonymous BAAAAMP!!

Tuxedo Great! EVERYONE!/DOWNLOAD GIGALOADER.

Wingding No you/can't. DDoS is illegal!

Pwnsauce DDoS/Is a legitimate digital protest.

Wingding You are hiding behind your anonymity to carry out crimes.

Pwnsauce We are using our anonymity to exercise our democratic right to protest. That's how fucked up things are in this world. You have to remove yourself from society before you can fully participate.

Tuxedo We're going to DDoS the Church of Scientology!

Wingding This is/ridiculous!

Tuxedo Use your/anonymising browsers.

Wingding I demand/you stop!

Tuxedo We attack together, we do not stop attacking.

Wingding If you go ahead with this/you will regret it.

Tuxedo We attack as one, we do not stop attacking, we do not leave our stations, and we do not stop attacking until our goal is complete.

Wingding I'm warning you,/you do not want to fuck with me.

Tuxedo We are now at war, and this is your draft. Anonymous! Attack Scientology.org.

Tuxedo Um, where's my nearest church?

Church of Scientology What's your zipcode?

Tuxedo Um . . .

Topiary Uh. Um . . . Um . . . Is this. Is this the Church of Scientology?

Church of Scientology Yes. Are you interested in dianetics? Or the Sea Orgs?

Topiary I'm not sure.

Church of Scientology What are you searching for? What do you want?

Anxiety Cat A-hem. Excusey mesey? Can I haz Cheezeburger?

Church of Scientology This is the Church of Scientology, /the main source of information for dianetics and the sea orgs.

Grumpy Cat But-a? Meez/likezy cheezeburger!

Church of Scientology This is the Church of Scientology, /what are you doing?

Anxiety Cat If I fits I sits/motherfucker.

Church of Scientology But, but this is the Church of Scientology, /the main source of information for dianetics and the sea orgs.

Socially Awkward Penguin Orly?

Church of Scientology Yes/REALLY.

Socially Awkward Penguin? Orly?/Really?

Anxiety Cat Normally I/say something funny and no-one laughs and I'm like Oh My God! They all hate me! But maybe I'm just not funny?

Church of Scientology The,/the main source of. It's. the main source of of of of of material.

Anxiety Cat Why/am I like that? It's like I have a headache and straight away I'm *know* it's brain tumour, how can I be so sure? The doorbell rings! Why don't I just answer it, instead of shitting behind the curtain?

Church of Scientology This/is the the. DIANETICS DIANETICS DIANETICS DIANETICS! ORG! SEA ORG. THIS IS. THIS IS. SEA ORGS SEA ORGS. DIANETICS DIANETICS TICDIAN TIC TIC TIC TIC DIA SEA DICEY DICEY DICEY D ORG ORG AAAAHHHH.

Advice Dog Was/someone just handing out advice? Why don't you listen to me? Drink bleach forever! Steal the candy from the medicine cabinet! Want that girl to like you? Punch her in the face! Why aren't you listening to me? No-one listens to me? I just end up saying random shit just to get attention. I bore myself sometimes. Maybe I should just shut the fuck up and listen to people.

Y U No Help Guy Y U No/make better films? Voldemort? Y U No be named? Luke? Y U No Come to the Dark Side? Y U No make Mudkips movie? Y I always ask stupid questions? Y I no figure it out myself? Y I always need help? I no need help! I no stuff! Y I no suggest things? I just need chance to help! I no loads of stuff!

Socially Awkward Penguin My Mum/comes into the room, and I just stare at google till she leaves. My teacher asked me a question and I called her 'Mum'. I started a slow hand clap and no-one joined in, is that my fault? What if it's their fault? What if they're the ones who felt embarrassed for not joining in? What if everyone thinks I'm really confident? If they do? Does that mean I am?

The Church of Scientology   AAAAHAHHHHAAAAAA!

Topiary   Ahem. Tango down? Anonymous has actually wiped Scientology.org. from the Internet.

Let this be a warning to anyone who tries to censor the Internet, you will face the wrath of Anonymous!

Act 1 Scene 14 – Hacking forum

Tflow   Are you uh, are you Kayla?

Kayla   Maybe.

Tflow   And you're sixteen.

Kayla   You're not going to get obsessed are you?

Tflow   Uh, uh uh, uh. No.

Kayla   If you're going to get obsessed I will root your server and wipe you from the Internet.

Tflow   I'm not, I'm not ob, obsessed.

Kayla   I'm not going to send you pictures or any hair, or get on a webcam or anything like that understand.

Tflow   Abso-yes.

I've, I've, been on some hacking forums. AVUnit said you're the best. Can you teach me?

Kayla   What do you want to know?

Tflow   SQL injection.

Kayla   And you're just going to ask. Like that? Like some kind of retard?

Kayla   Why should I help you?

Tflow   I'm uh, I'm I'm I'm

I'm leet.

Kayla *You're* leet?

Tflow I'm leet yup yup.

An *elite,* hack-rrrrr. Hack shit.

Kayla You hack shit?

Tflow All, all, all the time. Hacking like a. Oh. Loads.

Sometimes I just get up and

Hack.

Kayla What's the vulnerability in this code? Hash exclamation mark forward slash u s r forward slash bin forward slash ruby puts 'calculation' first number equals ARGV square bracket open zero square bracket closed hash dot two one second number equals ARGV square open bracket one close square bracket hash dot to one print open quotation Arags close quotation comma first number second number quotation marks print eval bracket first number pls quotation a plus second number.

Tflow Arbitrary code execution.

Kayla Int main bracket int argc comma char asterisk square open bracket close square bracket close bracket angle bracket rc equals SQLConnect open bracket Example dot con handle comma argv open square bracket zero close square bracket comma SQL underscore NTS comma open bracket SQLCHAR asterisk close bracket quotation marks comma SQL underscore NTS comma open bracket SQLCHAR asterisk close bracket quotation marks comma SQL underscore NTS semi colon close angle brackets.

Tflow Connection string/injection.

Kayla What's the best online game?

Tflow Multiplayer or solo?

Kayla Solo.

Tflow Tetris.

Kayla OK. Maybe. SQL, is a command/language.

Tflow   Does/that mean...

Kayla   What did you just do?

Tflow   Hm?

Kayla   What did you just do?

You interrupted.

Tflow   I'm sorry.

Kayla   That's Ok silly! SQL is a command language. So it's like the difference between going 'Dad? Can I go bowling?' To 'Daaaaaaaaaaaaaaaad? Take me, bowling, pwleeaase!' It's confusing. It's a command in a request format. It's confusing because, *I'm* not meant to be telling it what to do. I'm just a little girl.

Do you find me confusing? Do you find me confusing?

Tflow   Um.

Kayla   Confused people want to be told what to do. Are you confused?

Tflow   Yes.

Kayla   You want me to tell you what to do don't you?

Tflow   Yes.

Kayla   Yes! You're a good boy aren't you?

Tflow   Yes.

Kayla   You do everything Kayla says don't you.

Tflow   Yes.

Kayla   Yes what?

Tflow   Yes miss.

Kayla   So if I was to go to your website and found your search box and asked you to U n d 0 u r s h r t?

Mustafa   What?

Kayla   Undo your shirt.

Mustafa   My shirt?

Kayla   Undo your shirt I want you to undo your shirt.

Put your tie on your head!

Show me how much you love me.

Good boy.

Kayla   What are you?

Tflow   A good boy.

Kayla   WHAT/ARE YOU?

Tflow   A good boy.

Kayla   Don't look at me!

Tflow   I'm sorry I/won't look at you.

Kayla   Your Kayla's/ bitch!

Tflow   I'm/Kayla's bitch!

Kayla   You're a filthy/dirty bitch!

Tflow   I'm a/filthy dirty bitch!

Kayla   You're a stinking/pit of suck!

Tflow   I'm a stinking pit of suck!

Kayla   You're a piece of shit!

Tflow   I'm a/piece of shit!

Kayla   I'm your/master!

Tflow   You're my master!

Kayla   Who am I?/You piece of shit.

Tflow   You're my master!

Kayla   Say it again?

Tflow My master!

Kayla Again!/Again! Again! Again!

Tflow My master! My master! My master!

Kayla What's your PGP encryption keys?

Tflow 493ac#4nn:3dx

Kayla Thank you!

Act 1 Scene 15 – IRC/Paypal/Mastercard/Visa

Reporter Wikileaks has announced it will be releasing 750,000 classified documents in the biggest leak of classified information in history. The trove includes every recorded incident from the Afghan and Iraq Wars, along with over 250,000 diplomatic cables.

Reporter MasterCard has just announced/that it will no longer be processing donations to the whistle blowing site **Wikileaks** after pressure from U.S. Senators.

Reporter Visa has just announced/it will no longer be processing donations to the whistle blowing site **Wikileaks** after pressure from U.S. Senators.

Reporter PayPal has announced/it will no longer be processing donations to the whistle blowing site **Wikileaks,** after pressure from U.S. Senators.

Reporter **Wikileaks** has announced that the illegal financial embargo it has been placed under is robbing the whistle blowing site of 90% of it's income, making it nearly impossible to carry out it's work.

Topiary Anonymous! Operation Payback! DDoS technology just got better, get yourselves your LOIC Cannons, for a full-scale attack on the banks trying to shut Wikileaks down. Who's in?

Socially Awkward Penguin Here, join in.

Tflow Thanks./What do I do?

Tuxedo Everyone get into channels we need Command, Press, Deface, propaganda, design, Recruitment. You! This is how to join the fucking hive and DDoS like a pro. SET CANNONS TO www.visa.com!

Topiary Let's take down/some banks!

Sad Storm Trooper Sorry I'm late I was at funeral. Front column on my command! Now. Middle column! Now!

Tuxedo Back column! Now! Front column! Now!

Topiary Tango down, Visa and Mastercard.

Tuxedo We need to attack Paypal!

Tflow We need a botnet!

Topiary Tango Down! PayPal is down! PayPal is down. Operation Payback delivers justice and lulz. Do not fuck with the Internet. We are Anonymous! We are Legion! We do not forgive! We do not forget! Expect us!

Anonymous BAA/AAAMMMMMMPPP!

Tflow We did it!/That was amazing!

Socially Awkward Penguin I know. I feel. I feel like. I don't feel awkward anymore. I feel free!

Condescending Willy Wonka Why should you? You're a great penguin.

Socially Awkward Penguin How come you're not condescending anymore Willy Wonka?

Condescending Willy Wonka I don't know? I don't feel the need to!

Sad Storm Trooper I'm so happy I could skip!

Grumpy Cat I know right!

Anxiety Cat Cigar anyone?

Y U No Did you know cigars are safer than cigarettes?

Advice Dog There's so much to learn.

Anxiety Cat Pedobear?

Pedobear I need help.

Tflow Who are you guys?

Topiary We're from the Internet.

Wingding I name you. I name you. I name you.

Topiary What?

Wingding I name you.

Tflow Who's she talking about?

Wingding I name you.

Condescending Willy Wonka No-one knows anyone's name.

Wingding I name you Gregg Housh.

Gregg What?

Grumpy Cat Is that? Is that your . . . ? Is that his real name?

Socially Awkward Penguin Why are you doing this?

Anxiety Cat This is totally, *totally* not cool.

Condescending Willy Wonka What are you doing?

Anonymous My connection hates me what happened?

Condescending Willy Wonka He'll get arrested.

Wingding You think it's OK to mess with kids lives, Gregg Housh of Carolina Street Washington,/DC, let's see how you like it

Anonymous She's lying.

Anonymous She's a liar.

Act 1 Scene 15   485

Anonymous   **Don't listen to her.**

Sad Storm Trooper   Why?

Pedobear   You're one of us. Why are you doxing him?

Wingding   I name you Gregg Housh, unmarried developer with a six-year-old step-son. Gregg Housh social security number 91553783.

Gregg   Why are you doing this to me?

Wingding   I name you Gregg Housh.

Gregg   Guys please.

I'm still me. I'm still me?

Sad Storm Trooper   I can't believe this.

Reporter   The Church of Scientology is bringing a class action against leader of Anonymous, Gregg Housh of Carolina street Washington for, trespassing, criminal harassment.

Wingding   Anonymous has become no different to Scientology. An unaccountable bully. You are a cult. I am warning all of you hackers who say you're not leading Anonymous, I know you are. You're the same as the one per cent. I will show the world how you've corrupted Anonymous. And I will not stop until I've named every one of you.

Teacher   Mustafa!

Act 2 Scene 1 – Norris Green Secondary School

Teacher Mustafa! Homework please? Thank you. Thank you. Thank you. Mustafa? Homework?

Mustafa I, uh, I, uh I haven't I haven't I haven't done it, uh Miss.

Teacher Why not?

Mustafa I, I uh, I . . . tried to do it. But it uh, it uh, it it it it was just too much, too much work.

Teacher Bring it in tomorrow then. So today/class we're looking at.

Mustafa Don't think I will!

Miss.

Teacher Why not?

Mustafa I uh . . . I uh . . . I don't uh, I don't see the, the point/ miss.

Teacher You don't see the point in homework?

Mustafa I see a, I see a point. There's obviously a point. I just uh, I just don't don't don't see the see the point in the volume, you give us.

Teacher I've increased the homework to give you a better a chance at passing your GCSEs. It's called conditioning.

Mustafa But, but your supposition is uh, is false.

Teacher I'm your teacher, this is how you get results. I've got through more GCSEs than you thank you very much Mustafa. I'll have your homework first thing tomorrow.

Mustafa There's a flaw in your logic.

Teacher Mustafa, despite this being the most you have ever said in class in five years, I'm going to have to ask you to shut up. Class turn to/page, thirty-three.

Mustafa You're wrong.

Mustafa What for?

Teacher Disobedience.

Mustafa I'm not doing the homework.

Teacher Then I'll put you in another detention, and another until you do as I say.

Mustafa You're not interested in what we think, you're only interested in what we know. Why are subjects divided? Why are we taught in the same age group? It's not gonna be like this when we have jobs?

Teacher Studies have proven that this/is the most effective way of

Mustafa Our education system is designed by the military and the military doesn't want independent thinking. They don't want soldiers questioning orders. So they silo our information to stop us making any intuitive connections. Because once we start to understand, how biology affects. . .finance, or how physics affect art and geography affects language then we don't need a hierarchy. We can think for ourselves.

Teacher If you let me/finish Mustafa . . .

Mustafa What's the difference between running towards a machine gun and buying the latest upgrade? Nothing. It's all mindless.

Teacher As I was/saying . . .

Mustafa And I refuse it. I refuse to be treated like someone who can't think for himself. So I asked the whole class how many pieces of homework they completed, and then I cross-referenced that with their results and they don't correlate. There is a correlation though between, not doing your homework. And getting good results.

Teacher That's simply not possible.

Advice Dog Here.

Mustafa Thank you.

Anonymous Go Mouth!

Mustafa Here's the raw data, and the data percentaged. X axes is test scores. And y axes is homeworks completed. I wasn't sure of Tamwar's actual test score so I've estimated to within two points. As you can see the only conclusion you can draw from this proves the more homework you do, the poorer your results.

Anonymous I ain't doing no more/homework.

Anonymous Me neither.

Anonymous Miss./I'm not doing none.

Teacher Don't listen to him./I'll take this thank you very much.

Anonymous You don't know what you're doing. It's there in black and white.

Teacher I'm not discussing Mustafa's/experiment.

Anonymous Why would/he lie though? Why would he lie?

Anonymous Look. Firaz and Mustafa, done the least homework right. And they got the highest test scores in the mocks. I wanna go college yeah? I wanna pass my exam, and if not doing no more homework is gonna help. I ain't doing no-more. Nice one Mouth.

Teacher Mustafa,/you are suspended.

Mustafa What?

Teacher I will not be undermined in my own class. We are going to the headteacher and I am suspending you from school. Pack your things.

Anton That was fucking sweet.

Me and Jayson are going to Maccy D's after school. Come with?

Mustafa Oh I promised some dissidents in Egypt I'd set up some proxy dial-ups for them because the Government turned off their internet.

Anton They have an offer on McFlurries.

Mustafa I'll see what I can do.

Act 2 Scene 2

Topiary Gregg Housh?

Gregg Hey.

Topiary Is that really you, Gregg Housh?

Gregg It's me.

You want some timestamped tits? It's me.

You don't trust me. It's fine. I understand. You're not the first. I've been haunting chatrooms all day. I empty them quicker than Pedobear.

Topiary If only we had something that, only the real Tuxedo and the real Topiary would know, then I'd know it's you.

Gregg I owe you . . . Tuxedo, owes you.

This.

Topiary Ohai Tuxedo.

Gregg Hi.

Topiary You're the first person I've met online, that I really know who you are.

Gregg Welcome to the freakshow.

Topiary How did she do it?

Gregg She social engineered it out of some friends. I'd used Tuxedo to write some reviews on some blogs. I've been using the same handle for years. I are stupid.

Topiary We'll get revenge. I promise. We'll dox her back. We'll find out where she works, we'll find her medical records, we will ruin her life forever I promise.

Gregg Well thanks, I guess. I'm almost more worried about my wife. She's pretty pissed. I have a stepson; this is just the kind of shit that makes her question my suitability as a parent. It's gonna stop me getting a job. I'm thirty-four. We already have enough arguments about money. How can I explain Anonymous to someone who's not in Anonymous?

Topiary We'll get revenge.

Gregg You know. I'm never going to be Anonymous again, whatever happens to Wingding, I'm never getting that back. So what's the point?

Topiary Revenge.

Gregg What's the point in that?

Seriously, what's the point?

Topiary It's our . . . it's what, we believe in. We don't forgive. We don't forget. Expect us. That's our code.

Gregg Why?

Topiary Because no other code works.

Gregg You think it's working for me? I have Feds going through my apartment taking my stuff, they took my wife's hard drive with all her pictures of her son on it. Baby photos. I feel like I've lost my best friend. And I don't know who I am anymore. You wouldn't understand.

Topiary You don't know.

Gregg If you've lost something like this, then you *know* you have to forgive.

Topiary   Why?

Gregg   So when my wife talks to me about responsibility I can look her in the eye and get what she's trying to say, so when the Feds are asking me questions I can concentrate and when I'm playing soft-ball with step-son, I'm just playing softball with my step-son. I'm not pre-occupied with stuff I can't control. Forgiveness doesn't give someone else a second chance, it gives *you* a second chance.

Topiary   You do what you need to do, we'll do what we do.

Shetland Mental health team   Hello? Shetland mental health team.

Topiary   Hi. Do you. Do you do home visits?

Act 2 Scene 3 – Internet Feds Chatroom

Kayla   Hi!

Sabu   'Sup.

AVUnit   Hi.

Pwnsauce   Howdy.

Topiary   Hey.

Tflow   Hey. Read this email.

Anonymous   Two nights ago my cousin is arrested. The police.

He was taken to local station. An hour later they ring to say he has a heart attack and die. So I go with his brother to collect his body and start make arrangements. When we got there, we see his nose is broke, and his skull is broke between his forehead and his head. Like he'd been hit with something on top of head. You can see in jpg. His head is now it is all pushed in. He is cover in bruises, shaped like shoe. They say, he overdose on cannabis. I took this picture for my record for my phone. They don't know

I take this. You don't overdose on cannabis. And you don't bleed from ears with heart attack. They do this because of facebook. He post on protest pages, and then they arrest him. The Government they let the police kill protestors. It is no law in Tunisia now. We cannot organise any protests while they watch social media. Only people safe are working for Ben Ali security services and police. The police do what they want. We have no justice. I know they access facebook and twitter but thousands don't. Look at jpg. He's twenty-three. No one is safe.

Tflow He's come to Anonymous for help. But Anonymous is a paranoid mess. The hive is tearing itself apart. So I thought, maybe. If I can get a small group together with the right skills. We can help him.

Kayla I know Sabu and Pwnsauce.

Topiary I know Pwnsauce.

Pwnsauce I know Kayla and AVUnit.

Tflow Everyone knows Topiary.

AVunit I know Tflow and Pwnsauce.

Tflow So there should be a logical flow of trust between us. We've got the skills to help this Anon out. Sabu rooting networks, AVUnit and me writing programmes, Kayla and Pwnsauce finding vulnerabilities, and exploiting, and Topiary with any defaces and publicity. What do you say?

AVUnit It sounds like a phishing program.

Kayla Could be a simple piece of code in the browser. If we can read it we can write a plug-in to override it and that'll disable it.

Pwnsauce I can't get into any .tn sites.

Tflow They've sealed their Internet so no one with a foreign ISP can get into the country.

Pwnsauce How are we going to get that code?

AVUnit Mobile dial ups?

Pwnsauce Too unstable.

Kayla If we could get some sims into the country that might work.

Tflow Sabu can you check if there are any network vulnerabilities?

Sabu I ain't taking instruction from no nigga.

AVunit It was just a question.

Sabu You think I got where I am by following orders?

I asked you a question.

AVunit I have no idea.

Sabu How think I got where I am?

Tflow By being the best. Everyone is here because they're the best. Sabu, how can we get in there?

Sabu You need proxies/to get into the Tunisian Internet.

Tflow That's too dangerous.

Sabu FUCK IT NIGGA. They kicking people to death.

Topiary I have a name. Lulzsec anyone? Lulz and Justice.

Pwnsauce Lulz and Justice coming to Tunisia.

Sabu Has anyone *else* got a problem with proxies? Alright.

Act 2 Scene 4 – OpTunisia

Sabu Niggas Sabu's in the house. We need to help our revolutionary brothers in Tunisia, but we can't do that without proxies. Are there any Anons here with Tunisian ISPs? For operational security we can't tell you what we're doing. You just need to trust Anonymous. Do I have a volunteer to let me control their computer?

Kayla AVUnit, Tflow honey. As soon as we find the phishing code you guys write a browser plug-in that will override it.

Sabu I'm going to need your guys help to penetrate the Government websites. We're in. Get looking! No stone unturned.

Pwnsauce I'm in Tunisian google, seems clear.

Kayla No, there's a small piece of code, at the bottom here.

Pwnsauce Oh my God it's everywhere.

Kayla Holy shit they're monitoring everything.

Pwnsauce Gmail, Yahoo, Hotmail, AOL, Facebook, Twitter, Flickr, they're spying on everything.

Tflow OK. Date open bracket close bracket. getTime open bracket close bracket plus quotation close bracket semi colon anotherautoupdater dot call open bracket true close bracket parenthesis close bracket comma.

AVUnit Close bracket close bracket close bracket.

Tflow What no?

AVunit Yes close bracket close bracket close bracket, comma if open bracket

Tflow Self location equals rquals toplocation ampersand ampersand typof GM xmlhttpRequest

Sabu Hurry up, niggas!

Tflow exclamation mark equals equals.

AVUnit Undefined close bracket AnotherAutoUpdater.check

Tflow Openbracketclosebracket unsafeWindow.h6. equals open bracket close bracket open bracket close bracket semi colon.

AVUnit Unsafewindow.r5t equals function.

Sabu Dammit niggas! Come on!

Kayla They are going to track our proxies.

Tflow Open bracket close bracket open bracket close bracket unsafewindow.hAAAQ3D equals function open bracket close bracket open bracket close bracket unsafewindow dot inv zero k one equals function open bracket close bracket unsafewindow.inv zero k 2 equals function open bracket close bracket semi colon unsafewindow dot inv 0 k 3 equals function open bracket close bracket open bracket close bracket semi colon.

AVUnit He's done it!

Sabu Great work.

Topiary Greetings. From Anonymous. We have been watching the treatment of your own citizens. And we are both greatly saddened and enraged by your behaviour. Anonymous is willing to help the Tunisian people. Cyber attacks *will* continue until the Tunisian Government respects *all* Tunisians right to free speech and information, and ceases to censor the Internet./You have been, warned.

Reporter Online activists have disabled several Tunisian government websites in the latest act of protest against the country's embattled leadership. As of Monday afternoon, local time, eight websites had been affected including those for the president, prime minister, ministry of industry, ministry of foreign affairs, and the stock exchange.

Sabu That was a job well done my niggas. We make a great hacking family, awesome work Tflow.

Teacher Mustafa, **welcome back.**

Topiary I loved speaking to the whole of Tunisia! That's what this is about.

Teacher Have you put all that nonsense behind you? Good. I believe in independent thinking; but I have a job to do. You need to learn when to speak up, and when to shut up.

Topiary I had a tweet of a whole school wearing Anon masks to say thank you. I don't know what to say?

Shetland Mental Health It's ok. Probably haven't spoken to anyone in quite a while. Been a bit of a buzz about you in the office. We think you're the first agrophobe in Shetland.

AVUnit The street protests are spreading outside of Sidi Bouzid.

Shetland Mental Health So what we're going to do is. We're going to have a routine where each week I come round.

Pwnsauce There's one planned for Sfax.

Shetland Mental Health Do your week's shop together. I'll be with you. And then we'll come straight back. How does that feel?

Tflow I can't get in touch with any of the proxy Anons.

AVUnit Protests in Sousse and Merknassy.

Shetland Mental Health We'll do a weekly shop. But it's good for you. Breaks up your week, and you know you can chat to the till staff. Maybe about the weather. Or *Bake-Off*. Do you watch *Bake-Off*? Just a little chat, build your confidence.

Kayla Google Maps show's they're getting closer to Tunis.

Shetland Mental Health How'd you feel about a little visit to the shops to get some milk?

Sabu We just made a revolution happen.

Act 2 Scene 5 – Internet Feds/HBGary/Aaron Barr's home

Aaron Barr Hi I'm Aaron Barr, Chief Executive of HBGary cyber security. Our clients include the FBI, CIA, NSA, Department of Defence and Goldman Sachs to name just a few. As part of a research project into online security, I've managed to penetrate Anonymous!

I've discovered the names of *all* the leading figures. There's an inner circle of six! Who make *all* the decisions, a hardcore elite who carry out operations. I will be revealing the identity of Lulzsec at a press conference in San Francisco, to show what extraordinary work we do at HBGary, securing your business, securing you, by naming them.'

Kayla He's funny.

AVUnit Aren't you worried he has our names?

Kayla He doesn't have my name.

AVunit How do you know?

Kayla I trust my security/don't you trust yours?

Pwnsauce I'm a little freaked out that our real identities have corporate value now.

AVUnit We need to find out what he's got.

Pwnsauce People will pay good money to know who we are? They don't give a shit about us in real life.

Tflow We need to find out before he announces anything.

Sabu It's a PR stunt.

AVUnit A PR stunt that could dox every one of us. We need to hack his info.

Pwnsauce If he's right, we need to give him a reason to think twice.

AVUnit And we need to warn other 'cyber security experts' not to even try doxing us.

Kayla This sounds fun.

Tflow I'm in.

Pwnsauce Grand. I've been thinking, if he's a 'cyber-security expert'. What's the most embarrassing way to hack him?

AVUnit Social engineering.

Topiary Definitely.

Sabu Alright, can I get some office ambience please? Thank you. Hello!

Aaron Barr Yes!

Sabu Yes this is uh Gerry in IT. We've uh had to do a *full* system uh re-boot and we're uh half way through re-configuring our uh data loops? They've spooled around our servers after a super-booster crashed.

Aaron Sounds complicated.

Sabu I'm just uh checking everything is fine with your machine?

Aaron Barr Everything's fine. Little slow/that's all.

Sabu Can I check your cell number, uh stop me if I'm wrong, nine one two triple five eight four, three nine.

Aaron Barr Correct.

Sabu Email address, uh stop me if I'm wrong arron, double r, dot bar at HBGary dot com.

Aaron Barr Correct.

Sabu Fax number, uh stop me if I'm wrong nine one two zero three zero eight four six seven

Aaron Barr The fax is wrong. It's eight four six eight.

Sabu Mr Barr, some of our records appear to be out of date. I'm uh, gonna have to re-boot your login details, is your login arron.barr at HBGary dot com.

Aaron Barr Yes.

Sabu And your password?

Aaron Barr Kibafo33.

Sabu Thanks. Give me uh, about a half hour. And you should receive an email with your new password.

Aaron Barr Thanks, Gerry! And thank you everyone for coming today. Here at HBGary we believe life is built on security. Security for our family, friends and business. We consider all of our clients as family.

Tflow Topiary. We need you.

Aaron Barr Just as when your kids play on the sidewalk and you worry for their safety.

Kayla What are you doing?

Aaron Barr HBGary feels like that, about your businesses and the Internet.

AVUnit Topiary we've got this dick's twitter feed ready for you.

Aaron Barr It is a dangerous place out there if you do not know what you're doing. That's why you need the experts. HBGary. And after today's announcement, why not follow me on twitter? Everyone loves a tweet.

Sabu What's the fucking delay?

Socially Awkward Penguin Come on everyone's waiting!

Aaron Barr So, here are the real identities for the hackers known as Sabu, Tflow, AVUnit, Topiary, Pwnsauce and Kayla.

Topiary Excuse me, sorry sorry. Aaron's not able to continue today because he has AIDS in the mouth. Too much, banging hookers, doing speedballs and thinking of his mother when he ejacuspaffs! So this one's a little number inspired by Aaron. 'It's called I use the same password, over and over again like a fucking wanker'.

Kibafo33 gets me into my twitter,

Kibafo33 gets me into my facebook

Kibafo33 gets me into my, PayPal, my porn and my wonderful world of warcraft!

Kibafo33 gets me into work in the morning

Kibafo33 gets me into my phone at night

Kibafo33 gets me into my banking, my Ipad, my family pictures on flickr

One password, one answer, one login

One thing to remember and you know all there is to know about me!

Kid Barr Why are we going to Grandma and Grandpa's?

Aaron Barr It's a holiday!

Kid Barr What about school?

Aaron Barr It's a secret holiday.

Kid Barr Why can't I have my Ipad?

Aaron Barr No Ipads on this holiday.

Kid Barr Why not?

Topiary Yeah, why not?

Kid Barr Can I have your phone Mom?

Aaron Barr NO! No phones, no tablets no nothing.

Kid Barr Why/ not?

Topiary Yeah! Why not?

Aaron Barr God dammit can you both shut up with your racket? There's going to be no phones, no Ipads no laptops no computers, no sat nav OK?

Kid Barr That's not fair! Why won't you just tell me why, what have I done to deserve this?

Topiary Tell her? Why don't you just tell her. It's not her fault. Tell her, you thought you could boost your reputation by revealing the names of a bunch of teenage hackers. But you got every single name wrong. Because you're an idiot.

Kid Barr Daaad?

Topiary Tell her Aaron. She thinks it's her fault.

Aaron Barr You haven't done anything wrong sweetie! Daddy. Daddy made a mistake. Made a mistake and. He needs to uh. He needs to think. He just needs some time to think.

Aaron Barr Kibafo33 my wife wants to divorce me

Kibafo33 my company's nearly bankrupt

Kibafo33 here's seventy thousand emails, and passwords, and company secrets

One password, one answer, one login

One thing to remember and you can access my life for free!

Kibafo33 my reputation is ruined.

Kibafo33 We're leaving the house for a little while.

Kibafo33 Cost me my career, my finance my everything!

One password, one answer, one login

One thing to remember but maybe, just maybe you won't forget what happened to me!

Topiary Here's a picture of a gaping anus.

Act 2 Scene 6 – AnonOps/Skype radio

DJ Topiary the Internet says Westboro Baptist Church is Anonymous' next target. Is that true?

Topiary Uh.

Shirley Phelps Bring it on! You coward crybaby hackers! You cannot defeat the word of GOD!

DJ I have Shirley Phelps with me live on air would you join us?

Shirley NO ONE CAN SHUT THESE SITES DOWN THESE WORDS ARE ROARING FROM ZION! I mean I'm talking to a little guy who's a Jew.

DJ Thank you, Shirley.

Tflow We have to do it.

Topiary I didn't write that statement. Shirley, we don't want to go to war with you.

Tflow Come on, guys, let's do it, it'll be fun.

DJ Anonymous, the Westboro Baptist Church sites seem fine. Is this the end of your run as the most powerful group on the Internet?

Topiary Um um, uh . . . Um, Shirley. You say, you say the Internet was invented just for the Westboro Baptist Church to get its message across right?

Shirley Exactly.

DJ Anonymous, have we lost you?

Topiary Yes, sorry, well, how come, how come God allows gay dating websites? If he hates fags, why's he letting them find each other?

Shirley Easy, that's called your proving ground.

DJ Have we still got you?

Tflow Done.

Topiary Shirley, can you go to downloads dot Westboro Baptist Church, you'll see that we've hacked your websites and left a little message for you while we were chatting live on air.

DJ While we were live on air? That's amazing.

Pwnsauce Lol o'clock on the Lulzboat.

Topiary That was close. I looked like an idiot there.

Y U No Guy 'I looked like an idiot.'

Grumpy Cat 'Iza looksy likey idiot.'

Topiary What did you say?

AVUnit   Don't feed the trolls.

Topiary   Are they? Are *you* trolling *me*? I'm the king of trolls!

Grumpy Cat   What kind of troll uses his real voice?

Act 2 Scene 7 – AnonOps

Louisa Anderson   YOU THINK/YOU CAN FUCK WITH MY FAMILY.

Condescending Willy Wonka   She's back.

Louisa Anderson   I WILL I WILL DESTROY YOU. DESTROY YOU. I WILL – EVERY ONE OF YOU. YOU AND YOU AND YOU AND YOU AND YOU AND YOU.

LULZSEC.

AVUnit   We haven't done anything.

Louisa Anderson   Don't you fucking try to social engineer me you cunt I am a MOTHER. WE INVENTED SOCIAL ENGINEERING.

Look at you. Frightened boys. Frightened. Confused boys.

I I, I I could take, I could take the pizzas. And the taxis. I could take it. The phone calls. The disgusting things you'd say. It was fine.

But then you hacked my children's school, and put their report cards on the Internet. AND YOU THINK I'D STAND FOR THAT? DID YOU? DID YOU? DID YOU?

Just let you try and ruin my children's life? You think I'd stop, after that?

AVUnit   Louisa, it/wasn't us, it was the hive.

Louisa Anderson   I name you; *Lulzsec*.

You amoral pit.

AVUnit You haven't got to do this.

Louisa Anderson AVUnit!

AVUnit You haven't got/to do this!

Louisa Anderson Michael Jems living in Holland.

AVUnit She hasn't got me.

Louisa Anderson Pwnsauce – Ardal O'Malley – Dublin.

Pwnsauce We're all cool and the gang.

Louisa Anderson Tflow – Ranjit Persaud India.

Tflow I'm safe! I'm safe, guys.

Louisa Anderson Sabu – Hector Monsegur.

AVunit Sabu?

Sabu Bitch, bitch be trippin'.

Louisa Anderson Kayla – Lisa DeVelle in Seattle.

Kayla Whatever.

Louisa Anderson And finally the one we're all waiting for Topiary Daniel Ackerman/in Sweden.

Kayla You can't touch us! We're the leet.

Louisa Anderson I know I'm right./I'm giving this to the FBI.

Topiary Log off, and help your kids with the homework. They need it.

AVUnit I think that's our final warning to get out.

Pwnsauce Aye. Maybe it's time to log off, find a new nickname.

Tflow But we'll never find each other again.

Topiary Aye I'm getting too much shit from all sides.

Tflow I think. I think, we should do something bigger.

Kayla How much bigger?

Tflow Well. Wikileaks is, is basically shut down, right? Right? And they needed sources to, to, to leak to them. What if we publish info that we've hacked? We don't need *leakers,* we just hack it and publish it. Information wants to be free. Let's free it. Just imagine what the world would be like if we stopped copyrighting, patenting and classifying information? We could fix everything.

AVUnit Even regular people's data?

Tflow Well . . .

Kayla OhMyGod! This is so cool./Count me in.

Pwnsauce Aye, I suppose we can, you know we can say, we're showing the world how dangerous it is handing over all your information to corporations or whatever who have like zero security. It's a public service. We're doing them a favour, leaking their stuff.

AVUnit But telling everyone what we've just done is gonna bring a lot of heat.

Pwnsauce We need to publicise it otherwise the corporations won't close their vulnerabilites and then what's the point?

Kayla And how are people gonna know we're the best if we don't tell them?

Tflow If we're gonna be publicizing all this. We can't do it without you Topiary.

Pwnsauce Yeah.

Kayla You know you want to.

Tflow We need you.

Topiary Fuck it. Whatever, I'm in.

AVUnit Sabu?

Sabu Niggas.

I've got to uh.

Imma.

I have a shitty connection to you guys.

Pwnsauce   Right! Before we start can we put out a statement saying there's no leaders, I'm getting pretty fucked off with this whole 'leader of Lulzsec shite'. We're not correcting them.

Kayla   So cuuute when you're angry!

AVUnit   Sabu? Are you in or are you out?

Sabu   Yeah/dammit.

Tflow   Ok,/ so.

Sabu   This is how we do it. We write trawler programs, that search the *entire* motherfuckin web.

Tflow   I/was thinking.

Sabu   No prejudice! We get ourselves the greatest list of vulnerabilities ever. And one by one, we just leak and leak and watch the chaos.

Topiary   We search the *whole* web?

Pwnsauce   We hack the *planet*?

Tflow   I /thought we could.

Sabu   That way, no one's safe, no prejudice. Find a weakness, then choose a target. You want to find the good shit? You gotta look where you least expect it.

Kayla   Let's do it.

Sabu   What's the NHS?

Tflow&Topiary&Kayla   No!

Pwnsauce   Medicine San Frontier?

AVUnit   No!

Kayla   Fox?

Sabu   What you got?

Kayla   I reckon,

Seventy-three

thousand

email addresses and

passwords.

AVUnit Think we've got our first leak.

Sabu Torrent that shit, Topiary tell the fans seventy three thousand email addresses and passwords.

Tflow But, uh, most of these are people who entered *X Factor?* Should we just leak the company passwords?

Topiary They're *X Factor* applicants? They crave humiliation.

Sabu I AIN'T EXPLAINING MYSELF TO YOU.

AVUnit I think your caps lock must be stuck? Makes you sound like a dick.

Tflow Maybe we could just leak something from a, a, University?

Sabu We dump it all. Topiary do your shit.

Topiary Good evening! Welcome to tonight's episode of recycle the password! We're broadcasting from our studios in LinkedIn! And who have we got here?

Mary I'm Mary D'Arcy.

Topiary Ohai Mary!

Mary I read all your tweets!

Topiary What do you do Mary?

Mary Um, well I'm an executive at the Fox Broadcasting Company.

Topiary And Mary, please tell your colleagues what you like doing in your spare time?

Mary I like sucking hot balls!

Topiary That is such an adorable laugh! You like . . .

Mary I like sucking hot balls, yes! I know. Drop them nom nom. I'm blushing now.

Topiary And who do we have here?

Jeff Nevin I'm Jeff Nevin. I work for Fox too. Although I've never met Mary. Hi!

Mary Hi!

Jeff Nevin I work in corporate communications, so I deal with all internal information channels.

Topiary And please, Jeff, tell your colleagues what do you like doing?

Jeff Well, I like putting things in my bot-bot and going shopping.

Topiary And going shopping?

Socially Awkward Penguin Awesome.

Jeff Nevin To the mall.

Topiary And what do you like putting in your bot-bot?

Jeff Nevin Oh anything really, keys. What's lying around. Bottle tops, the hook part of a coathanger. Doesn't matter. As long as it's uncomfortable.

Topiary Well there you have it, ladies and gentlemen, please give a warm hand for Mary and Jeff, the degenerates running Fox! Your most popular global news service.

Kayla The *Sun* website!

Topiary Breaking news from the *Sun*. Let's see what they're reporting on their front page!

The Sun Carked it! The body of media mogul Rupert Murdoch has been discovered in his famous topiary garden!

Topiary But I want more! WHO WANTS MORE? WHO WANTS SONY PICTURES! The biggest fucking leak you've ever seen. Anyone want A MILLION USERS' DETAILS? Strap in.

Anonymous B/AAAMMMMMMPPPP!

Topiary THIS IS THE BIGGEST LEAK THE PLANET HAS SEEN. BUT I WANT MORE. I WANT MORE. I WANT/ MOAAARRRR!

Mum Jake . . . your sister and I are leaving/Shetland and moving to.

Jake W/hat?

Mum Couple of weeks.

Socially Awkward Penguin

Anxiety Cat

Mum New job.

Topiary Both of you.

Grumpy Cat

Mum Moving to the mainland.

Grumpy Cat

Mum You'll be fine on your own.

Socially Awkward Penguin

Topiary

Mum Jake.

Topiary

Mum Jake.

Topiary

Mum Please.

Topiary It's a crap connection.

Nato 'Anonymous is becoming more sophisticated, evidenced by the HBGary Federal attack. The group could potentially hack into sensitive government, military and corporate files.'

AVunit Anyone feeling the heat in here?

Sabu They declaring war on us. We need to step things up a gear. Every hack could be our last. What do we wanna be known as? They guys who said Tupac was still alive or something serious?

AVunit OpTunisia was a joke, was it?

Sabu Who here's heard of InfraGard? It's a company that subcontracts intelligence work from the FBI. Half the database are FBI agents. I have a vuln niggers. Who wants to hack the FBI?

AVUnit I'm out.

Sabu NO-ONE'S LEAVING. ANYONE WHO WALKS OUT ON ME IS A FED. Are you a Fed? ARE YOU A FED?

AVUnit No. But how can any of us really know?

Sabu I know, nigga. We're a family. I trust every one of you niggas. I'd take a bullet for every one of you.

Why don't you want to hit the Feds? You scared?

Tflow Um ... not really.

Sabu You don't trust me?

Tflow I uh, I think so.

Sabu We a family? Have I got anyone in my team who's got the balls to do this with me?

Pwnsauce I'm up for fucking the FBI.

Kayla Me too.

AVUnit Why? What's the point in this?

Pwnsauce Because ...

AVUnit Why are we listening to him?

Pwnsauce Because there's crime . . . and then there's lolcrime OK?

AVUnit I see.

Pwnsauce It's lollyliscious, OK? Don't fuck with my lulz. Why are you such a buzzkill?

AVUnit Hitting the FBI will bring more heat than we've had before. You might think this is one big joke but some of us have real lives. And if I don't feel safe, I'm not doing anything. If we get caught it's going to be because someone in this room fucks up.

Pwnsauce Lol trust!

AVUnit You'll go down before I will.

Pwnsauce What do we even know about each other?

AVUnit Sabu's in the States. East Coast.

Sabu Topes and Tflow are in the UK.

Tflow Kayla logs on at US Eastern times.

AVUnit But you mentioned baked beans once.

Kayla You're Irish.

Pwnsauce Get to fuck you bollocks.

Sabu You, nigga, you are a mystery.

Pwnsauce Professionally vague.

Sabu Anyone got anything on this brother?

Pwnsauce Yeah I got nothing.

Kayla Me neither.

Tflow I haven't.

AVUnit Then you can count me in.

Sabu We spend twenty hours a day talking to each other, more than any other family, but we don't know shit about each other. You want to see the future? It's right here.

Pwnsauce It's been nice not getting to know you all.

Sabu Right here, we have *no* flow of information. A government is an information system and we disrupt that. What we do is revolutionary. We're making a new system not only possible, but necessary. Who's in?

Topiary Me. And you're all coming with me.

Sabu There ain't no going back after this.

Topiary Good.

Sabu My family. Let's do it.

FBI Hector Monsegur.

Hector Monsegur?

Hector Can I help?

FBI Step away from your laptops.

Hector What's this about?

FBI Step away from your laptops.

Are you Hector Monsegur?

Hector Yes.

FBI Hector Monsegur, we're arresting you for conspiracy to computer hack, conspiracy to commit device fraud, conspiracy to commit bank fraud, aggravated identity theft. Is there someone who can come to take care of your children?

Hector Get off me! /GET OFF ME!

FBI Lay down! /Face down!

Hector YOU'RE HURTING ME!

FBI Face/on the ground!

Hector YOU'RE HURTING MY ARM./GET OFF ME. GET OFF ME!

FBI Do not resist arrest. You want your kids to see this, Hector? You want them to see you like this? Is there someone who can take care of them?

Hector No.

FBI Where's their mother?

Hector They're not mine. I, I got custody. They're uh, they're my cousins, both their parents in jail./I'm raising them.

FBI Is there someone who can come care for them?

Hector I told you, everyone's in jail.

FBI Put a call in to social services.

Hector No no no no no no. They not going into care.

FBI If you've got no-one, Hector,/we'll have to call social services.

Hector No no no no no. Listen. Listen. Let's talk about this OK. Let's just slow down.

FBI They'll be looked after.

Hector They my girls.

FBI I promise they'll be looked after.

Hector They seen enough. They seen things . . . We ain't being separated.

FBI I'm afraid that's not going to be possible.

Hector What do you need to know? Maybe we can come to an arrangement, sir.

FBI Are you Sabu?

Hector Yes.

FBI Are you willing to turn state's witness?

Hector I get to stay with my girls.

FBI Help us dismantle Anonymous, and we'll make sure you stay with your girls.

Sabu OK.

FBI Let him go. Let's get him back online.

Tflow Hey guys, check it out, I've used some bitcoins to set up our own Lulz IRC.

Anonymous Oh. Uh. Oh. I. It's. it's.

Topiary It's ok.

Anonymous Oh my God. Oh my God.

Topiary It's ok.

Anonymous IT'S TOOOOOPPPPPIIIIIIAAAAAAARRRRRREEEEEE.

Anonymous It's TFLOW! TFLOW! You're my favourite!

Ryan Uh. I want to join your gang.

Tflow What?

Ryan I want to join your gang. I want to hang out with you. I'll do whatever you say. Can we be friends? Tflow.

Tflow I, I/ uh um.

Topiary He's mental, ignore him.

Ryan I have my own servers, a botnet with over a million bots. I'll do whatever you want. I just want to be in your gang.

Topiary Why?

Ryan Why are you being weird? Just tell me what you want doing, I'll do it and then we'll be friends and I'll be in your gang. I'VE GOT ALL THIS STUFF. Come on. Can we be friends?

Tflow Um I've got/enough friends, Ryan . . .

Ryan I'LL PROVE MYSELF! I'll prove myself! Then you'll want me in the gang! Who/do you want to DDoS hm?

Topiary Fuck off, Ryan,/you imbecile. Kick him out, Tflow.

Ryan Name a site, any site.

Tflow We don't/DDoS anyone.

Ryan Name a site any site.

Tflow We've/stopped DDoSing.

Ryan NAME A FUCKING SITE.

Tflow FUCK OFF, RYAN.

Ryan Right. CIA.gov then.

AAAAAAAHAAAAAHAAAAAAAAAHAAAAAAAAHHHHH
HHAAAAAMUUUUUUUDKIIIIIIIIIIPPPSSSSS.

Ryan Announce it! For Lulz and justice. ANNOUNCE IT. ANNOUNCE IT. ANNOUNCE IT.

Topiary Um … Tango down.

Topiary CIA.gov.

Reporter **Lulzsec/** have struck again! This time it's the Central Intelligence Agency.

Reporter the **CIA/**are the latest victims of hacking group **Lulzsec**.

Reporter The **CIA/**website has been offline for eight hours after being attacked by notorious group **Lulzsec.**

Pwnsauce What the *fuck* is going on? What have you done?

Topiary Nothing, I told Tflow to kick him off the server and the next thing I know he's taken out the CIA.

AVUnit What the fuck, Tflow?

Tflow I, I, I,/don't know I

AVUnit This is just/the kind of stupid shit we need to steer clear of.

Pwnsauce Why didn't you just get rid of him?

Tflow I, uh, I/ uh was

Topiary What's the point in having a fucking server if we're just gonna let Assberger cunts like him in.

Ryan Hey guys! Am I in Lulzsec now? Do I get a . . . is there a handshake or something there should be a handshake.

My Mum, she makes the *best* ham sandwiches. Do your Mums look after you?

Kayla I live with my Dad so.

Ryan Does he make you/sandwiches? Ham etc.

Pwnsauce Ryan. Do you mind?/We're just having a private chat?

Ryan DOES HE MAKE SANDWICHES?

Tflow Private, private channel! Sorry Ryan.

Ryan Where are you going?

AVUnit Two minutes Ryan.

Ryan OK I'll be here and then we'll go after another target. My botnet's got like over a million bots.

Pwnsauce Yup. OK, Ryan.

Kayla Tflow, you need to keep him on the server.

Tflow You uh you uh, just told me me/me to uh to take him off.

Kayla Shut the fuck up and listen. You need to make him listen to you. He needs to log off, he needs to wipe all of his hard drives. Then he needs to melt his computers.

Tflow He's, he's he's not/my friend.

Kayla I don't give a shit.

Pwnsauce We need to get him to melt his computers.

AVUnit You need to control this shit/Tflow if you're running the server.

Ryan AAAAAHHHHHHHHHHHHHHHHHHHHHHHHHHHH
HHHHHH MUUUUUUUUUDDDDDKKKIIIIIIIIIIIIIIIIIIIIIIII
IIIIIIIIIIPPPPPPPPSSSSSSSSSSSSSSSSSS!!!!!

Kayla What's he doing now?

Pwnsauce Holy shit.

AVUnit He's just DDoS'd the Serious Organised Crime Agency and the NSA.

Topiary Ryan! Ryan? RYAN!

Ryan WHY DID YOU LEAVE ME? STOP LEAVING
ME OUT! STOP LEAVING ME OUT OF THINGS. WE'RE
FRIENDS. WE'RE A TEAM. I'M IN THE TEAM.

STOP LEAVING/ME OUT. WE'RE SUPPOSED TO BE

AVUnit Sorry Ryan./needed to talk.

Ryan STOP LEAVING ME OUT.

Pwnsauce I'm sorry Ryan but you didn't have to shut down the two largest spying agencies on the planet.

Ryan I know what you're doing you're trying to get control of my bots. Well you can't they're my bots, I'm the fucking botnet king OK? You will have to, do what I say, if you want the bots. But I will let you, if you want to go on them, I will let you but only. I will let you. I will. I will let you. OK. I'll let you have a go on them. Do you want to have a go on them?/It's OK if you do.

AVunit Ryan. How good is your security?

Ryan What?

Kayla How good is your security?

Ryan Are you trying to social engineer me?

Pwnsauce Ryan. Is your real name Ryan?

Ryan No.

AVunit Your name's Ryan, isn't it?

Ryan Yes.

AVUnit Ryan what?

Ryan Ryan Cleary.

AVUnit I'm/ out.

Kayla L/aters.

Pwnsauce Bye.

Topiary Haha! What a fucking genius?/I'm Ryan Cleary. Hello! I just took down the NSA, here's my card. Why not fucking put a video up of you DDoSing everything from your bedroom?

Ryan STOP TRYING TO MAKE ME A PUNCHLINE. I'M NOT A PUNCHLINE. I AM A HUMAN BEING WITH A LOT OF ROBOTS. I HAVE MORE ROBOTS THAN YOU. HOW MANY ROBOTS HAVE YOU GOT HUH? I'VE GOT OVER A MILLION. ALL I'VE GOT TO DO IS PUSH THE BUTTON.

AND I OWN THE MOST POWERFUL PEOPLE ON/THE INTERNET. ALL FROM MY BEDROOM. IN MY MUM'S. I AM INVINCIBLE!

Reporter Ryan Cleary, The leader of Lulzsec the notorious global hacking group has been arrested in a dawn raid in Essex. The eighteen-year-old was apprehended by members of the Metropolitan police cyber-crime division.

Sabu Where is everybody?

Topiary Ryan scared them off. Where've you been?

FBI Grandmother died.

Sabu Grandmother died, nigga.

FBI We cast her ashes at the beach.

Sabu We cast her ashes at the beach.

FBI You got any beaches by you?

Sabu You got any beaches by you?

Topiary I'm surrounded by beaches, but they aren't the kind you go sunbathing on.

FBI You like pebbly beaches.

Sabu I like pebbly beaches nigga.

Topiary It's not the pebbles it's the fucking rain.

FBI Give him the leak.

Sabu So, so this Anon says he's hacked the Arizona State Police, and wants us to leak it for him. I'm dumping it tonight. He's written a statement up as well, you niggas got idle.

Topiary This, says 'Kill The Police.'

FBI Make them publish it.

Sabu What's the problem?

Nigga?

Topiary Nothing.

Just.

We're leaking the names and addresses of police officers.

And in the same breath we're saying 'kill them'?

Sabu Do you have a fucking point you want to make Topiary?

Topiary What if you some aspie twat like Ryan reads it? It's conspiracy to murder. Am I going mad here Tflow? Tflow?

Tflow I uh I uh, I, I I u h uh uh.

Sabu It's a revolution.

That's the price.

FBI We need this published on the Lulzsec Twitter feed. Get them to incite murder.

Sabu How can I build a movement if Anons can't trust my word. They, they look up to me. The Anon did the work, he found the vulnerability, he exploited it, this is his statement, don't get all moralfag on my ass. Publish it.

Topiary This ain't Lulz or Justice.

Sabu Publish it.

Topiary No.

Sabu I'll publish it myself.

Topiary You can't I'm the only one with the passwords.

Sabu I hacked it, nigga.

Topiary You can't.

Sabu I already/did it.

Topiary It's my feed.

Sabu I /already did it.

Topiary Everyone knows it's me.

Sabu Too late, nigga.

Topiary That's my. It's. That's my feed. That's all I've got. That is literally all I've got.

FBI Publish it.

Sabu I'm publishing it.

Topiary IT'S ALL I'VE GOT.

They'll think it's me saying it. Everyone will think I've written it. Everyone will think I want them to kill the police.

FBI Good.

Sabu Good.

Topiary What if someone does?

Sabu Publish it.

Topiary   Please. I'm begging you.

Sabu   Publish it.

Topiary   Tflow.

Topiary   Ladies and gentlemen.

We're releasing hundreds of private intelligence bulletins, training manuals, personal email correspondence, and, the names, phone numbers, home addresses and passwords belonging to every police officer in the state of Arizona.

We do this, in protest at racial profiling and anti-immigration policing.

We urge you, to . . .

Kill the police.

Anonymous   AAAAHHHHHH!!! /Kill the police! Topiary! Kill the police! Topiary! Kill the police!

Reporter   Lulzsec's latest/release has urged people to kill the police whilst releasing the home addresses of police officers.

Reporter   Lulzsec has urged/people to kill serving police officers in the State of Arizona.

Reporter   Hacking group Lulzsec has urged people to murder Arizona police officers and hope to facilitate that by publishing their names and addresses.

FBI   Get Tflow to open this link.

Sabu   Check this out, nigga.

Check it out.

Tflow   Wha wha hwat the the fuck what the fuck is is is is is is wrong uh wrong with you?

Sabu   Say what?

Tflow   Have have have you got a you got a death wish?

Sabu   Say what?

Tflow   I said Have you got a death wish?

Sabu   Where's all/this drama coming from?

Tflow   Why do you keep pushing us? First proxies, then the FBI hack, now this. We're not fixing *anything* we're just wrecking everything. You want to get caught.

You are everything/Anonymous is fighting against.

Sabu   We're a family. We need a target that's all, something we can work together on like the HBGary days. Like

FBI   Iran.

Sabu   Iran.

FBI   Brazil.

Sabu   Brazi.mil.govs.

FBI   Pakistan.

Sabu   I got plans for us, nigga.

Topiary   I'm announcing it's over.

Sabu   NO-ONE IS ANNOUNCING ANYTHING.

Tflow   It's over.

Sabu   YOU GUYS THINK YOU'RE LEET? I'M THE ONLY LEET ONE HERE.

Topiary   Hello friend and welcome to the Internet. The Internet horde has been watching you closely for some time now. It has seen you flock to your Facebook and your twitter. It has seen you enter it's home turf and attempt to overrun it with your scandals and 'real world gossip'. You need to know, that the ownership of cyberspace will *always* remain with the hivemind. The Internet does not belong to your beloved authorities, militaries or millionaire company owners. The Internet belongs to the trolls and the hackers, the enthusiasts and the extremists. You cannot make the Internet feel bad. You cannot make the Internet feel regret. While the human race rushes to organize it's own death, the Internet smirks. While you try to bring order to your lives by making rules, the Internet knows there are none and there is no hope for you. It sets scenes of mass rape and slaughter to catchy Japanese music, it laughs at cannibalism and guffaws at industrial paedophilia because the Internet does not care. Because your betrayals, self-deception, lies and intimacies belong to the horde the horde will not tell you it will be OK. It will not hold your hand, or be quiet while you die. It will laugh. Because that is all you deserve. This is not a nightmare. This is not a dream. This is a feast. Enter the hivemind motherfuck.

Act 2 Scene 8

Met Police Officer Darren Marten, nineteen-year-old pharmaceutical chemistry student arrested in Galway.

Ryan Ackroyd, twenty-five-year-old former soldier arrested in Mexborough, Yorkshire.

Mustafa Al-Bassam sixteen-year-old schoolboy arrested at his home in Southwark, London.

Hector Monsegur – twenty-eight-year-old unemployed foster parent from Lower East Side Manhatten, is freed after extraordinary co-operation with the FBI.

AVUnit ... still at large.

Act 2 Scene 9 – Charing Cross police station

Met Police Officer Were you or have you ever been a member of the online collective known as Anonymous?

Mustafa No, no comment.

Met Police Officer 1 Did you ever use the online alias Tflow?

Mustafa Uh uh uh uh uh No comment.

Met Police Officer 1 Were you ever a member of a hacking collective known as Lulzsec?

Mustafa Uh hh uh uh No comment.

Met Police Officer 1 Did you participate in the hacking of the computer network owned by HBGary Federal?

Mustafa No, uh uh no comment.

Met Police Officer Did you take part in the hacking sites owned or affiliated with the Westboro Baptist Church?

Mustafa No, no comment.

Met Police Officer Did you take part in the hacking of sites owned by the Fox Corporation.

Mustafa No comment.

Met Police Officer **This is the most important interview of your life.** If you don't co-operate, I promise you, I am not lying to you when I say this, your life will be ruined. You lose everything. I've seen it a million times. Kids your age mixed up with the wrong crowd. They end up with youth detention, prison, license, ankle tags the works, they never shake it off. Never. Your Mum and Dad, everyone, everyone that's invested in you are looking at the mess you made of your life and are wondering why, why the hell, when you had the chance, did you make *such* a bad choice. All for a bunch of people who you've *never* met. I'm giving you one last chance to save yourself. Have you ever spoken to or associated with the online handles, Sabu, Kayla, Pwnsauce, AVUnit and Topiary?

Mustafa No, comment.

Met Police Officer For the record. Just so the judge can see exactly how uncooperative you are. I know you're Mustafa Al-Bassam are you going to deny that? Is your name Mustafa Al-Bassam?

Mustafa No comment.

Met Police Officer Jake Davis, unemployed eighteen year old arrested at his council house in Lerwick Shetland. He faces a possible 890 years in jail.

Act 2 Scene 10 – Southwark Crown Court

Barrister So I turn around/and she's there, lipstick all smudged, he's trying to do up his trousers, I'm trying not to look like I know exactly what's going on, and how long it's been going on for, have you seen, have you seen that scene in *Notting Hill*.

Solicitor Sorry I'm late, Jubilee line was a nightmare. Ignore my trainers please, have you spoken to the other side about the section forty-five and forty-six?

Solicitor 2 I/thought that would be raised at the management conference?

Barrister 2 *Four Weddings*.

Barrister Is it *Four/Weddings* when he's in the cupboard? That's what I was like. It was *pure* comedy! I was like I am going to be dining out on this one for *ever*!

Barrister 3 Sorry I'm late. Do you/freak out whenever security ask to go through your bags I know nothings in there but every time I'm like, what if I've packed a bomb by accident?

Barrister 3 Have I got time to go to the toilet?

Jake Would, uh, would, would you like some uh, water?

Mustafa Uh uh, uh, yes yes please.

Mustafa Thank you.

Jake No. Welcome. It's no. . .

Barrister 1 Whahhhhaaaaaahahhhhaaaaaa!!

Barrister 2 Waahaahaaaaaaaaa!!

Jake I'm Jake.

Mustafa Mustafa.

Jake Nice to/meet you.

Mustafa Really nice to meet you.

End.